Communications
in Computer and Information Science 2157

Rationale

The CCIS series is devoted to the publication of proceedings of computer science conferences. Its aim is to efficiently disseminate original research results in informatics in printed and electronic form. While the focus is on publication of peer-reviewed full papers presenting mature work, inclusion of reviewed short papers reporting on work in progress is welcome, too. Besides globally relevant meetings with internationally representative program committees guaranteeing a strict peer-reviewing and paper selection process, conferences run by societies or of high regional or national relevance are also considered for publication.

Topics

The topical scope of CCIS spans the entire spectrum of informatics ranging from foundational topics in the theory of computing to information and communications science and technology and a broad variety of interdisciplinary application fields.

Information for Volume Editors and Authors

Publication in CCIS is free of charge. No royalties are paid, however, we offer registered conference participants temporary free access to the online version of the conference proceedings on SpringerLink (http://link.springer.com) by means of an http referrer from the conference website and/or a number of complimentary printed copies, as specified in the official acceptance email of the event.

CCIS proceedings can be published in time for distribution at conferences or as post-proceedings, and delivered in the form of printed books and/or electronically as USBs and/or e-content licenses for accessing proceedings at SpringerLink. Furthermore, CCIS proceedings are included in the CCIS electronic book series hosted in the SpringerLink digital library at http://link.springer.com/bookseries/7899. Conferences publishing in CCIS are allowed to use Online Conference Service (OCS) for managing the whole proceedings lifecycle (from submission and reviewing to preparing for publication) free of charge.

Publication process

The language of publication is exclusively English. Authors publishing in CCIS have to sign the Springer CCIS copyright transfer form, however, they are free to use their material published in CCIS for substantially changed, more elaborate subsequent publications elsewhere. For the preparation of the camera-ready papers/files, authors have to strictly adhere to the Springer CCIS Authors' Instructions and are strongly encouraged to use the CCIS LaTeX style files or templates.

Abstracting/Indexing

CCIS is abstracted/indexed in DBLP, Google Scholar, EI-Compendex, Mathematical Reviews, SCImago, Scopus. CCIS volumes are also submitted for the inclusion in ISI Proceedings.

How to start

To start the evaluation of your proposal for inclusion in the CCIS series, please send an e-mail to ccis@springer.com.

Audronė Lupeikienė · Jolita Ralyté ·
Gintautas Dzemyda

Editors

Digital Business and Intelligent Systems

16th International Baltic Conference, Baltic DB&IS 2024
Vilnius, Lithuania, June 30 – July 3, 2024
Proceedings

Editors
Audronė Lupeikienė 🆔
Institute of Data Science and Digital
Technologies
Vilnius University
Vilnius, Lithuania

Jolita Ralyté 🆔
CUI
University of Geneva
Carouge, Switzerland

Gintautas Dzemyda 🆔
Institute of Data Science and Digital
Technologies
Vilnius University
Vilnius, Lithuania

ISSN 1865-0929   ISSN 1865-0937 (electronic)
Communications in Computer and Information Science
ISBN 978-3-031-63542-7   ISBN 978-3-031-63543-4 (eBook)
https://doi.org/10.1007/978-3-031-63543-4

Preface

We are pleased to welcome you to the proceedings of the 16th edition of the International Baltic Conference on Digital Business and Intelligent Systems (Baltic DB&IS 2024), which took place in Vilnius from June 30 to July 3, 2024.

Baltic DB&IS is an international event that focuses on the advances of computer science in digital business and intelligent systems and provides a rich environment for exchange of research findings and emerging ideas among scientists, practitioners and doctoral students from the Baltic Sea region, Europe, and the rest of the world. Since its first edition in 1994 in Trakai, Lithuania, the conference is held every second year in one of the three Baltic countries, Lithuania, Latvia and Estonia. This edition was co-hosted by four Lithuanian academic institutions: Vilnius University, Vilnius Gediminas Technical University, Lithuanian Academy of Sciences and Lithuanian Computer Society, and celebrated the 30th anniversary of the conference.

Over these 30 years, the theme and topics of the conference have gradually evolved from database and information systems engineering to business digitalization and the development of intelligent systems, with the aim of addressing current challenges and trends. In an era of rapid technological change, where digitalization permeates every facet of our lives, businesses must navigate the complex interplay between innovation and adaptation. This conference serves as a forum to explore cutting-edge research, share ideas, and envision the transformative potential of intelligent systems in reshaping the digital business landscape.

The program of Baltic DB&IS 2024 included four remarkable keynote speeches: "Towards Active Inference for Distributed Intelligence in the Computing Continuum", by Schahram Dustdar, from the Distributed Systems Group, TU Wien, Austria; "Unlocking Insights: Empowering Decision-Making in Data-Driven Environments", by Maribel Yasmina Santos, from the Department of Information Systems, University of Minho, Portugal; "Reducing the Administrative Burden in Healthcare: Ontological Conversation Interpretation for Generative Medical Reporting", by Sjaak Brinkkemper, from Utrecht University, the Netherlands; and "Information Security in Digital Business and Intelligent Systems", by Raimundas Matulevičius, from the Institute of Computer Science, University of Tartu, Estonia.

The conference received 36 submissions, of which 13 were accepted as full papers (acceptance rate of 36.1%) and 3 as short papers. They are included in this volume of the Baltic DB&IS 2024 proceedings. Each paper went through a thorough single-blind peer review process and received at least three reviews from the international Program Committee, which included 50 members from 21 countries. We are deeply thankful to the Program Committee members for their fair and competent contribution in selecting papers and providing constructive feedback to the authors.

The papers included in this volume present original research contributions in the fields of business digitalization and development of intelligent business systems. They propose new approaches, algorithms, methods and tools as well as analyze and evaluate the existing ones. The use of artificial intelligence techniques such as machine learning, deep learning and natural language processing is recurrent in many contributions. They face various software engineering, digital business and societal challenges such as efficiency of digital business systems, concurrent engineering, sustainability, eco-design, learning and education, data collection and processing, image processing and security.

Organizing the conference was a great pleasure, since we had an excellent Organizing Committee. We thank all its members for their time and dedication to help make this conference a success. Special thanks go to our sponsors and to the Baltic DB&IS 2024 Steering Committee.

We also thank Springer for their assistance in the production of the conference proceedings and Microsoft CMT for providing an efficient conference management system.

Finally, we thank all the authors for sharing their work and findings and all the attendees for their lively participation and fruitful discussions. We hope you will enjoy reading this volume.

June 2024

Audronė Lupeikienė
Jolita Ralyté
Gintautas Dzemyda

Organization

General Chair

Gintautas Dzemyda   Vilnius University, Lithuanian Academy of Sciences, Lithuania

Program Committee Chairs

Audronė Lupeikienė   Vilnius University, Lithuania
Jolita Ralyté   University of Geneva, Switzerland

Doctoral Consortium Co-chairs

Diana Kalibatienė   Vilnius Gediminas Technical University, Lithuania
Tarmo Robal   Tallinn University of Technology, Estonia

Steering Committee

Janis Bubenko (Honorary Member) (1935–2022)   Royal Institute of Technology and Stockholm University, Sweden
Arne Sølvberg (Honorary Member)   Norwegian University of Science and Technology, Norway
Guntis Arnicāns   University of Latvia, Latvia
Juris Borzovs   University of Latvia, Latvia
Gintautas Dzemyda   Vilnius University, Lithuania
Jānis Grundspeņķis   Riga Technical University, Latvia
Hele-Mai Haav   Tallinn University of Technology, Estonia
Diana Kalibatiene   Vilnius Gediminas Technical University, Lithuania
Mārīte Kirikova   Riga Technical University, Latvia
Innar Liiv   Tallinn University of Technology, Estonia
Audronė Lupeikienė   Vilnius University, Lithuania
Raimundas Matulevičius   University of Tartu, Estonia
Tarmo Robal   Tallinn University of Technology, Estonia

Program Committee

Guntis Arnicans	University of Latvia, Latvia
Romas Baronas	Vilnius University, Lithuania
Justyna Berniak-Woźny	Systems Research Institute of the Polish Academy of Sciences, Poland
Stefano Bonnini	University of Ferrara, Italy
Dominik Bork	TU Wien, Austria
Juris Borzovs	University of Latvia, Latvia
Antoine Bossard	Kanagawa University, Japan
Robert Andrei Buchmann	Babeş-Bolyai University, Romania
Vytautas Čyras	Vilnius University, Lithuania
Rebecka Deneckère	Université Paris 1 Panthéon-Sorbonne, France
Flavius Frasincar	Erasmus University Rotterdam, Netherlands
Johann Gamper	Free University of Bozen-Bolzano, Italy
Shahram Ghandeharizadeh	University of Southern California, USA
Giovanni Giachetti	Universidad Andrés Bello, Chile
Jānis Grabis	Riga Technical University, Latvia
Janis Grundspenkis	Riga Technical University, Latvia
Hele-Mai Haav	Tallinn University of Technology, Estonia
Mirjana Ivanovic	University of Novi Sad, Serbia
Hannu Jaakkola	Tampere University, Finland
Mārīte Kirikova	Riga Technical University, Latvia
Arne Koschel	Hannover University of Applied Sciences and Arts, Germany
Olga Kurasova	Vilnius University, Lithuania
Dejan Lavbič	University of Ljubljana, Slovenia
Innar Liiv	Tallinn University of Technology, Estonia
Timo Mäkinen	Tampere University, Finland
Virginijus Marcinkevičius	Vilnius University, Lithuania
Saulius Maskeliūnas	Vilnius University, Lithuania
Raimundas Matulevičius	University of Tartu, Estonia
Laila Niedrite	University of Latvia, Latvia
Oscar Pastor	Universitat Politècnica de València, Spain
Jens Myrup Pedersen	Aalborg University, Denmark
Jaroslav Pokorny	Charles University, Czech Republic
Tarmo Robal	Tallinn University of Technology, Estonia
Ben Roelens	Open University of the Netherlands, Netherlands
Jose Raul Romero	University of Cordoba, Spain
Gunter Saake	University of Magdeburg, Germany
Kurt Sandkuhl	Rostock University, Germany
Ulf Seigerroth	Jönköping University, Sweden

Michał Śmiałek	Warsaw University of Technology, Poland
Janis Stirna	Stockholm University, Sweden
Vjeran Strahonja	University of Zagreb, Croatia
Marek Szelągowski	Systems Research Institute of the Polish Academy of Sciences, Poland
Bastian Tenbergen	SUNY Oswego, USA
Ernest Teniente	Polytechnic University of Catalonia, Spain
A Min Tjoa	TU Wien, Austria
Damjan Vavpotič	University of Ljubljana, Slovenia
Inta Volodko	Riga Technical University, Latvia
Markus Westner	OTH Regensburg, Germany
Robert Wrembel	Poznań University of Technology, Poland
Andrejs Zujevs	Riga Technical University, Latvia

Organizing Committee

Kristina Lapin	Vilnius University, Lithuania
Virginijus Marcinkevičius	Vilnius University, Lithuania
Saulius Maskeliūnas	Vilnius University, Lithuanian Computer Society, Lithuania
Snieguolė Meškauskienė	Vilnius University, Lithuania
Jolanta Miliauskaitė	Vilnius University, Lithuania
Laima Paliulionienė	Vilnius University, Lithuania
Valerija Paškauskienė	Lithuanian Academy of Sciences, Lithuania
Martynas Sabaliauskas	Vilnius University, Lithuania

Abstracts of the Keynote Speeches

Towards Active Inference for Distributed Intelligence in the Computing Continuum

Schahram Dustdar(iD)

Distributed Systems Group, TU Wien, Vienna, Austria
dustdar@dsg.tuwien.ac.at

Keynote Abstract

Modern distributed systems also deal with uncertain scenarios, where environments, infrastructures, and applications are widely diverse. In the scope of IoT-Edge-Fog-Cloud computing, leveraging these neuroscience-inspired principles and mechanisms could aid in building more flexible solutions able to generalize over different environments. A captivating set of hypotheses from the field of neuroscience suggests that human and animal brain mechanisms result from a few powerful principles. If proved to be accurate, these assumptions could open a deep understanding of the way humans and animals manage to cope with the unpredictability of events and imagination.

Unlocking Insights: Empowering Decision-Making in Data-Driven Environments

Maribel Yasmina Santos ⓘ

Department of Information Systems, School of Engineering, University of Minho, Guimarães, Portugal
maribel@dsi.uminho.pt

Keynote Abstract

In today's data-driven landscape, strategic deployment of data architectures is pivotal for facilitating decision-making in data-intensive applications. From streamlining data ingestion to enabling complex analytics workflows, these architectures support extracting actionable insights from vast and varied datasets. This talk explores the intersection of data architectures and decision-making, highlighting their close relationship in driving business value and innovation, and discusses common data architectures such as traditional data warehouses, massive storage in data lakes, emerging data lakehouses, and the decentralised data mesh, highlighting their role in fostering data science and analytics capabilities, and in enabling informed decision-making in our increasingly data-centric world.

Reducing the Administrative Burden in Healthcare: Ontological Conversation Interpretation for Generative Medical Reporting

Sjaak Brinkkemper[iD]

Utrecht University, Utrecht, The Netherlands
S.Brinkkemper@uu.nl

Keynote Abstract

The administrative burden in routine healthcare processes is high, but for communication among care providers the reporting about patient consultations in hospital information systems (HIS) is very essential. In order to reduce this burden we have started the Care2Report research program (www.care2report.nl) that aims at a generative HIS reporting based on multimodal (audio, video, bluetooth) recording of a consultation, followed by knowledge representation, ontological conversation interpretation, and finally the generation and uploading of the report in the patient medical record in the HIS. Novel generative pre-trained transformers (e.g. ChatGPT, Gemini, Llama) provide innovative means for conversation dialogue interpretation and abstractive summarization. In this keynote I will present the aims and goals of the Care2Report research program and its startup Verticai (www.verticai.nl), the various linguistic intelligence pipelines, its current functional and technical architecture, and the achievements so far. The linguistic pipeline research will be demonstrated by (i) the generation of medical guideline ontologies for the matching of the consultation audio transcript, (ii) the optimization of prompt engineering with output difference taxonomy and (iii) the medical action recognizer based on convolutional neural networks. We end with an outlook of the current research projects and experiments in healthcare institutions.

References

1. Faber, W., Bootsma, R.E., Huibers, T., van Dulmen, S., Brinkkemper, S.: Comparative experimentation of accuracy metrics in automated medical reporting: the case of otitis consultations. In: Proceedings of the 17th International Joint Conference on Biomedical Engineering Systems and Technologies (BIOSTEC 2024), vol. 2, pp. 585–594. SCITEPRESS (2024)

2. van Zandvoort, D., Wiersema, L., Huibers,T., van Dulmen, S., Brinkkemper, S.: Enhancing summarization performance through transformer-based prompt engineering in automated medical reporting. In: Proceedings of the 17th International Joint Conference on Biomedical Engineering Systems and Technologies (BIOSTEC 2024), vol. 2, pp. 154–165. SCITEPRESS (2024)
3. ElAssy, O., de Vendt, R., Dalpiaz, F., Brinkkemper, S.: A semi-automated method for domain-specific ontology creation from medical guidelines. In: Augusto, A., et al. (eds.) BPMDS EMMSAD 2022. LNBIP, vol. 450, pp. 295–309 (2022). Springer, Cham. https://doi.org/10.1007/978-3-031-07475-2_20
4. Maas, L., et al.: The Care2Report system: Automated medical reporting as an integrated solution to reduce administrative burdening healthcare. In: Proceedings of the 53rd Hawaii International Conference on System Sciences IEEE (2020)

Information Security in Digital Business and Intelligent Systems

Raimundas Matulevičius🆔

Institute of Computer Science, University of Tartu, Estonia
raimundas.matulevicius@ut.ee

Keynote Abstract

Nowadays, digitalisation and intelligent infrastructure change human activities and industrial systems. Disruptive technologies, such as cloud computing, blockchain, AI/ML systems, and others, have become applicable in various domains, including self-driving vehicles, e-health, innovative city applications, and industrial automated systems. The intensive use of these technologies also generates and manages a lot of data and information, which should be used for the intended purposes, made available when needed, and integral to making correct decisions. This means that security should be treated as the first level of citizens in digitalised processes and intelligent infrastructures. This talk will consider the assets and values of digitalised systems and intelligent infrastructures. Specifically, it discussed the need to protect them against unauthorised access, harm, and risks. It highlights how one can apply disruptive technology to protect intelligent infrastructures. However, it also discusses the security weaknesses of this technology and countermeasures to mitigate them.

Contents

Models, Methods, and Tools
for Digitalization

Exploring Goal Relationships in Satellite Assembly Line Design

Anouck Chan⬛, Thomas Polacsek(✉)⬛, and Stéphanie Roussel⬛

DTIS, ONERA, Université de Toulouse, 31000 Toulouse, France
{anouck.chan,thomas.polacsek,stephanie.roussel}@onera.fr

Abstract. With the emergence of satellite constellations in recent years, satellite assembly lines have to respond to new demand : produce multiple copies of the same satellite at short production rates, manage multiple production rates for different constellations, but also continue to produce specific satellites in a single copy over longer time horizons. Designing versatile assembly lines that can assemble multiple types of satellites is a major challenge for manufacturers. Such lines must be designed within the existing infrastructure and with the specific required machines and tools, which must be shared between assembly activities for all types of satellites. In this work, we are interested in eliciting the goals of a versatile assembly chain from the perspective of goal-requirement modelling. More specifically, we want to determine which goals might conflict with each other. To do this, we propose to elicit the different goals and then use a constraint programming approach to compute if some goals are difficult to satisfy together.

Keywords: goal-requirement modelling · assembly line · automatic calculus

1 Introduction

Satellites are complex systems composed of various components such as solar panels, communication systems, propulsion systems and scientific instruments. While satellite production historically involved low-volume, the recent demand for satellite constellations has necessitated a shift towards high-volume manufacturing. This new demand creates a need for the exploration of alternative production methods. A satellite constellation is a group of satellites working together in a coordinated manner to achieve a specific purpose. These constellations offer a wide range of functionalities including observation, communication or scientific research. *Communication constellations* enable high-speed internet access across the globe and are composed of thousands of small satellites in low Earth orbit, *global navigation satellite systems* provide precise positioning and timing information for navigation and various location-based services, *Earth observation constellations* are equipped with sensors to observe and monitor the Earth's surface, atmosphere and oceans. They provide insights for environmental

© The Author(s), under exclusive license to Springer Nature Switzerland AG 2024
A. Lupeikienė et al. (Eds.): DB&IS 2024, CCIS 2157, pp. 3–17, 2024.
https://doi.org/10.1007/978-3-031-63543-4_1

monitoring, disaster management and resource management. Examples include the *Copernicus Sentinel* constellation and the *Dove* constellation of small satellites, showcasing the diverse applications of these coordinated satellite systems.

Despite potential variations in the specific requirements of different satellite types, their similarities in assembly processes and components make them suitable for shared production lines. This shared approach is facilitated by the common aspects of both the assembly procedures and the components in the different satellite categories. Many essential components, such as solar panels, attitude control systems, and propulsion systems, are common in different satellite types. In addition, the assembly processes also show a high degree of similarity for diverse satellite types. Processes can include tasks such as structural component integration, payload instrument or communication payload installation, and rigorous testing and verification procedures. Consequently, the assembly line can be designed to handle the assembly of these common components reducing the need for specialised equipment and processes.

While the fundamental principles of assembly line design can be applied to satellite production, the unique requirements and complexities of satellite manufacturing necessitate a nuanced and specialised approach. This necessitates expertise and careful consideration of factors like customisation and technological complexity. Therefore, constructing different satellite types on a singular assembly line presents a significant challenge that can provide economies of scale and efficiency benefits. By maximising the utilisation of manufacturing equipment and resources, manufacturers can achieve cost reductions and faster production cycles. However, designing such an assembly line requires the understanding of the trade-offs involved. Should the line be flexible and adaptable to accommodate technological advancements, evolving customer requirements, and fluctuating market trends? Should it be easy to scale the production up or down in response to market dynamics? Should the focus be on minimising capital costs by sharing resources across multiple satellite constellation projects, or reducing operating costs? Defining clear and prioritised objectives is crucial before designing such an assembly line. An optimised line requires a clear understanding of the criteria being optimised, as well as the identification of potentially conflicting objectives that necessitate strategic trade-offs. Furthermore, setting clear goals and requirements is essential for the design of a versatile satellite assembly line. By defining specific objectives and criteria upfront, manufacturers can ensure that the line is designed to effectively address the key challenges and opportunities inherent in the satellite manufacturing process.

Goal-Oriented Requirements Engineering (GORE) is an approach that focuses on capturing and defining the objectives, the goals, of stakeholders to drive the development of systems [16]. Unlike requirements, goals are not necessarily mandatory but rather desires, desirable objectives. It is therefore possible for goals to be in opposition. One major contribution of GORE is to finely characterize the interactions between goals. Frameworks such as *NFR (Non-Functional Requirements)* [5,15], iStar [6,19] and *GRL (Goal-oriented Requirement Language)* [1] proposed to model these links between goals. These relationships help to define the dependencies, conflicts and synergies between different goals within the system being modelled. Understanding these relationships is critical to ensure that the requirements derived from the goals are coherent and consistent. Usually, goal relationship elicitation involves collaborative efforts among stakeholders and requirements engineers. In the context of a project to investigate the versatile satellite assembly line feasibility, we have used a goal-based approach. Goal elicitation has enabled us to define what a *good* versatile assembly line could be. In order to be able to choose between these goals, it is also necessary to determine which goals reinforce each other and which goals are difficult to combine. However, defining such relations in our context was far from trivial. For example, given the complexity of the interactions involved in satellite manufacturing, determining if the satisfaction of the objective *keeping to a production schedule* has an impact on the satisfaction of *kneed to avoid storage space* is not simply a matter of expert judgement. Therefore, in order to find non-trivial relationships between goals, we have used automatic computation. As we shall see, we have not carried out a systematic and exhaustive study, but we have laid the foundations of an approach that could enrich traditional GORE approaches. On the basis of real industrial data, using our approach based on automatic computation, we have been able to find conflict between goals that were not elicited by the experts.

The paper is structured as follows: in Sect. 2, we present the challenges of designing a satellite assembly line and how we have encountered the problem of defining what constitutes good design. We will then explore how goal modeling can assist us, in Sect. 3, and present a goal model for a versatile satellite assembly line in Sect. 4. Section 5 is dedicated to our proposal to automatically calculate possible interactions between goals. Section 6 presents related work on the integration of calculus and goal models. Finally, we conclude in Sect. 7 with a brief discussion on the limitations of the methods and future work.

2 Design a Good Assembly Line

In our context, an assembly line is a set of physical work stations, composed of jigs and fixtures. Each type of satellite requires a specific set of operations to be performed. These operations require the use of dedicated jigs, fixtures and tools. Satellites under construction are moved from station to station according to the operation that needs to be performed.

Our use case aims to create a versatile manufacturing facility capable of assembling a variety of satellites, including two satellite constellations and two specific earth observation satellites. The assembly line should be designed with modularity in mind, allowing seamless integration of different satellite components and subsystems. It should allow multiple satellites to be processed in parallel, optimising production efficiency and reducing lead times. In addition, flexible workflow configurations could be a key issue, allowing easy reconfiguration of assembly processes to accommodate different satellite designs and production schedules. Moreover, cost reduction through the sharing of jigs, test facilities, and specific tooling is a strategic approach that can significantly reduce overheads and improve efficiency.

Integration jigs and fixtures are used to hold components in place during assembly and integration. Jigs and fixtures are often custom-designed to accommodate the specific geometry and requirements of each satellite type. Satellite components are delicate and often need to be handled with care. Equipment such as robotic arms, lifting devices and handling carts are used to safely transport components within the cleanroom. A cleanroom is a controlled environment in which the concentration of airborne particles such as dust, microbes, aerosol particles and chemical vapours is kept within specified limits. In practical terms, a cleanroom is an area of the production line equipped with high-efficiency particulate air (HEPA) filters to remove airborne particles. The airflow within the cleanroom is carefully controlled to ensure that particles are continuously removed from the environment and that contaminants are not introduced into sensitive areas.

In assembly, alignment and measurement tools play a critical role in ensuring that components are accurately positioned and aligned according to design specifications. For example, interferometers are used to measure distances and surface flatness with high precision using interference patterns created by beams of light. For very sensitive tasks, vibration isolation systems could be used. These features are designed to minimise external disturbances that could affect the precision and quality of the assembly processes.

In addition, throughout the assembly process, a range of test equipment is used to ensure that each component works correctly. This equipment can be very expensive. For example, blackout enclosures are specially designed chambers with opaque walls to block external light sources. These enclosures create a dark environment suitable for carrying out optical tests without interference from ambient light. In fact, satellite optical devices such as imaging sensors, cameras and telescopes require precise measurements and evaluations that can be affected by ambient light.

In practice, as part of our case study, we are aiming to design an assembly line capable of manufacturing three different types of satellite (we are working on a real industrial delivery schedule). Type 1 and Type 2 satellites are part of the constellation and have to be delivered at regular intervals, on specific dates. Type 1 satellites must be delivered every two months and Type 2 satellites every three months. In the end, on a two years period, four Type 1 and five Type 2 satellites must be produced. Type 3 satellites are *one-off* satellites, they do not have to be delivered at regular intervals but have a final delivery date. The factory where the assembly line will be installed already has tools and machines. So, in the first stage of our work we want to study the feasibility of a versatile plant based on the resources available. Minimising and maximising performance criteria or resource consumption are not part of our objectives.

We have encoded our problem as a constraint optimisation problem (using CpOptimizer 20.1 [11] and the open-source solver ACE [13]). For this first application, we have no objective function (*i.e.* there is no criterion to optimise), and only criteria to satisfy. We obtain the assembly line whose schedule is given in Fig. 1. If the computer finds no solution, it means that building an assembly line is impossible. In the figure, each line represents the schedule for assembling a satellite. The colours yellow, blue and pink represent Type 1, 2 and 3 satellites respectively. The yellow, blue an pink vertical bars represent the dates by which a Type 1, 2 or 3 satellite must be delivered. So we see that it is possible to build a versatile factory, but is it a good factory? How to define *good*?

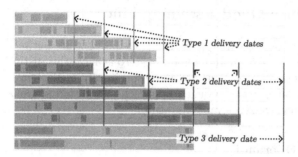

Fig. 1. Case Study, Assembly Line Scheduling

3   Goal Modeling

To define *good*, we can focus on the storage. In our solution, presented Fig. 1, satellites are manufactured well in advance of their delivery dates. Perhaps it is better not to store them and to assemble them as late as possible? Secondly, weonly considered with the existing tools and facilities. It may be possible to go faster with additional equipment, such as HEPA or interferometers. In fact this can be useful to reduce bottlenecks, but it increases the investment. It may also be interesting to minimise the amount of equipment used. This equipment could be used on another assembly line, thus reducing investment costs. These are just a few examples of the goals that could define a good versatile satellite assembly line.

In order to define what is a good assembly line, we opted for goal modelling, drawing upon the principles of *Goal-Oriented Requirements Engineering (GORE)*. This selection was motivated by several factors.

The goal modelling framework helps us to organise these elements by establishing relationships and guiding the elicitation of intermediate goals through *why* and *how* questions [12]. Then significant portion of the acquired goal has fuzzy description and ambiguity in determining their satisfaction. Because they are vaguely defined goals with no clear-cut criteria for their fulfillment, soft goals are particularly well suited to modelling this type of objective [7]. A third reason is that conflicts may arise amongst the elicited goals, where satisfying one might hinder the fulfilment of another. Additionally, redundancy may emerge due to differing elicitation methods employed by experts or the need for refined formulations and additional precision. Therefore, a flexible framework that accommodates redundancy and conflict expression was crucial.

Given these three main reasons, coupled with prior positive experiences in modelling, we choose goal modelling diagram, specifically the *Goal-oriented Requirements Language (GRL)* framework, as the foundation to design an versatile assembly line performance model [1].

4   Goals for a Good Assembly Line

In the context of our research, it is crucial to differentiate between a mere functional assembly line design and a good one. To achieve this distinction, we must identify a set of evaluation elements, more specifically, goals. Our goal model was constructed through a two-pronged approach: elicitation sessions with domain experts and a review of relevant literature.

4.1   Modus Operandi

We conducted elicitation sessions with various groups of domain experts, depending on their availabilities and our specific needs. The initial session involved domain experts explicating the specificities and main challenges associated with satellite assembly lines. Next sessions followed another format. At first, based on a selection of previously elicited objectives, model experts presented potential assembly line designs to domain experts. Figure 1 is an example of such a presentation, focusing solely on mandatory goals. Then, model experts proposed potential objectives through drafts of assembly line designs that could be carried out if these goals were to be met. Employing visual representations facilitated domain experts' comprehension of the impact of goals on assembly line designs and enabled them to remain at the appropriate level of description. Both representations served as a springboard for expert discussions. Hypotheses were validated or rejected.

4.2   Model Description

The assembly line performance goal model, depicted in Fig. 2, has 34 goals: 8 hard goals and 26 softgoals. In addition, we have specific goals: mandatory goals (in grey on the Figure). These goals could be interconnected through contribution link or correlation link. Contribution links indicate the desired influence of one element on another. Within our model, we utilise two types of contribution: *Help* and *Make*. In addition, we add a correlation link, *Unknown.* As opposed to desired impacts, correlation relationships describe the potential side effects of fulfilling an element [2,3].

Help relationship is a type of dependency between goals that indicates one goal's achievement or satisfaction contributes positively towards the achievement of another goal. In our model, if the goal *need for new resource is reduced* fulfil,

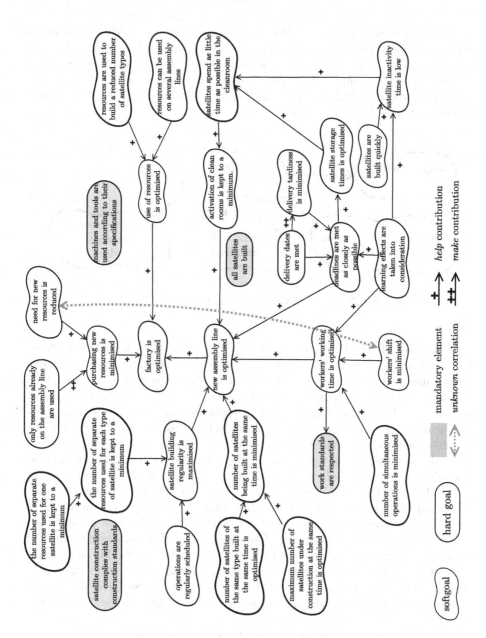

Fig. 2. Goal model of factory performance

it contributes to the satisfaction of *purchasing new resources is minimised* . It contributes, but it doesn't imply. The *Make* relationship is stronger. Indeed, *Make* relationship between two goals indicates that the successful attainment of one goal is a prerequisite the achievement of the other goal. This relationship implies that the goal being made depends on the accomplishment of the goal that is making it happen. In our model, *only ressources already on the assembly are used* obviously implies that *purchasing new resources is minimised*. The *Unknown* correlation indicates the existence of a relationship between goals, but we are unable to determine its nature.

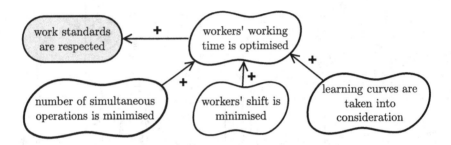

Fig. 3. Goals related to work in goal model Fig. 2

We do not give an exhaustive description of all the goals in our model here. For example, we can focus on goals related to working time (Fig. 3). A *Help* arrow connects the softgoal *workers' shift is minimised* to *workers' working time is optimised* . In this context, a shift refers to time slot assigned to an employee and can vary from 6 to 12 h. Here, this contribution link signifies that minimising the duration of workers' shifts contributes to optimising their working time. However, achieving the minimum shift duration for all workers does not guarantee the optimisation of their working time. Fulfilling other elements, such as minimising the *number of simultaneous operations*, might also be necessary. In our work, we only used *Unknown* correlations, represented by two-way dashed arrows. In Fig. 2 there is only one correlation link between *workers' shift is minimised* and *need for new resources is reduced.* This link implies that pursuing the satisfaction of the softgoal *workers' shift is minimised* with the aim of optimising workers' working time might lead to a decrease in the satisfaction of need for *new resources.* Conversely, trying to fulfil the softgoal *need for new resources*, might also decrease the satisfaction of *workers' shift is minimised.* Due to the unquantifiable nature of this impact, we employ the unknown qualifier for the link.

Despite the knowledge of the experts, it became clear that there must be links, which were not elicited. Given the complexity of our system, it seems impossible to find all the relations between objectives using human expertise alone. As we will see in the next session, alternative methods, such as automated calculus, were needed to establish these links.

5   Automatic Calculus to Find Possible Interactions

The previously presented goal model facilitates the conceptualisation of an *ideal* assembly line desig, *i.e.* an assembly line that satisfies all the established goals. However, the realisation of this ideal design might be hindered by the presence of conflicting goals. Achieving complete goal satisfaction within a singular design might algorithmically difficult to obtain or even infeasible due to inherent conflicts or the comlexity associated with such designs. Identifying these conflicts offers several advantages : the selection of consistent group of goals we can decline in requirements of the assembly line, the identification of specific goals that need further refinement from domain experts, potentially involving preference ordering and trade-offs and the identification of groups of goals that necessitate the development of specialised tools to facilitate their integration within the assembly line design.

5.1   Approach

We have built an operational research algorithm to generate high-level assembly line designs. This program computes designs that satisfy a selected set of objectives formed by combinations of goals from the model. If the program rapidly computes a design, we infer the absence of conflicts between the given goals. Conversely, if the program requires more than a predetermined time limit to find a solution, or fails to find one altogether, we conclude that the objectives concerned are likely to influence each other. In such cases, a correlation link is added between the involved goals within the model. It is important to acknowledge that the time limit employed for correlation detection is arbitrarily defined and can be adjusted based on the desired level of accuracy. We consider finding a design within two hours to be *fast* and exceeding one day to be *slow*, but domain experts said that even several days might be considered as *fast* in assembly line design.

5.2   Practical Uses of Our Approach

For our application, we have datasets provided by a satellite manufacturer. These datasets encompass the assembly processes for three distinct satellite types (Type 1, Type 2 and Type 3), involving 147 resources. Each satellite requires 40 to 90 individual operations for its construction and there is a 18 month planning horizon. We have developed a constraint programming algorithm. Studied goals within the model is translated into a corresponding constraint within the algorithm. These constraints can be enabled or disabled depending on the specific set of goals we intend to evaluate. The algorithm receives a dataset description as input and outputs a detailed assembly line description. This description includes the operation schedule for each satellite along with the required time and resources. We utilise two constraint satisfaction solvers: CpOptimizer 20.1 [11] and ACE with PyCSP3 [13,14].

Finding Possible Interactions Between Mandatory Goals. Our first application focused on satisfying the mandatory goals highlighted in grey within Fig. 2 and Fig. 4. These goals represent essential requirements that must be fulfilled in the final assembly line design. The model comprises four mandatory goals.

- *All satellites are built*, four Type 1, five Type 2, and two Type 3 satellites, must be fully assembled by the end of the 18-month horizon.
- *Satellite construction complies with construction standards*, the construction process of satellites must be compliant to operations needed, their duration and order. The machines and tools needed by the operation have to be available.
- *Work standards are respected*, the process must comply with regulations of the Labour Code, like daily working hours, breaks, holidays, and ergonomic considerations for the workforce.
- *Machines and tools are used according to their specifications*, t he utilisation of machines and tools must respect their designated specifications. This includes respecting the number of simultaneous operations allowed on a single machine/tool, as well as machine setup times.

By considering these four mandatory goals, the developed algorithm successfully generated a functional assembly line design in 19.55 s. This rapid computation time suggests the absence of negative correlation links between these specific goals.

This initial application is a starting point. We can now add other goals and analysing the resulting assembly line design and computation times.

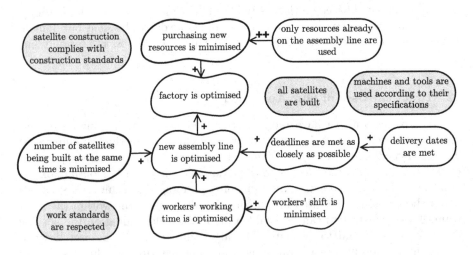

Fig. 4. Goals from Fig. 2 evaluated in Sect. 5

Finding Possible Interactions Between Delivery Dates and Resources Limitation. A second application aimed to evaluate the impact of introducing two additional goals:

- *Goals delivery dates are met*, the construction of each satellite is achieved before their respective delivery deadlines. Earlier completion is allowed.
- *Only resources already on the assembly line are used* the assembly line design only utilises resources that are already available on it.

These goals were chosen because they represent the first goals elicited by the domain experts and these constraints are frequently encountered in Operational Research [8]. By including these two additional goals with the four mandatory ones, the algorithm was able to generate an assembly line design in 174 s (less than 3 min). Figure 1 shows the resulting schedule. From this illustration we can notice that the design ensures that all satellites are constructed with the appropriate number of bars associated at each type. The schedule respects all delivery deadlines. For instance, in the case of Type 1 satellites, the first horizontal yellow bar ends before the first vertical delivery date, which means that the satellite is built before its delivery date, the second bar ends before the second vertical delivery due date, etc. The rapid computation time of 174 s suggests that there are likely no significant negative correlation links between these six goals.

Workers' Shift. A third application consisted to evaluated mandatory goals with the softgoal *workers' shift is minimised*. To model this softgoal, we fixed a maximum daily working shift of 6 h for each employee and each day. The algorithm was unable to return a feasible assembly line design. This outcome indicates that our definition of minimal worker shifts might be incompatible with satisfying all mandatory requirements. To express this conflict, we introduced correlation links between the *workers' shift is minimised* softgoal and the four mandatory goals within the model. This means that there is a need for a trade-off between *workers' shift is minimised* and the mandatory goals.

Simultaneous Satellite Building, Resources and Worker' Shift. The fourth application studied the impact of the three goals, *Goals delivery dates are met, number of satellites being built at the same time is minimised* and *need for new resources is reduced.*

- *Number of satellites being built at the same time is minimised*, the number of satellites being built simultaneously on the assembly line has to be reduce.
- *Need for new resources is reduced*, the utilisation of existing resources is prioritised and the need to acquire additional resources for the assembly line is minimised.

The algorithm successfully generated an assembly line design within 13.5 s when considering these two goals with the four mandatory goals. This rapid

(a) Mandatory goals, simultaneous satellite and minimising resources

(b) Mandatory goals, simultaneous satellite, minimising resources and worker' shift

Fig. 5. Schedule of assembly line

calculation implies the absence of negative correlation links between these six goals. The associated schedule is illustrated Fig. 5a.

Then we integrated the *workers' shift is minimised* softgoal, the computation time needed around 4 days, 17 h, and 30 min (Fig. 5b). The increase in computation time suggests that the satisfaction of the softgoal is likely to have an impact on the achievement of the six other goals. We have therefore added appropriate correlation links to the model to express these conflicts.

We carried out more applications in order to add the correlation links that we see in Fig. 6. It should be noted that not all the goals have been evaluated and that our choice of modelling also has an impact on the result obtained. The goal model obtained is therefore just one of the potential goals models we could obtain.

6   Related Work

The field of Goal-Oriented Requirement Engineering (GORE) offers several examples where researchers have combined goal models with computational approaches to achieve optimal solutions. These approaches address complex system design problems by establishing a set of desired goals and using computational methods to identify solutions that best satisfy these goals.

Propagation methods, as described in [1,7,10], play a key role in evaluating the impact of achieving specific goals on strategic goals. Each relationship within the goal model is associated with a propagation function, which determines how the satisfaction level of one element influences another. However, potential conflicts can arise during the design process. To address these conflicts, researchers have defined specific rules. For instance, in the context of Non-Functional Requirements (NFRs), [15] proposes a method where satisfaction states are ordered. And, for example, elements receiving conflicting contributions from an and-refinement (all subgoals need to be satisfied) are assigned the lowest satisfaction level.

Solver-based approaches offer another avenue for exploring optimal solutions. In [17], Nguyen combines goal models with Satisfiability Modulo Theories and

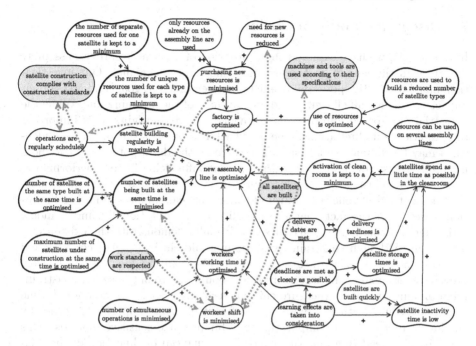

Fig. 6. Goal model of factory performance with automatically calculated correlation links

Optimisation Modulo Theories to identify the maximal set of goals that can be simultaneously satisfied. Similarly, Horkoff and Yu present a method in [9] for defining feasible and optimal solutions based on an iStar goal model and a SAT solver. Baatartogtokh *et al.* in [4] model goal satisfaction as a *Constraint Satisfaction Problem (CSP)*. They then integrate this model with the *Evolving Intension Framework* propagation method to evaluate element state labels based on various objective functions. This approach makes it possible to identify solutions that not only satisfy the greatest number of goals in an specific goal model, but also optimise the set of satisfied goals based on different criteria.

Furthermore, [18] by Sumesh and Krishna proposes a method for achieving an optimal set of goals for the system under consideration. Their definition of optimality not only maximising the number of satisfied goals, but also ensuring the robustness of the final solution. This robustness is evaluated by assigning fuzzy values to both the propagation links and the goal satisfaction levels, and then employing sensitivity analysis techniques. These techniques assess the impact of slight modifications in goal satisfaction on the overall solution, allowing for a more nuanced understanding of the trade-offs involved. However, it is important to note that the information obtained from sensitivity analysis is currently not fed back into the goal model itself.

7   Discussion and Conclusion

In this article, we have explored the conception of a versatile satellite assembly line through the lens of goal-requirement modeling techniques. Our investigation aimed to identify potential conflicts between different goals and assess their impact on the overall efficiency and effectiveness of the assembly line. While the industrial data-based approach has provided valuable insights, it is important to acknowledge its limitations. One drawback is that the scope of conflicts identified may be confined to the specific context of the data, potentially overlooking broader systemic issues or external factors influencing factory performance. However, the industrial data-based approach offers a pragmatic and contextually relevant method for eliciting and understanding real conflicts. Another limitation arises from the fact that the inability to computationally find a model satisfying two conflicting goals does not formally demonstrate the existence of a problem. Although constraint programming aids in identifying conflicts and assessing their feasibility, the absence of a feasible solution does not conclusively prove inherent goal conflicts. Future work should aim to optimise our constraint programming approach to ensure efficient resolution within an acceptable time frame. We could further explore how different elements impact each other by employing more refined computational techniques like sensitive analysis. This analysis could lead to a quantitative or more nuanced qualification of the relationships between these elements.

In conclusion, leveraging computational techniques to analyse goals enables stakeholders and requirements engineers to gain insight into goal relationships, dependencies, and potential conflicts. By identifying inconsistencies and exploring alternative solutions, these techniques facilitate the development of coherent, consistent, and stakeholder-aligned requirements. This holistic approach is essential for optimising the design and operation of versatile satellite assembly lines and ensuring their effectiveness in meeting stakeholder objectives.

References

1. Amyot, D., Ghanavati, S., Horkoff, J., Mussbacher, G., Peyton, L., Yu, E.: Evaluating goal models within the goal-oriented requirement language. Int. J. Intell. Syst. **25**, 841–877 (2010)
2. Amyot, D., Horkoff, J., Gross, D., Mussbacher, G.: A lightweight GRL profile for i* modeling. In: Heuser, C.A., Pernul, G. (eds.) ER 2009. LNCS, vol. 5833, pp. 254–264. Springer, Heidelberg (2009). https://doi.org/10.1007/978-3-642-04947-7_31
3. Amyot, D., Mussbacher, G.: User requirements notation: the first ten years, the next ten years (invited paper). J. Softw. **6**(5), 747–768 (2011)
4. Baatartogtokh, Y., Foster, I., Grubb, A.M.: Visualizations for user-supported state space exploration of goal models. In: 2023 IEEE 31st International Requirements Engineering Conference (RE), pp. 281–286 (2023)
5. Chung, L., Nixon, B.A., Yu, E., Mylopoulos, J.: Non-Functional Requirements in Software Engineering. International Series in Software Engineering, vol. 5. Springer, Heidelberg (2000)

6. Dalpiaz, F., Franch, X., Horkoff, J.: istar 2.0 language guide. CoRR arxiv:1605. 07767 (2016)

7. Giorgini, P., Mylopoulos, J., Sebastiani, R.: Goal-oriented requirements analysis and reasoning in the tropos methodology. Eng. Appl. Artif. Intell. **18**(2), 159–171 (2005)

8. Hartmann, S., Briskorn, D.: An updated survey of variants and extensions of the resource-constrained project scheduling problem. Eur. J. Oper. Res. **297**(1), 1–14 (2022)

9. Horkoff, J., Yu, E.: Finding solutions in goal models: an interactive backward reasoning approach. In: Parsons, J., Saeki, M., Shoval, P., Woo, C., Wand, Y. (eds.) ER 2010. LNCS, vol. 6412, pp. 59–75. Springer, Heidelberg (2010). https:// doi.org/10.1007/978-3-642-16373-9_5

10. Horkoff, J., Yu, E.S.K.: Comparison and evaluation of goal-oriented satisfaction analysis techniques. Requir. Eng. **18**(3), 199–222 (2013)

11. Laborie, P., Rogerie, J., Shaw, P., Vilím, P.: IBM ILOG CP optimizer for scheduling: 20+ years of scheduling with constraints at IBM/ILOG. Constraints **23**, 210–250 (2018)

12. van Lamsweerde, A.: Goal-oriented requirements engineering: a guided tour. In: 5e IEEE International Symposium on Requirements Engineering, pp. 249–262 (2001)

13. Lecoutre, C.: ACE, PyCSP3-XCSP3 (2023). https://github.com/xcsp3team

14. Lecoutre, C., Szczepanski, N.: Pycsp3: modeling combinatorial constrained problems in python (2020)

15. Mylopoulos, J., Chung, L., Nixon, B.A.: Representing and using nonfunctional requirements: a process-oriented approach. IEEE Trans. Softw. Eng. **18**(6), 483–497 (1992)

16. Mylopoulos, J., Chung, L., Yu, E.S.K.: From object-oriented to goal-oriented requirements analysis. Commun. ACM **42**(1), 31–37 (1999)

17. Nguyen, C.M.: Efficient Reasoning with Constrained Goal Models. Ph.D. thesis, University of Trento (2017)

18. Sumesh, S., Krishna, A.: Sensitivity analysis of conflicting goals in the i* goal model. Comput. J. **65**(6), 1434–1460 (2022)

19. Yu, E.S.K.: Towards modelling and reasoning support for early-phase requirements engineering. In: Proceedings of ISRE'97: 3rd IEEE International Symposium on Requirements Engineering, pp. 226–235. IEEE (1997)

Eco-Conscious Software Development: A Comprehensive Guide for Sustainable Practices

Ryan Vernex and Rébecca Deneckère(✉)

Centre de Recherche en Informatique, Université Paris 1 Panthéon-Sorbonne, Paris, France
denecker@univ-paris1.fr

Abstract. According to the World Health Organization, climate change is identified as a significant threat, primarily driven by excessive greenhouse gas emissions. While the natural greenhouse effect is essential for maintaining a habitable planet, human activities contribute to an overproduction of these gases, leading to accelerated global climate warming. In response to this, the concept of Green IT emerges, encompassing Information and Communication Technologies that mitigates environmental harm. Although Green IT is commonly associated with hardware, its software aspect plays a critical role in controlling energy consumption. This work try to answer to this challenge by offering a guide to improve the development process with a sustainable approach through a literature review and interviews of several professionals.

Keywords: Eco-design · Development · Guide · Sustainability · Sustainable policy

1 Introduction

According to the World Health Organization (WHO), climate change is one of the main threats of the century. The primary actor in this phenomenon of climate disruption is the excessive emission of greenhouse gases. Even if the greenhouse effect is essential for the planet to be habitable for humans, human activity tends to excessively increase their production. The immediate consequence is an excessive absorption of heat, inevitably leading to global climate warming. According to [1], Information and Communication Technologies (ICT) accounted for 4% of the global greenhouse gas emissions in 2020. This report also predicts an increase to 14% by 2040. It is in this context that the concept of Green IT makes sense. There is a strong relationship between ICT and sustainability [2] and Green IT refers to "all ICT whose use helps reduce the harmful effects of human activity on the environment." Today, Green IT is primarily recognized for its positive impacts on infrastructure and hardware [3].

However, the software aspect represents a crucial domain because it controls the use of hardware and, consequently, the energy consumption of devices. Thus, [4] emphasizes the importance of developing products that manage their consumption. There are a lot of

A. Lupeikienė et al. (Eds.): DB&IS 2024, CCIS 2157, pp. 18–33, 2024.
https://doi.org/10.1007/978-3-031-63543-4_2

works addressing this problem. For instance, [5] addresses the topic of ecology in software engineering. This work primarily focuses on metrics and measurement methods for the consumption of web services applications. Their research objective is to propose a solution that can guide architectural decisions for a project utilizing web services. Similarly, [6] propose a ranking of programming languages based on their ecological characteristics. It also attempts to establish a connection between energy consumption, runtime, and memory usage. Thus, the language with the best energy performance is not necessarily the one that executes the fastest. Hassmann and Westner [2] proposes a literature review focalized on the past ten years research that treat the topic of sustainability and ICT. This work emphasized the need to have a holistic approach to sustainability in ICT. This context leads us to the following research question: *How to guide the application development process towards a sustainable approach?*

The research methodology is explained in Sects. 2 and 3 analyses the results. An eco-design guide is described in Sect. 4 and a description of the evaluation is made on Sect. 5. We conclude in Sect. 6.

2 Research Methodology

Our research adopted a design science approach to develop a sustainability guide for software development. We followed the seven guidelines preconized by [7].

- Guideline 1: Design as an artefact. Our objective was to define a guide to lead the development process towards a more sustainable approach.
- Guideline 2: Problem relevance. Sustainability is a contemporary challenge, and there are numerous works related to this issue in the context of software development.
- Guideline 3: Design evaluation. Our initial evaluation involved expert feedback, and we are planning a more comprehensive assessment to validate and refine the proposed guide.
- Guideline 4: Research contributions. We are proposing a guide for sustainability in software development. We have identified three levels of involvement for sustainability and structured our findings into these three levels.
- Guideline 5: Research rigor. To ensure rigor, we conducted a thorough review of existing literature to define the guide's elements. Additionally, we conducted interviews to validate and enhance the guide's effectiveness. Details of our protocol methods are elaborated further in this section.
- Guideline 6: Design as a search process. The creation of our guide involved synthesizing pertinent information from the literature review and insights provided by domain experts.
- Guideline 7: Communication of research. The resulting guide provides a holistic view accessible to stakeholders involved at different levels of sustainability engagement.

We followed the process illustrated in Fig. 1. Each step is described in the rest of the section.

Define Research Question. Our main research question is *How to guide the application development process towards a sustainable approach?* To this end, we studied how to measure the usage of resources in ICT solutions (what resources, what measurements, which tools), what solutions currently exist to limit the usage of resources in ICT solutions, and we propose a guide summarizing our findings.

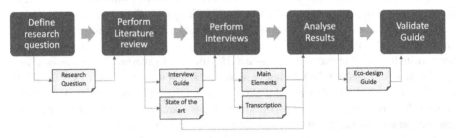

Fig. 1. Research process

Perform Literature Review. The literature review allowed us to identify existing tools for measuring resource consumption and then analyze eco-design methods that have already been applied. We used the Scopus API to search through the database and obtain the papers corresponding to the following set of inclusion criteria:

(1) use of specific keywords like "energy" and "consumption" and "software development", or "green" and "software" and "process" with the use of two keywords strings: TITLE-ABS-KEY(energy) AND TITLE-ABS-KEY(consumption) AND TITLE-ABS-KEY(software development) AND PUBYEAR > 2021 AND (SUBJAREA(COMP) OR SUBJAREA(ENGI)), and TITLE-ABS-KEY(green) AND TITLE-ABS-KEY(software) AND (TITLE-ABS-KEY(process) OR TITLE-ABS-KEY(practice)) AND PUBYEAR > 2021 AND (SUBJAREA(COMP) OR SUBJAREA(ENGI));
(2) the paper proposes methods or tools for the development process with a sustainability axis;
(3) the paper is a primary research;
(4) the paper is in English.

Perform Interviews. In order to support and challenge the results obtained in the state of the art, we confronted them with the opinions of professionals. This method brings a crucial qualitative aspect to the proposal of our guide. We chose participants who work daily in the context of Green IT and the profiles differ based on their various professions. Table 1 shows a quick presentation of each participant.

The interviews aimed to gather as much information and added value as possible to enrich the research. In this context, we conducted semi-structured interviews [8]. Each interview was constructed around three parts.

– Context Reminder: First and foremost, it seemed essential to put the interlocutor in or back into the context. Thus, we systematically explained the issue, the outline, but above all, the goal of the research. This brief presentation of the context allowed the interviewees to better position themselves and guide their responses to connect with the context.

- Presenter Presentation: Subsequently, the interlocutors introduce themselves, their role, and what they think they can contribute during this exchange.
- Rebound Phase: Once the interlocutor is introduced, we ask the predefined questions. Based on the responses, we can follow up on specific topics by seeking more details or by directly posing new questions. For instance, some of the questions were the following: what are the most relevant resource consumption measures in the context of a development project? What measurement tool(s) have you already used? What is your definition of eco-design? What eco-design method/process have you already experimented with? How can it be improved?

Table 1. Interviewees.

	Role	Missions
1	Green IT manager at BTI—advisory	- Support clients (B2B context) in their green IT initiatives
2	Sustainable IT analyst at Accenture	- Compile a set of tools related to responsible digital practices, focusing on open-source and free software - Responsible for supporting companies in the evolution of their eco-responsible initiatives
3	Full-stack developer at CarbonScore	- Develop a B2B SaaS tool that enables all employees of the client company to track real-time indicators such as CO_2 emissions or water consumption
4	Consultant	- Engage in the development of companies' responsible digital initiatives

All the interviews had been carefully recorded and transcribed by hand.

Analyze Results. We studied the interviewees responses to answer the research question and elaborate our guide to lead the development process by respecting sustainability requirements. We ensured inter-rater reliability by cross-referencing remarks from the interviewees and retaining only those that aligned across multiple responses. Our principle was to give greater weight to remarks that were consistently mentioned by multiple interviewees, as they were deemed more significant in our analysis.

Validate Guide. Following the exploration of the ideas highlighted in the first round of interviews, we developed our proposal of a guide. It was therefore relevant to seek validation for this work. Semi-structured interviews also allow us to build on the responses and address new questions. This approach adds fluidity to the exchange and, most importantly, enables us to extract the maximum value that the participants can provide. Here are the different steps of this exchange with the same interviewees as in the first round:

- Reminder of the context: Several months had passed since the initial exchange with each of the interviewees, so we had to reintroduce the research context and the general problematic.
- Presentation of the research work: We provided a detailed presentation of the eco-design guide. During this presentation, we strongly encouraged our interlocutors to interrupt us if they had any questions or misunderstandings. It allowed us to rephrase or better elaborate on certain points.
- Questioning/critique phase: Once the presentation was complete, we gathered our interlocutor's feedback on the proposal. We also invite them, if necessary, to suggest other research angles that we may not have addressed but could be interesting.

3   Measurement of Energy Resource Consumption and Potential Solutions

The literature review and initial round of interviews emphasized the significance of precise resource consumption measurement in software development, particularly in defining the measures used and recommending the tools for these measurements. Furthermore, the state of the art also presents a range of solutions aiming at reducing this consumption and two of the interviewees insisted on the use of a specific business model aiming at improving the sustainability aspects.

3.1   Measure the Resources Consumption

Information and communication technologies generate significant resource consumption throughout their life cycle. In recent years, technological innovation, coupled with increasingly intense marketing strategies and a continuously growing demand, has massively contributed to a rapid turnover of electrical/electronic equipment [9].

Measure types. In this section, we will identify and analyze relevant measures in the context of software development projects. We will take the opportunity to explain the impact of each of these measures to understand how to exploit them to the fullest. We classified the measures used in the literature, following the typology proposed in [3]. There are 6 categories of measures: (a) related to component consumption (hard drive, screen), (b) related to code analysis, (c) related on runtime, (d) based on estimates, (e) related to the development process, and (f) others. On this classification we can select three measures directly linked to the development part: (b), (c), and (e).

- Measures related to code analysis. These measures consider several indicators, as:

  - the number of executed instructions,
  - the number of direct sub-classes, or inheritance richness,
  - the lack of cohesion on methods: Number of pairs of functions with shared instance variables subtracted from the total number of pairs of functions without shared instance variables, and
  - the weighted methods per class: sum of complexities of methods defined in a class [10].

- Measures on runtime. The indicators used to evaluate these measures are:

  - the energy consumption during execution, often expressed in kilowatt-hours (kWh) [11],
  - the number of network exchanges: it means requests and responses; reducing unnecessary data exchanges can contribute to better energy efficiency,
  - the refresh rate[1]: if too high, this can lead to overuse of the CPU and memory, and
  - the response time: reducing response times improves the overall efficiency of the application and can potentially result in lower energy consumption [12].

- Measures related to the development process. They are taking three indicators into account:

  - The number of iterations required to complete the development of a feature/module. A too high number would imply greater resource consumption and thus indicate a potential issue in the design.
  - The level of documentation (quantity and quality). A rich documentation can enhance the overall productivity of a development team. However, unnecessary, redundant or overly detailed documentation is time consuming so should be avoided too.
  - The automated testing structure. A good test coverage ensures the longevity of the product and enables greater efficiency.

Measuring tools. Today, more and more tools are emerging in the IT environment to help measure resource consumption. All interviewees emphasized that the chain of responsibility includes all stakeholders of the software, from users to management. We can then categorize the tools based on the scope they cover, that is, the scale at which the tool can be exploited: either at the user level, the development level, or the management level, as shown in Fig. 2.

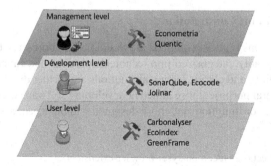

Fig. 2. Measuring tools examples

---

[1] https://www.makeuseof.com/test-monitor-refresh-rate-best-sites/.

User level. Let's start at the lowest scale, at the level of awareness of an individual user. Several tools exists, directly addressed to the user. There is the Firefox browser extension named Carbonalyser[2]. This tool provides real-time information about the electrical consumption and associated greenhouse gas emissions of your internet browsing. This type of tool primarily aims to provide transparency to users of a product to raise awareness about its associated consumption. On the same way, EcoIndex[3] calculates the environmental performance of a site and its environmental footprint (weight of greenhouse gas emissions and water consumption generated by the page) [10]. Other tools rely on a measurement system that takes into account user scenarios, like GreenFrame[4].

Development level. Many measurement tools are accessible to application designers with the aim of better managing the ecological footprint of the developed systems [13]. Sonar[5] has developed the SonarQube tool to detect clean code structures. Bad code may have a negative ecological impact so it is important to identify the cleanliness of the used code. Plugins can also be added to SonarQube, as Ecocode, a collective project aiming to reduce environmental footprint of software at code level. Based on a list of static code analysers it will highlight code structures that may have a negative ecological impact. Noureddine et al. [14] proposes Jolinar, a tool for measuring the energy consumption of an IT system. This tool is accessible to technical profiles (developers, architects) but also to less technical profiles through an intuitive interface. Noureddine et al. [14] shows that the choice of using an algorithm in an application can be crucial for the product's energy consumption.

Management level. The entire responsibility should not rest solely on the developers. Indeed, it is important that project managers, often higher-ups, are aware of this aspect and make decisions accordingly. Tools exists also for this level of responsibility, such as Econometria,[6] Quentic,[7] etc.

It is important to note that all the tools and methods mentioned in this section represent only a tiny portion of what exists in the market today. In summary, we can see that the ecological impact of any IT system is everyone's concern, and each person can contribute to the overall improvement of the process.

3.2   Solutions to Limit Consumption

In the literature, various types of solutions are available for addressing this issue. These solutions can be broadly categorized into technical solutions and functional solutions. To enhance readability and clarity, technical solutions are further divided into two parts based on their general purpose: those aimed at developing software with a primary goal of limiting resource consumption, and those designed without a primary focus on Green IT principles.

---

[2] https://theshiftproject.org/en/carbonalyser-browser-extension/.

[3] https://www.ecoindex.fr/.

[4] https://greenframe.io/.

[5] https://www.sonarsource.com/products/sonarcloud/.

[6] https://ecometrica.com/.

[7] https://www.quentic.com/.

Technical solutions for software whose primary goal is resource consumption limitation. Limiting resource consumption is crucial for sustainable development and environmental protection. By efficiently managing resources, we reduce waste, promote environmental sustainability, and contribute to economic resilience. This approach aligns with the principles of a circular economy, emphasizing the reuse and recycling of materials to minimize environmental impact. Recognizing the importance of resource consumption limitation is vital for maintaining a balance between human development and environmental well-being. We can find several solutions of this type in the literature, such as Power API, SmartWatts, JoularJX, etc.

Power API is a tool developed by the University of Lille. It is intended to serve as a toolbox for measuring the power consumption of a program. Applications built using PowerAPI are referred to as PowerMeters [15]. A PowerMeter can then measure the power consumed by a machine or a group of machines. This calculation can be done either in real-time or retrospectively once the monitored software is no longer in use. This type of tool can be very relevant in a Cloud context for managing the power allocated to the containers used. Indeed, by measuring and analyzing real-time consumption, it is possible to adapt configurations such as the CPU of a container. The SmartWatts software also proposes a concept of this type [15].

JoularJX[8] is a tool that allows tracking the evolution of energy consumption by method. The real added value here is the granularity of the process. It is interesting for the developer to know which method is responsible for a potential excess consumption.

Technical solutions for software not primarily designed with a Green IT perspective. Here, it is interesting to explore how the usage of such software can be modeled to achieve Green benefits. Let's take the example of Kubernetes.[9] It is an open-source container orchestration system widely used to automate the deployment, scaling, and management of containerized applications. Its primary function is the management of deployments and their configurations. However, Kubernetes also offers the possibility of configuring automatic scaling of its clusters. This feature allows optimizing resource utilization without compromising application performance.

Functional solutions. There are functional/organizational solutions that can be used in a software. For instance, the "Software Carbon Intensity (SCI)" methodology is proposed.[10] It is based on energy consumption, carbon intensity, and additional carbon emissions related to the amount of carbon emitted during the construction and recycling of the hardware used. The goal of this measurement is to provide a relevant indicator of the eco-design level of a product. The SCI then helps make decisions regarding the system design of an application to directly influence related carbon emissions.

---

[8] https://www.noureddine.org/articles/joularjx-2-A-leap-forward-in-green-software-analysis.

[9] https://kubernetes.io/.

[10] https://sci.greensoftware.foundation/.

3.3 Sustainable Business Models

The development of sustainable business models represents an innovative element of business strategy. Various industries and business categories have employed these models to concurrently address their economic, environmental, and social objectives. There is an increasing amount of works on sustainable business model (a simple search on the Scopus database with the keyword "sustainable business model" shows around 1000 results only for the last 4 years. Nosratabadi et al. [16] proposes four main types of solutions: designing a sustainable value proposition, designing sustainable value creation, designing sustainable value delivering, and generating sustainable partnership networks for creating and delivering such sustainable value which can meet the social, environmental, and economic benefits at the same time.

Böttcher et al. [17] highlight four types of business models that depend on the context: Sustainable Software Solution, Sustainable Product-Service System, Sustainability intelligence, and Digital Sustainable Platform.

- *Sustainable Software Solution.* This involves selling software with features that can impact the client's resource consumption. This model is most commonly found in a B2B context and corresponds to what is called "IT for green" solutions. Let's look into the following example: a company currently offers a range of training and advice on various ways to save water consumption. Here, the business model could evolve by introducing software that allows customers to measure the evolution of their water consumption. In doing so, this company takes advantage of securing and retaining its customer base. It is the same kind of business model utilized by CarbonScore, the company presented by our 3rd interviewee.
- *Sustainable Product-Service System.* This model combines the sale of products and services by offering sustainable options for both. A simple example of this business model is the rental of a product rather than its sale. Often, the company takes advantage of this to sell additional IT services related to the product. For instance, A company sells phones with interchangeable components (as the Fairphone[11] company). Here, a service related to the product is its maintenance, often involving simply replacing one of the product's components rather than the entire device.
- *Sustainability intelligence.* These solutions integrate data analytics with sustainability techniques to offer transparency in companies' ecological sustainability assessments. This kind of solution helps to support sustainable decision-making and identify new sustainability improvement opportunities.
- *Digital Sustainable Platform.* This involves the establishment of a circular exchange platform, often aimed at individuals. This platform can be used to address specific environmental issues and help promote a circular economy. The Too Good To Go platform is a very good example of a circular economic platform.

However, as highlighted by our interviewees, it is important to be wary of potential negative rebound effects from this type of platform.

---

[11] https://www.fairphone.com/.

4 Eco-Conscious Software Development Guide

In this section, we present a guide that draws its logic from both the analyzed state of the art and the interviews conducted with professionals in the field. Sustainability in the development process impact three aspects: the business model, the development and the management. The highlighted idea here is the necessity of combining these three different aspects to effectively establish sustainable development within a company. It is essential to note that, in the context of initiating responsible digital transformation, it is possible to have implemented only two or even just one of these aspects. For instance, the transformation can start with choices made by the management and subsequently evolve over time to complete implementation and business model aspects.

4.1 The Importance of a Sustainable Business Model

We highlighted the importance of implementing a sustainable business model in Sect. 3. A business model outlines how value is created, delivered to customers, and captured by the company. It serves as a mediating framework that aligns overarching business strategies with operational processes, playing a crucial role in achieving a competitive advantage that directly influences a company's performance [17].

Sustainable business models influences all the stakeholders, as shown in Fig. 3.

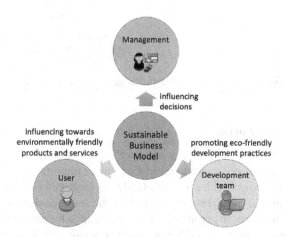

Fig. 3. Influences of a sustainable business model

The holistic approach depicted in this figure helps illustrate how the various aspects of eco-design interconnect to create a sustainable ecosystem in the development and use of products and services. Sustainable business models influence the decisions made by the management; they also influence the development team by promoting development practices which satisfy sustainable requirements; but they also influence the users in their choices of sustainable products and services.

4.2 Impact Sensitive Management

Management must also consider sustainability. By applying the company's sustainable policy, certain impact requirements must be considered throughout the development process.

We illustrate the management activities to consider these impacts by using the MAP formalism [18] to show the high level of abstraction of the process (see Fig. 4). The management has to satisfy two main intentions: to define and to validate the impact requirements.

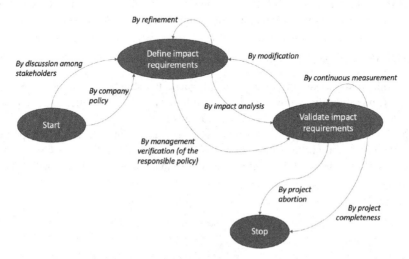

Fig. 4. Impacts requirements management process model

Define impacts requirements

By discussion among stakeholders. The manager's role is to bring together all project stakeholders. This step is necessary to inform and, more importantly, clarify the objectives inherent to the project with each stakeholder. Indeed, before the implementation begins, it is crucial that all stakeholders align on the same goals. To achieve this, it is relevant for the manager to organize dedicated meetings for these discussions. During these exchanges, managers of different involved teams discuss the possibilities of implementing the solution based on the resources and skills of their respective teams.

By company policy. A sustainability or responsible policy outlines an organization's commitment to integrating environmentally friendly, socially responsible, and ethical practices into its operations. It includes reducing environmental impact, promoting fair labor practices, transparent governance, sustainable supply chains, circular economy principles, and innovation for environmentally friendly products. This policy reflects a long-term commitment to social and environmental responsibility, meeting the expectations of stakeholders, including consumers, investors, employees, and society.

By modification. If the requirements are not completely validated, it is possible to update the project and the impact requirements. In this case, the management will need to undergo another impact analysis to ensure that the changes align with the policy.

Validate impact requirements. During the project framing, the manager is responsible for ensuring that it adheres to the eco-design guidelines established by their leadership and aligned with the sustainable business model.

By management verification. The project validation is not subject to an impact analysis. This scenario can occur when the project in question is directly aligned with the goal of improving the environmental footprint of the company.

By impact analysis. The manager can delegate team members to conduct an impact analysis. This task may resemble a traditional feasibility study for a project.

By continuous measurement. As soon as the implementation of the solution begins, the manager must ensure the monitoring of environmental impact indicators. It involves verifying predefined indicators, especially during the impact analysis. To ensure the relevance of these measures throughout the project, it is necessary to repeat them periodically. For example, in a project following monthly delivery cycles, it may be relevant to measure the impacts before each production release.

Stop. There are two ways to stop this process. Either the project is aborted (*By project abortion*) or everything has been going well and the impact requirements have all been validated correctly for this project (*By project completeness*).

4.3 Approaches for Eco-Conscious Development

In this section, we address best practices and processes to be applied by members of the development team. We present two different processes based on the context: either the solution is completely new or it is a solution already existing but requiring a redesign to enhance sustainability.

Redesign of an existing solution. Here, the goal is to propose a relevant process in the context of redesigning an application solution already in use within a company. The objective is to maintain the application, add new features, and potentially decommission other functionalities. The first step is to list all existing functionalities of the system. Then, for each functionality, an assessment is needed with the aim of making a decision. The following decision tree (Fig. 5) serves as a guide for this decision-making process.

This diagram includes some tools mentioned earlier to illustrate some tool possibilities. The use of this tree is valuable for classifying needs for each part of the project (here separated into functionalities).

Implementation of a new solution. This involves a thorough analysis of the stated need. The comprehensive analysis of the specifications should enable the establishment of various implementation scenarios. These scenarios may differ, particularly in the choices of application design. It may, therefore, be relevant to conduct feasibility studies upfront based on the various implementation possibilities. Table 2 shows that there are three possible decisions for choosing the implementation of a feature, depending on the

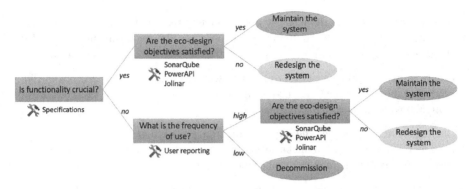

Fig. 5. Decision tree on the functionalities

importance of the functionality and its environmental impact. The feature can either be automatically implemented or discontinued, but it can also be studied more in-depth.

Table 2. Decision matrix for functionalities.

Functionality importance	Bad impact	Average impact	Good impact
Facultative	To phase out	To phase out	To study deeper
Useful	To phase out	To study deeper	To implement
Crucial	To study deeper	To implement	To implement

For each feasibility study, we establish the list of features that matched with the matrix above. Subsequently, the results of each study can be compared, and a decision can be made on the most interesting combination of functionalities. To make this decision, it is necessary to present the various possible scenarios to end-users. Involving users in the design process helps facilitate the decision-making on the scenario to implement. At the same time, it provides users with a better understanding of development choices, especially regarding features that are not feasible.

4.4 A Multi-level Approach for Improved Sustainability

We can illustrate the proposed guide with a multi-level approach, as shown in Fig. 6. This figure shows the interactions between the different levels and how the diverse activities can impact the artefacts and the next activities. Moving from top to bottom, we have the business model, management, and implementation levels.

We start from the left at the business model level. The initial and arguably most crucial step is critically analyzing the existing business model within the company to recognize opportunities for improvement and alignment with one of the patterns discussed above. Once we've chosen the pattern that best fits, we initiate the transition toward this new business model. This marks the descent into the management domain.

The leadership team articulates the new model through the initial projects stemming from it. Then, the task then falls to the management, to select the team, manage implementation resources, and breathe life into the first project.

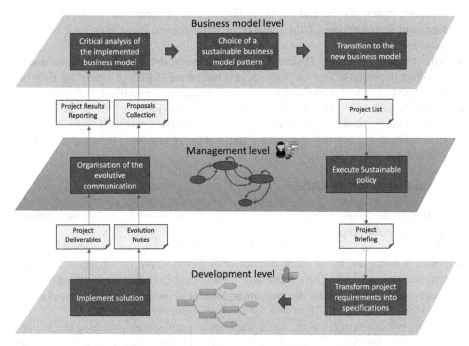

Fig. 6. Interactions between the different levels

The implementation team's primary mission is, of course, to develop the solution. However, it extends beyond that, initiating a bottom-up logic. Implementation teams may possess insights that those at higher levels, whether in management or leadership, might not have. Therefore, it's valuable to gather their opinions and ideas to potentially evolve the business model.

It becomes the management's responsibility to orchestrate this evolving communication, ensuring it travels upward to the highest level—back to the business model—and then engaging in discussions for continuous improvement. This process ultimately forms a loop that continues.

In addition to this summary diagram highlighting the interactions between the three levels, it is interesting to detail the content and purpose of each of the artifacts:

- The project list: Once a business model pattern is selected, the management begins to establish projects that address the needs arising from the new BM. The projects are then allocated among the different management teams.
- The project briefing: For each project, the manager must carry out a document. Including various elements: Identification of different stakeholders, Distribution of responsibilities among people, Definition of project objectives, Identification of the risks, and Definition of all project deliverables to be provided.

- Project deliverables: This refers to all the documents to be provided at the end of the project. Numerous elements may be included depending on the project context: Documentation, Product user manual, Specifications, Functional prototype, and so on.
- Evolution notes: At the end of the project, the implementation team produces a document summarizing all the remarks or improvement ideas submitted by team members.
- Project results reporting: Following project delivery, the management team needs to collect the results. This involves success indicators (KPIs). A report can then be generated based on a predefined time period (3 months, 6 months, 1 year).
- Proposals collection: This involves translating the previously established evolution notes by the implementation team. Managers must first assess the feasibility of the ideas submitted. They can also support these ideas by providing resource plans able of translating these ideas into projects.

5   Evaluation of the Guide

We validated the guide through another round of interviews to gather the experts' perspectives on the proposed guidelines.

This allowed us to validate certain elements that had not been discussed with all respondents during the initial round of interviews. For example, the impact of having a specific business model was only addressed by two of our interviewees, but this proposal was appreciated by all during the evaluation. Similarly, the process recommended for management was refined to align with the feedback from our respondents.

All interviewees endorsed the multi-level figure proposal, emphasizing the importance of having this holistic view of the problem and highlighting the relevance of the proposed cycle.

6   Conclusion

The aim of this study was to provide a guide to lead the development process towards a more sustainable approach.

We looked into the literature in order to define the key elements to a sustainable development, interviewed four experts, and presented our guide, the result of our study. This guide is based on exchanges between the three layers: business model, management, and implementation. It stresses about the importance to use a sustainable business model to guide a sustainable approach. It looks more closely on the managing process of impacts requirements at the management level. It offers guidelines in the implementation of a solution, if the main goal is to transform an existing solution into a more sustainable one or if it is to implement a brand new solution.

To continue this work, we first plan to execute a more complete evaluation of the proposed guide to complete our study. We then plan to conduct a systematic literature review to extract best practices in this domain (for instance, does open-source collaboration or the use of agile methodologies offers a more sustainable approach to the development?). These practices will be linked to the guide, enhancing its capability to provide more effective guidance within the context of eco-design.

References

1. TheShiftProject: Déployer la sobriété numérique, Rapport TheShiftProject (2020)
2. Hassmann, T., Westner, W.: Conceptualizing sustainability in the context of ICT. In: A literature review analysis. Conference on Computer Science and Intelligence Systems (FedCSIS 2023), Warsaw, Poland (2023)
3. Ergasheva, S., Khomyakov, I., Kruglov, A., Succi, G.: Metrics of energy consumption in software systems: a systematic literature review. IOP Conf. Ser. Earth Environ. Sci. (2019)
4. Lami, G., Fabbrini, F., Fusani, M.: A methodology to derive sustainability indicators for software development projects. In: International Conference on Software and System Process (2013)
5. Kiesl, F.: Metrics for Measuring Greenability in Web-based Software Systems. Johannes Kepler University Linz (2021)
6. Pereira, M., Ribeiro, F., Saraiva, J.: Towards a Green Ranking for Programming Languages. Universidade do Minho (2017)
7. Van der Merwe, A., Gerber, A., Smuts, H.: Guidelines for conducting design science research in information systems. In: Annual Conference of the Southern African Computer Lecturers' Association. Springer International Publishing, Cham (2019)
8. Edwards, R., Holland, J.: What is Qualitative Interviewing?, p. 128. Bloomsbury Academic (2013)
9. Wang, F., Kuehr, R., Ahlquist, D., Li, J.: E-Waste in China, A Country Report. United Nations University (2013)
10. Watson, A.H., Wallace, D.R., McCabe, T.J.: Structured Testing: A Testing Methodology Using the Cyclomatic Complexity Metric, vol. 500, No. 235. US Department of Commerce, Technology Administration, National Institute of Standards and Technology (1996)
11. Singh, V.K., Dutta, K., VanderMeer, D.: Estimating the energy consumption of executing software processes. In: 2013 IEEE International Conference on Green Computing and Communications and IEEE Internet of Things and IEEE Cyber, Physical and Social Computing, pp. 94–101, Beijing, China (2013)
12. Sun, X., Zhang, Q., Medina, M.A., Liu, Y., Liao, S.: A study on the use of phase change materials (PCMs) in combination with a natural cold source for space cooling in telecommunications base stations (TBSs) in China. Appl. Energy 117, 95–103 (2014)
13. Josephson, C., Peill-Moelter, N., Pan, Z., Pfaff, B., Firoiu, V.: The sky is not the limit: untapped opportunities for green computing. ACM Sigenergy Energy Inform. Rev. 3(3), 33–39 (2023)
14. Noureddine, A., Islam, S., Bashroush, R.: Jolinar: Analysing the energy footprint of software applications (demo). In: The International Symposium on Software Testing and Analysis (2016)
15. Fieni, G., Rouvoy, R., Seinturier, L.: Smartwatts: Self-calibrating software-defined power meter for containers. In: 2020 20th IEEE/ACM International Symposium on Cluster, Cloud and Internet Computing (CCGRID), pp. 479–488. IEEE (2020)
16. Nosratabadi, S., Mosavi, A., Shamshirband, S., Zavadskas, E.K., Rakotonirainy, A., Chau, K.W.: Sustainable business models: a review. Sustainability 11(6) (2019)
17. Böttcher, T.P., Empelmann, S., Weking, J., Hein, A., Krcmar, H.: Digital sustainable business models: using digital technology to integrate ecological sustainability into the core of business models. Inf. Syst. J. (2023)
18. Rolland, C., Prakash, N., Benjamen, A.: A Multi-Model View of Process Modelling, Requirements Engineering, vol. 4, no. 4. Springer-Verlag London Ltd. (1999)

Towards a New Method for Designing Manufacturing Capabilities

Anouck Chan[1] (ID), Janis Stirna[2(✉)] (ID), Jelena Zdravkovic[2] (ID), Thomas Polacsek[1] (ID),
Simon Hacks[2] (ID), Janis Grabis[3] (ID), and Claudio Favi[4] (ID)

[1] ONERA, Toulouse, France
{anouck.chan,thomas.polacsek}@onera.fr
[2] Stockholm University, Kista, Sweden
{js,jelenaz,simon.hacks}@dsv.su.se
[3] Riga Technical University, Riga, Latvia
grabis@rtu.lv
[4] University of Parma, Parma, Italy
claudio.favi@unipr.it

Abstract. Many industries are experiencing the challenges and opportunities associated with the rapid pace of technological change. In manufacturing, the adoption of new materials and manufacturing processes is a common concern, for example, the use of new composite materials offer significant advantages in terms of energy efficiency and performance. However, their use poses challenges in terms of manufacturing and assembly. On the side of technological advances, the exploration of digitalisation, automation and robotics to improve efficiency is a strong trend. However, implementing these technologies requires investment and significant changes to existing assembly processes. To meet these challenges, fostering collaboration between design and manufacturing, as well as between manufacturer and its suppliers is often seen as the key solution for various industries. In this work, we present how capability modelling can help both parties to describe their demands and offers with respect to needed and provided quality properties such as set-up times or ecological footprint. These serve as input for a digital business ecosystem in which the pareto-optimal factory design can be chosen supported by a digital platform integrating the manufacturer and its suppliers.

Keywords: Capabilities for manufacturing · Digital business ecosystem · Manufacturing as a service · Concurrent engineering

1 Introduction

Manufacturing has been profoundly influenced by emerging digitalization technologies including Industrial IoTs, smart manufacturing, digital twins, AI, and cybersecurity [1]. Several global trends, such as climate change, globalisation of supply chains, shift towards servitiation, and a redistribution of power between established economies and upcoming powers are also heavily influencing the manufacturing business domain [2].

A. Lupeikienė et al. (Eds.): DB&IS 2024, CCIS 2157, pp. 34–49, 2024.
https://doi.org/10.1007/978-3-031-63543-4_3

To remain competitive under such evolving technological and business conditions, manufacturing companies need to be flexible towards changing demands and external factors, as well as capable for exploiting the new digital technologies to their highest extent. Many manufacturing companies need, for example, to improve *manufacturing design* to reduce climate footprint, as well as to make *manufacturing execution* more efficient by being able to reorganise the production capabilities to new and often ground-breaking products, according to new market conditions, or for meeting some urgent needs that are emerging crisis related [3]. One for the key rationales for coming up with new approaches in design and execution, supported by novel digital technologies, is making an impact on future manufacturing by smoothing the cooperation between factories and suppliers and other actors involved in the production. This can be achieved, among other things, by transitioning from siloed manufacturing units or companies toward collabora-tive engineering—for facilitating manufacturing as a service. Cooperation allows for the early identification of potential problems in the design that may affect the manufacturing process, which can help to make adjustments before production (i.e. execution) begins, reducing the risk of costly errors; as well as it enables the optimisation of manufacturing processes.

This aim requires reorganising the existing and the development of new capabilities, also being able to reproduce previous effective outcomes. From the IT perspective, such challenges call for having new methods, accompanied with software architectures and tools that would support design and execution of manufacturing capabilities, including algorithms calculating needed adjustments according to various data parameters, internal and external to manufacturing companies and their partners networks.

An effective way to enable manufacturing companies to address these challenges is to make a better use of manufacturing capabilities. Currently they are too dependent on the business context for which they have been designed and too tightly coupled to the fea-tures of the produced product so the extent of their application and reuse in other contexts and for other products is limited. So far, the research on capability-based system devel-opment has considered configuration of capability components according to changing environment and business indicators [4], but those solutions are not encompassing the setting spanning several, even many organizations that collaborating and co-designing, nor approaches to their reuse; for these needs Digital Business Ecosystem (DBE) model has been recently in consideration by different researchers and practitioners [5].

DBEs are interconnected networks of organisations, individuals and technologies that collaborate and transact within the digital setting [6]. They are characterised by their complex and evolving nature due to the involvement of diverse actors each having unique interests, responsibilities, and requirements, while interacting through a wide range of digital assets and activities, including online platforms, digital services, and data exchanges that need to be continuously integrated and interoperable. These charac-teristics, in turn, boost the magnitude of the involved entities and tasks, leading to various challenges and difficulties in efficient DBE management [7, 8]. Yet, [9] finds that DBE studies with different kind of actors are few, while well-designed industry ecosystem architectures are not many. Because enterprise modelling techniques have been proven for enabling analysis of complex business settings, they may complement DBE design by bringing agility and resilience to it [5].

To this end, the goals of this paper are:

- *to report the cases of three manufacturing companies and summarise the challenges that they currently face in product design and execution*
- *outline an approach for developing an integrated and extendable method and platform for configurable factory (i.e. manufacturing design and execution).*

The rest of the paper is structured as follows. Section 2 presents a background to manufacturing and capability management. Section 3 presents the research approach. Section 4 presents a summary of the industrial challenges and initial requirements. Section 5 presents the envisioned method. In Sect. 6, conclusions are provided.

2 Background to Manufacturing and Capability Management

2.1 Manufacturing

Objectives and constraints within factories influence the design of a product—the link between the two aspects often leads to collaborative, concurrent or simultaneous engineering [9]. These approaches suggest involving different engineering teams working simultaneously and collaboratively to achieve the best possible design in terms of manufacturing. For instance, it is mainly used in the automotive supply chain, where the focus has long been on addressing manufacturability issues. In this context, approaches primarily address the physical components of a system and endeavors to design elements that can be assembled efficiently or have the optimal assembly sequence [10]. In aeronautics, some works propose to consider the impact of an aircraft design on its assembly line design in order to choose the optimal product design and assembly line [11]. Other methodologies focused on the conceptual design phase with the aim to optimize product architecture that increase the plant capabilities while keeping the physical constraints [12]. Starting from early requirements, they highlight the dependencies and, based on an optimization tool, they search for an optimal global system. In this context, a pivotal role is played by the well-known Design for Assembly (DFA) and Design for Manufacturing (DFM) approaches. DFM specifies a set of design rules to meet or improve production conditions, with the objective of increasing a product's manufacturability. DFM endeavors to create decision-making methods to incorporate manufacturing issues into product design choices [13]. Since the first approaches developed at the beginning of 1980 when analytical tools were made available to guide designers towards products that are easy to manufacture and assemble, these techniques created a revolution in the manufacturing industry and they evolved to a more concrete integration of product and process design [13]. The concurrent design of manufacturing and assembly systems is recognized as a modern industry challenge in reference to the I4.0 paradigm and the product customization requirements reflected in agile manufacturing [12]. The idea of coupling process and product design is also an emerging trend when environmental concerns need to be tackled. New design requirements emerged in terms of product de-manufacturing for the circular economy (e.g., repair, remanufacture, recycle), life cycle engineering (LCA, LCC, and SocialLCA) and supply chain management which foster the integration of product and process design (including manufacturing and de-manufacturing as well) [14].

Our study wants to tackle the challenge to close the gap between the product development process and the manufacturing system design, tackling the modern challenges of product customization, agile production and manufacturing reconfiguration, focusing on the emerging trends such as life cycle engineering, and circular economy.

2.2 Capability Management, Digital Business Ecosystem, and Digital Twins

Capability thinking has been widely adopted in the area of Enterprise Architecture Management for the purpose of organisational design, (see [15] for a comparison of capability use). It is an approach to designing enterprise-wide information systems on the basis of capability components [4]. Lately capability management has been extended by open data processing for the purpose of ensuring that business capabilities can be adjusted and configured dynamically at run-time [16]. Data stream processing is used to analyse data supporting capability management and analytical tools like digital twins used to evaluate the required adjustment. Capability thinking also is closely related to business ecosystem management [5].

Digital Twin (DT) is a notion intensively researched recently in computer science and business information systems, defined as a virtual representation of a physical object or system that uses real-time data to enable understanding, learning and reasoning using a bi-directional connection between the physical twin and itself [17]. Despite the rapid technological advancements and industry-wide discussions, technical implementations and adaptation of DTs are still being explored.

In the domain of production systems, DTs lead manufacturing into a new era of efficiency and intelligence. These virtual models offer a detailed and dynamic representation of physical production processes, enabling manufacturers to simulate, analyze, and optimize operations in real time. For instance, DTs facilitate a deeper understanding and control over production processes and hence improve efficiency of operations and decision-making [18]. DT, integrated within hybrid production systems, can significantly augment the responsiveness and adaptability of manufacturing operations to market changes and technological advancements [19]. Moreover, DTs can be applied in smart factories to achieve a more responsive and interconnected production environment [20]. Accordingly, DTs in production systems are not just a technological upgrade but a strategic asset that enables manufacturers to foresee challenges, streamline processes, and foster innovation, ultimately leading to enhanced competitiveness and sustainability in the fast-evolving industrial landscape.

Going beyond the state of the art, the study will propose the principles of resilient digital business ecosystem design for achieving configurable factories based on the capabilities the ecosystem needs, including with what performance indicators indicated by engineered DT, and what the actors offer and by what data is that documented.

3 Research Design

The research project follows the design science research (DSR) process proposed in [21] and is currently in the phase of problem explication and early requirements elicitation. Nevertheless, considering the iterative nature of the DSR we have already begun to construct the initial architecture of the envisioned design artefacts, namely, a method and a supporting platform for manufacturing design and execution. The initial problem and requirements have been investigated in collaboration with three companies (cf. Table 1) operating in different manufacturing sectors with respect to their needs of customizing manufacturing capabilities.

Table 1. Over of the companies involved in the investigation

	Company A	Company B	Company C
Industry sector	Aeronautics	Mechatronics	Construction
Primary products	Aircraft	Professional coffee makers and grinders	Timber frame houses
Type of company	Large	SME	SME
Stakeholders interviewed Unstructured interviews and discussions about the business needs	Three experts responsible for product design and for manufacturing design One executive from a company supplying aircraft components	COO responsible for product and manufacturing design	Experts and designers responsible for manufacturing design and execution

4   Industrial Challenges and Needs

Manufacturing processes are of two main phases, namely, manufacturing engineering and manufacturing execution. Manufacturing engineering is designing the production processes and technologies, while manufacturing execution is the actual production process. Concerning the manufacturing engineering phase, (1) factories need to be designed concurrently with the products and (2) the supplier onboarding process needs to be accelerated and standardised using a system engineering digital framework with a focus on the manufacturing system of interest. This phase should include manufacturing performance simulations and visualisations. This also requires support for the identification and assessment of the supplier capabilities in terms of the expected level of performance. This will also support the co-design of the product where the supplier is involved as a partner to propose any kind of improvement idea. This aspect of co-design also requires a discussion with respect to the trade-offs concerning the product and manufacturing designs.

Concerning the manufacturing execution phase, (1) performance of the production processes needs to be monitored, (2) supplier performance needs to be monitored, and (3) in case performance criteria are not met, corrective actions need to be executed. In the same fashion, when a factory is not used or when it has an excess of production capacity, it needs to be adapted to produce other types of products to not waste re-sources (raw materials or production resources). To adjust the manufacturing capabilities during manufacturing execution requires the analysis and optimization of a large number of criteria and parameters originating from an organisation's strategy and business design as well as operational execution performance.

Company A operates in an industry that has very high requirements for manufacturing quality, including for aircraft safety and its environmental footprint. Any kind of new manufacturing contract is based on a dedicated qualification process where the supplier has to demonstrate the manufacturing capability according to different criteria such as cost, ability to ramp-up, quality, sustainability parameters. The decisions concerning suppliers is made during the manufacturing engineering phase, supported by a digital factory. But once the production starts, Company A needs to have support for continuous performance monitoring during manufacturing execution, supported by a manufacturing execution system. Company A needs to prepare the manufacturing service suppliers to systematise the supplier onboarding process, to make then able to answer quickly to calls for tenders where variability and modularity are key competitive factors. From the supplier point of view their intention for which they need support is to be flexible and to supply high-quality components.

Company B produces premium coffee machines and grinders for professional use. Its manufacturing challenges include adapting to evolving market demands and integrating new, environmentally sustainable methods in manufacturing processes, to quickly respond to changing requirements, including related to circular economy business strategies, product repair, product upgradability. Due to the large number of variants the products are mainly made to order, and in some cases designed to order. The problems involve overcoming traditional manufacturing constraints and updating technological infrastructure. The manufacturing processes should also support the concept of life cycle engineering and product eco-design. The intension is to use recycled materials or material scraps from synergic industries and in that way participating in a sustainable production ecosystem. Company B also follows the principles for design for disassembly to foster circular economies by refurbished/repaired/upgraded machines. Company B seeks to develop a new, dynamic approach to manufacturing, incorporating digital tools and innovative processes that support rapid adaptation and ecological sustainability. This solution aims to make manufacturing more agile, efficient, and sustainable.

Company C produces timber frame houses, modules, and structures. Its orders often change in terms of volume and requirements. Increased demand requires additional resources and attracting subcontractors. Currently these tasks are managed manually. An additional need arises in situations when Company C does not have available technological solutions/equipment or it is not feasible to purchase such equipment (e.g., large-format woodworking machines). Currently subcontractor or partners onboarding is hard work done manually and the range of subcontractors ends up narrower than it could be. Moreover, there is a risk of lost revenues if a cooperation partner is able to produce the same with existing resources and at a lower cost. Company C needs to establish a capability-based process of manufacturing that involves suppliers as well as customers (e.g., real estate developers, entering a partnership).

The business needs of the surveyed companies concern both phases of manufacturing, namely, manufacturing engineering and manufacturing execution. Manufacturing engineering is designing the production processes and technologies, while manufacturing execution if the actual production process.

Concerning the manufacturing engineering phase, (1) factories need to be designed concurrently with the products and (2) the supplier onboarding process needs to be accelerated and standardised using a system engineering digital framework with a focus on the manufacturing system of interest. This phase should include manufacturing performance simulations and visualisations. This also requires support for the identification and assessment of the supplier capabilities in terms of the expected level of performance. This will also support the co-design of the product where the supplier is involved as a partner to propose any kind of improvement idea. This aspect of co-design also requires a discussion with respect to the trade-offs concerning the product and manufacturing designs.

Concerning the manufacturing execution phase, (1) performance of the production processes needs to be monitored, (2) supplier performance needs to be monitored, and (3) in case performance criteria are not met, corrective actions need to be executed. With the same aim in mind, when a factory is not used or when it has an excess of production capacity, it needs to be adapted to produce other types of products to not waste resources (raw materials or production resources). To adjust the manufacturing capabilities during manufacturing execution requires the analysis and optimization of a large number of criteria and parameters originating from an organisation's strategy and business design as well as operational execution performance.

5   Method for Capability Design and Management

A way towards addressing the challenges, is to provide means to select manufacturing capabilities according to the business objectives of the company and the features of the product at the same time when designing a factory, when reconfiguring a production process, or when designing a product. With regard to the existing manufacturing capabilities that need to be extended and optimised, this needs to be done on the basis of data such as process execution performance data, KPIs, and situational context data. This data needs to be processed and included as design requirements as well as they need to be considered when existing manufacturing processes need to be customised. An additional challenge to this is the need to be able to deal with data from suppliers and business partners, which should be able to specify what data they expose to others and monitor their data security. Doing these tasks efficiently also increases the resilience of manufacturing and, transitively, of the company and its suppliers. Being able to adjust to change in a speedy and controlled manner lies at the heart of capability thinking and capability management.

The envisioned approach will integrate business goal and task modelling, capability management, digital twins, virtual reality, as well as AI and optimization into a coherent approach to design and operation of manufacturing. Since a significant aspect of ensuring manufacturing flexibility is management and coordination of suppliers and business partners it will be supported by incorporating the principles of business ecosystem management as part of the capability modelling work.

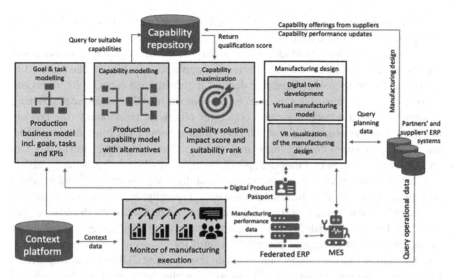

Fig. 1. Overview of the envisioned approach, method components and key artefacts

Figure 1 shows an overview of the envisioned approach. Following the principles of situational method engineering [22], it consists of a number of method components named by the key concepts that they address. The method for manufacturing design and execution also needs to be supported by a set of software components integrated in a *platform* the responsibility of which is the coordination and scheduling among the components. The method is envisioned to have (1) a baseline method targeting general needs of manufacturing design and execution, and (2) a set of method extensions targeting the specific manufacturing needs and business goals tailored for applications in specific industry sectors. The aim of the base method is to offer a generic and customisable method and the aim of the method extensions is to capture the lessons learned from real application cases. The baseline method is envisioned to have of the following components:

1. *Business goal and task modelling.* The purpose of this method component is to specify what are the business objectives of the product and the manufacturing process, KPIs on the business level. A business goal represents intentions that the company wishes to achieve or avoid on any level of abstraction (strategic or operational). KPI expresses a measurable indicator for monitoring a company's performance concerning goal achievement or capability performance. When a business is designed, goals are associated with KPIs that will measure their achievement. When the business is run this is realised by calculating KPI values from data originating, for example, from the ERP systems. This method component will also specify what are the manufacturing tasks, what are the detailed goals for the tasks and the detailed KPI to be measured and KPI target values for each business case manufacturing. Including the goals and expected KPIs that can be satisfied by involving external suppliers. A business ecosystem analysis will also be a part of this method component to consider the interactions of all actors involved in or affected by the manufacturing process

to ensure resilience of the process. This method component is based on an existing enterprise modelling method, namely, 4EM [23].

2. *Manufacturing Capability Modelling*. The purpose of this method component is to specify which organisation's capabilities or suppliers' capabilities can be used to deliver the business goals. Capability denotes the ability and capacity for an organisation to achieve a business goal in a certain context. It will be used for the purpose of analysing what a company can produce (or otherwise contribute to the production), for what purpose, within which performance parameters (measured by KPIs) and in which business context (measured by internal and external context data). Our view on capabilities is that they are specific to an actor who possesses the capability and that they are specific to a context for which they are designed/offered in which they perform within the specified parameters. Typically, manufacturing goals and tasks can be implemented by several capabilities and depending on the desired goal KPIs and historical capability performance data, several capabilities and capability configurations can be seen as potentially useful for choosing as the manufacturing solution. This method component is based on results of the CDD—Capability Driven Development method in particular [4]. In addition, this component will be supported by an existing method component on digital business ecosystem (DBE) modelling [5]. The DBE modelling will be called upon when a manufacturing company wants to establish a long-lasting resilient network of suppliers essentially making it a manufacturing capability marketplace. Such an approach would considerably lighten the process of supplier onboarding.

3. *Capability Maximization*. The purpose of this method component is to choose a suitable manufacturing capability configuration to fulfil the business goals. This method component will also populate the capability models with historical data coming from organisation's ERP systems, suppliers' data that they have chosen to expose together with their capability offerings, as well as with relevant external context data such as energy prices, weather data, security information etc. This method component will create an impact score for each capability configuration alternative. The impact score will indicate how a capability solution is able to achieve the set KPI targets. There are numerous data inconsistencies in the distributed manufacturing process that will need to be resolved using machine learning models and Large Language Models (LLM). The LLM will be trained using the data in the capability repository, material and equipment specifications as well as historical production data and data shared by manufacturing service providers. Machine Learning models will be used to deduce additional constraints for the capability maximisation model, which will be formulated as a multi-objective mathematical programming model selecting manufacturing services providers and equipment for the distributed manufacturing process. The specific aspects such as resilience, security, and sustainability will be represented by incorporating penalty terms in the objective function and additional constraints induced using machine learning. Thus, the model will be a hybrid analytical-machine learning optimization model, which incorporates both quantitative and qualitative decision-making aspects. The capability maximisation output serves as a basis for optimization of case specific production planning aspects such as facility planning and tactical production scheduling. Optimization and AI services will be used for the manufacturing process to reduce important aspects such as set-up times, security,

safety, as well as environmental footprint. The production planning models will use robust optimization techniques to account for limitation of data availability in the distributed manufacturing setting because not all parties involved share all information. Intelligent optimization methods such as genetic algorithms will be used to solve the models. The optimization interacts with the digital twin component to explore uncertainties with strong emphasis on resilience and evaluation of the impact of external context such as disruptive events. The machine learning module suggests the aspects to highlight the areas of exploration.

4. *Digital Twin Development.* The purpose of this method component is to create a digital twin for the chosen capability configuration and the associated manufacturing processes. The method component will support model-based digital twin development from the business goals and tasks model and capability models [24]. This task will establish the integration mechanisms with the data specifications (on a type level) that were specified in the previous steps with the actual data sources and interfaces from their sources. Calculation algorithms for data representation will also need to be specified here. The digital twins will be used to simulate the chosen manufacturing designs and their performance.

5. *Virtual reality.* The purpose of this method component is to visualise the manufacturing process and the manufacturing design thus creating a virtual manufacturing model. It will significantly enhance the visualization and understanding of manufacturing processes and designs. This virtual reality component allows for an immersive and interactive experience, enabling engineers and designers to explore and evaluate manufacturing setups and workflows in a simulated environment before actual implementation. It provides a platform for identifying potential issues, optimizing space and resource usage, and experimenting with different configurations without the costs and risks associated with physical prototyping. The input to the VR tool includes detailed 3D models of the manufacturing layout, machinery, and processes, as well as data on materials, workflow, and ergonomics. The output is a highly realistic, interactive VR environment where stake-holders can virtually navigate, interact with, and assess the manufacturing design, leading to informed decisions, reduced time-to-market, and increased efficiency in the manufacturing process. This technology not only facilitates better design but also promotes collaboration and training, allowing diverse teams to work together seamlessly and understand complex manufacturing scenarios intuitively.

The components of the envisioned method will be used in two interlinked processes of manufacturing (see Fig. 2), namely, (i) design and deployment, and (ii) execution and feedback. More specifically,

I. *Manufacturing design and deployment.* During this phase the manufacturing solution is designed. The process starts by analysing the company's business vision and product design to elaborate a goals and tasks model of the manufacturing solution. This model is then further elaborated by analysing which company's capabilities are possible to use to fulfil the tasks and which capabilities need to be purchased from external suppliers and business partners. Since several solutions are possible the capability constellations need to be maximised with respect to their past performance and the business KPIs or the company, which requires capability optimisation.

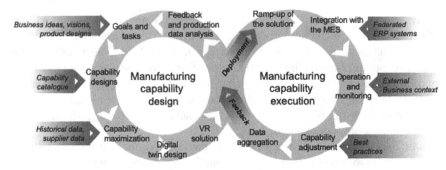

Fig. 2. The overall life cycle for manufacturing capability management

The available data that can be used for capability monitoring and optimization are also analysed during this phase. Once a capability solution has been chosen a digital twin and a VR solution is created to assess the manufacturing design. In some cases, the manufacturing solution is tested in a laboratory environment with simulated data. If the resulting solution's performance is satisfactory, then the solution is deployed, i.e., realised in the production environment.

II. *Manufacturing execution and feedback.* During this phase the manufacturing design is executed. More specifically, it is serialised and implemented in as many instances as necessary (ramp-up). This also requires integrating the envisioned platform with the MES and the ERP systems supporting the manufacturing process with relevant data. This phase will also require establishing connections with the suppliers and their information systems. The next step is to operate and monitor the performance of the process. This also requires monitoring of the external business context and taking in data originating from external sources. If undesired changes in the manufacturing performance are noticed or if the external context has changed to a state for which the capability was not designed, then capability adjustments need to be made, for instance, by using different best practices. This phase also collects and aggregates data that serves as feedback for the manufacturing capability design improvements.

5.1 A Meta-Model for a Modelling Language

The envisioned approach will use modelling for the purpose of capturing and documenting manufacturing designs and means of monitoring manufacturing execution. Hence a modelling method will be elaborated and for this purpose we present a meta-model of a modelling language. The language needs to support the method components one and two for the purposes of goal and task modelling as well as of capability modelling.

Figure 3 shows the overview of the modeling language. It consists of the following concepts:

- Capability: an ability and capacity that enable a company to achieve a goal in a certain context. A capability consists of a set of capability tasks that specify how it is implemented.
- Design solution: Is the combination of a capability, its tasks and a goal all of which have been chosen for a specific manufacturing design. That means the company has

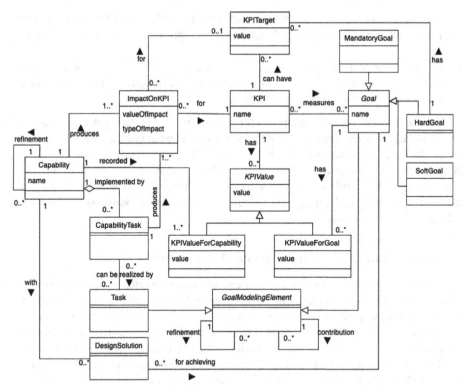

Fig. 3. Meta-model of the modeling language

selected a given capability and its implementation tasks allow to achieve the goal, and therefore the capability impacts on goal satisfaction.

- Task: Describes a set of actions to satisfy a goal. Task is an operationalization of a goal. Tasks can be used to express alternative ways of satisfying a goal. Some tasks are designed to be a part of a capability.
- Impact on KPI: Describes how the capability and its implementation tasks impact the target value of the KPI depending on the task chosen.
- KPI target: Expresses the level of qualification or quantification in terms of value that must achieved to satisfy the related goal.
- Goal: A situation that the company wants to achieve or avoid. Goals are of two types: Hard goals, the achievement of which can be measured by specifying KPITarget, and SoftGoals without explicitly defined criteria for achievement and measurement. Some HardGoals are seen as mandatory goals, for example the purpose of specifying business intensions that must be achieved.
- KPI: Key Performance Indicator expresses a measurable indicator for monitoring a company's performance concerning goal achievement or capability performance KPI is used to model the type of data to be used. Target values are modelled as KPI targets and runtime values as KPI values.
- KPI Value: represents a value for a given KPI.

- KPI Value for capability: is a value for each KPI on which the capability has an effect at a certain time of measuring. A set of values represent past performance of the capability.
- KPI Value for goal-KPI value for goal: is a value for each KPI used for measuring a particular goal at a certain time of measuring. A set of values represent historical data of how the goal has been satisfied.

The meta-model contains components that support manufacturing design on a general sense, e.g. to specify the needs of the company and what tasks are needed to make the product such as goals and tasks, components that are to specify the manufacturing design configuration such as capabilities offered by suppliers and a selected design solution starting which capabilities are used to deliver which tasks, as well as components used for monitoring and configuring manufacturing execution based on runtime data values, such as KPI values.

5.2 Manufacturing Design and Execution Environment

The manufacturing capability design and execution is supported by a computational platform. The platform should ensure the interoperability, scalability, and transferability and enable an optimized communication between the different actors in the manufacturing ecosystem. The envisioned platform (Fig. 4) is to be built on agreed and approved communication standards and account for those that are under on-going development.

The key functions of the modelling environment that serve as input for the optimization include capability modeling, which involves mapping and analyzing various manufacturing capacities. Visual modeling allows for graphical representation of these capabilities, enhancing understanding and communication. The environment also focuses on capability optimizing, and optimizing manufacturing processes for efficiency and effectiveness. Multi-criteria decision-making is supported, enabling complex decisions based on various operational factors. Manufacturing optimization is achieved through AI and data analytics, leveraging advanced technologies to refine and enhance production processes.

The platform's key functions revolve around the detailed specification of virtual manufacturing processes. This includes defining the input materials required, detailing the specific tasks involved, outlining the expected output product, and enumerating the resource requirements and sequencing of tasks.

In terms of data management, the platform features a federated data model with a domain-specific model. It allows for querying partners' ERP systems and managing master data. The control of access rights via tokens and management of data duplication and archiving are also integral, with partners having the autonomy to decide which data can be stored on the platform.

Further functionalities include partners' self-registration, role and data sharing setup, and real-time tracking of manufacturing processes. This encompasses querying transactional data and monitoring the status of processes. The platform also facilitates the population of digital product passports. Additionally, it provides a distributed manufacturing portal with workspaces for monitoring and accessing both platform and external components. These workspaces are tailored for specific use cases and integrate data spaces, mapping model specifications to frameworks like Gaia-X/IDS, and extracting data from relevant spaces. A key component is the capability repository and the use of a virtual twin that utilizes the platform's data infrastructure for accessing data.

The IT architecture of the platform is structured around a modular microservices-based approach, which segments the architecture into small, independently functioning services. Central to this architecture is the use of capability and decision-making models as web resources, accessible through an API gateway. This design simplifies interactions between different components and facilitates integration with external systems. Additionally, an identity management server is a crucial component, responsible for managing user identities and authentication. This server reinforces secure access and controls permissions within the platform.

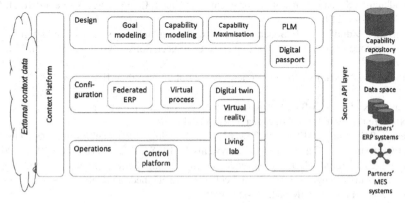

Fig. 4. Overview of the envisioned platform

6 Conclusions and Future Work

We have presented an outline of industrial requirements and an approach to support a holistic and efficient manufacturing process. Feature of the envisioned solution emphasizes customization, flexibility, and responsiveness to meet the requirements for high quality on-demand products and short production runs. A key innovation lies in its focus on sustainable and circular manufacturing practices, product co design, and dynamic reconfiguration of manufacturing executing, particularly relevant for small and medium-sized enterprises (SMEs). The capability-based management also supports exploration of novel business models of engaging with customers and suppliers suited for the digital age.

The proposed vision for a method consists of a number of tasks. Concerning future work, the next step is to modularise vision into components, more specifically, method chunks [25], and to define (1) pathways between the chunks, i.e. when to use them and why, (2) analyse which existing modelling approaches can be used to support the goals of each method chunk, as well as (3) which chunks need development of new modelling approaches.

References

1. Singh, A., Ramkumar, J., Vipin, B.: Digital manufacturing. In: Amit, R.K., Pawar, K.S., Sundarraj, R.P., Ratchev, S. (eds.) Advances in Digital Manufacturing Systems. Springer, Singapore (2023). https://doi.org/10.1007/978-981-19-7071-9_4
2. Gupta, C., Bhatia, S.: The inherent risk of climate change becoming a hindrance in a business supply chain. In: Grima, S., Sood, K., Özen, E. (eds.) Contemporary Studies of Risks in Emerging Technology, Part A (Emerald Studies in Finance, Insurance, and Risk Management), pp. 127–137. Emerald Publishing Limited, Leeds (2023). https://doi.org/10.1108/978-1-80455-562-020231009
3. Bin-yu, H., Xin, Y., Shusheng, Q.: Product low-carbon design, manufacturing, logistics, and recycling: an overview. Wiley Interdisc. Rev. Energy Environ. (2023). https://doi.org/10.1002/wene.479
4. Sandkuhl S., Stirna J.: Capability Management in Digital Enterprises. Springer (2018). ISBN 978-3-319-90423-8
5. Tsai, C.H., Zdravkovic, J., Söder, F.: A method for digital business ecosystem design: situational method engineering in an action research project. Softw. Syst. Model. **22**(2), 573–598 (2023)
6. Moore, J.F.: Predators and prey: a new ecology of competition. Harv. Bus. Rev. **71**, 75–86 (1993)
7. Senyo, P.K., Liu, K., Effah, J.: Digital business ecosystem: literature review and a framework for future research. Int. J. Inf. Manage. **47**, 52–64 (2019)
8. Senyo, P.K., Liu, K., Effah, J.: Towards a methodology for modelling interdependencies between partners in digital business ecosystems. In: LISS 2017, pp. 1165–1170. IEEE (2017)
9. Putnik, G.D., Putnik, Z.: Defining sequential engineering (SeqE), simultaneous engineering (SE), concurrent engineering (CE) and collaborative engineering (ColE): on similarities and differences. Procedia CIRP **84**, 68–75 (2019)
10. Hadj, R.B., Belhadj, I., Trigui, M., Aifaoui, N.: Assembly sequences plan generation using features simplification. Adv. Eng. Softw. **119**, 1–11 (2018)
11. Chan, A., Fernandes, P.A., Polacsek, T., Roussel, S.: The aircraft and its manufacturing system: from early requirements to global design. CaiSE **2022**, 164–179 (2022)
12. Formentini, G., Bouissiere, F., Cuiller, C., Dereux, P.E., Favi, C.: Conceptual design for assembly methodology formalization: systems installation analysis and manufacturing information integration in the design and development of aircraft architectures. J. Ind. Inf. Integr. **26**, 100327 (2022)
13. Lu, Q., Wood, L.: The refinement of design for manufacture: inclusion of process design. Int. J. Oper. Prod. Manage. **26**(10), 1123–1145 (2006)
14. Diaz, A., Schöggl, J.P., Reyes, T., Baumgartner, R.J.: Sustainable product development in a circular economy: Implications for products, actors, decision-making support and lifecycle information management. Sustain. Prod. Consump. **26**, 1031–1045 (2021)
15. Zdravkovic, J., Stirna, J., Grabis, J.: A comparative analysis of using the capability notion for congruent business and information systems engineering. Complex Syst. Inform. Model. Q. **10**, 1–20 (2017)
16. Kampars, J., Zdravkovic, J., Stirna, J., Grabis, J.: Extending organizational capabilities with open data to support sustainable and dynamic business ecosystems. Softw. Syst. Model. **19**(2), 371–398 (2020)
17. Dalibor, M., Michael, J., Rumpe, B., Varga, S., Wortmann, A.: Towards a model-driven architecture for interactive digital twin cockpits. In: Dobbie, G., et al. (eds.) Conceptual Modeling. ER 2020. LNCS, vol. 12400. Springer, Cham (2020). https://doi.org/10.1007/978-3-030-62522-1_28

18. Cimino, C., Negri, E., Fumagalli, L.: Review of digital twin applications in manufacturing. Comput. Indust. **113** (2019)
19. Schmid, S., Winkler, H.: Hybrid production management system in the context of industry 4.0. In: IEEE International Conference on Industrial Engineering and Engineering Management (IEEM). IEEE (2022)
20. Wang, Y., et al.: A digital twin model of smart factory production system. In: International Conference on Image, Vision and Intelligent Systems. Springer Nature Singapore, Singapore (2022)
21. Johannesson, P., Perjons, E.: An introduction to design science, 2nd edn. Springer Cham (2021)
22. Henderson-Sellers, B., Ralyté, J., Ågerfalk, P.J., Rossi, M.: Situational Method Engineering, 1st edn. Springer (2014)
23. Sandkuhl, K., Stirna, J., Persson, A., Wißotzki, M.: Enterprise Modeling—Tackling Business Challenges with the 4EM Method. Springer (2014). ISBN 978-3-662-43724-7
24. Sandkuhl K., Stirna J.: Supporting early phases of digital twin development with enterprise modeling and capability management: requirements from two industrial cases. In: Proceedings of EMMSAD 2020, pp. 284–299. Springer, LNBIP (2020)
25. Ralyté, J., Rolland, C.: An approach for method reengineering. In: Kunii, H.S., Jajodia, S., Sølvberg, A. (eds.) Conceptual Modeling—ER 2001. LNCS 2224. Springer (2001)

Indoor Environmental Quality Data Measurement, Management and Analysis: First Draft of the Conceptual Model

Guntis Arnicans$^{(\boxtimes)}$ ⓘ and Laila Niedrite ⓘ

Faculty of Computing, University of Latvia, Raina bulvaris 19, Riga 1586, Latvia
`guntis.arnicans@lu.lv`

Abstract. The indoor environmental quality (IEQ) has a significant impact on people's health and therefore deserves a detailed research to provide effective information technology (IT) support for IEQ control and management. Existing IEQ research includes different aspects of indoor air quality (IAQ), outdoor meteorology and air quality, as well as building characteristics and IT solutions used to measure different pollutants indoor and outdoor. Due to IEQ domain covers such different directions, an integrated and specialized view is necessary to support domain understanding and IT solutions development. The goal of our research is to develop a comprehensive view in IEQ domain based on studying of scientific papers and various regulations related to IAQ and IEQ as well as evaluating technical solutions used in these research studies, by collecting the used concepts. The IEQ domain concepts are described regarding following categories: Indoor Environment Quality Measurements, External Environment Impact, Building Characteristics, Sensors and Measuring Process, Pollutants, Management Aspects. Based on these concepts found during the studies we developed a number of conceptual models.

Keywords: Sensor data · Indoor environmental quality · Indoor air quality · Monitoring system · Conceptual model

1 Introduction

People spend the majority of life indoors [10] therefore the impact that have the indoor air quality (IAQ) on the people's health and well-being is significant and deserves a detailed and thorough research. However, the indoor air quality compared to the outdoor air quality has been significantly less researched [10].

Many outdoor pollutants can also be observed indoors, although differences in characteristics often appear. For example, the concentration of pollutants can be indoors much higher than outdoors [4, 10].

Not only the researchers but also the governments and institutions working on different regulations mostly have paid their attention to the outdoor air quality,

ⓒ The Author(s), under exclusive license to Springer Nature Switzerland AG 2024
A. Lupeikienė et al. (Eds.): DB&IS 2024, CCIS 2157, pp. 50–65, 2024.
https://doi.org/10.1007/978-3-031-63543-4_4

including World Health Organization (2021) and European Commission (2022), that defined the limits for a number of pollutants.

More and more researchers are turning not only to IAQ, but also to Indoor Environmental Quality (IEQ) research, which actually includes this IAQ aspect and additionally looks at others that describe the conditions within the buildings. Here we can indicate such additional aspects as lighting, including the availability of daylight, noise level and room acoustics, comfortable temperature, as well as the level of occupancy of rooms. Taking into account all aspects of IEQ, not only IAQ issues, the living and working conditions can be improved, the impact of these factors on human health can be diminished, by initiating actions corresponding to the measurements made and recommendations developed by various organizations.

Organizations and countries have a lot to do for establishing new regulations and guidelines to provide a secure working and living environment. Some state level regulations exist at different countries, some are issued by European Union. Due to lack of proper standards devoted to the air pollution indoors the Chartered Institute of Building Services Engineers (CIBSE) in UK in 2021 produced guidelines on Indoor Air Quality regarding the assessment, monitoring, modeling, and mitigation [10].

In their guidelines CIBSE [10] concluded that the existing research in IAQ problem area is very fragmented and each individual study usually covers only limited aspects of all factors influencing the indoor air quality, for example, studies are performed in different environments like schools and homes as well as they provide data only for some pollutants during a short time span. Only some research include data about activities undergoing indoors during observation period.

Such heterogeneity is caused by difficulties to organize a comprehensive observations indoors, that is also resource intensive [10], often the measurements in one room cannot be generalized to other rooms due to different environmental parameters.

Existing indoor models lack building- and occupant-specific parameters, as well as parametrization of ventilation, and other aspects like temperature, relative humidity, lighting, as well as air exchange of individual buildings [10].

Many research studies use for the pollution data collecting purposes low-cost sensors (LCS). Currently more sophisticated systems with much broader functionality than only data collecting have been developed and provide monitoring, management, visualization, and analysis functions. Different technologies, including the Internet of Things (IoT), Artificial Intelligence, and many others, can be used to implement such systems. IoT solutions can serve as a foundation for the development of efficient epidemic control as well as air quality control systems in smart cities [7]. IoT and AI solutions can also promote smart buildings' functioning by supporting heating, ventilation, air-conditioning, and occupancy tracking [33] to guarantee for all involved people safe indoor environment. Today, IoT-based building management systems (BMS) have quite a wide range of previous mentioned functionality. Nevertheless, comprehensive BMS including extensive data analysis functions are missing [22]. At the same time, many buildings without BMS must also deal with air quality issues, and therefore need a specialized indoor air quality monitoring system.

Systems, especially self-constructed ones, as shown by the fragmentation of research above, are based on a limited domain model. Therefore, when creating a new indoor environment quality control system, it is necessary to have a comprehensive domain model.

The goal of this paper is to develop such a comprehensive model based on two approaches, firstly, inspecting scientific papers and various regulations related to IAQ and IEQ domain and collecting the concepts used and secondly, summarizing the technical solutions used in research studies regarding the data items and models implemented. The evaluation of the obtained information and as a result the creation of the domain model is based on the previous experience of the authors [1,25], during development of an epidemic control system.

The rest of the paper is organized as follows. Section 2 gives an overview of a motivating example. Related work is presented in Sect. 3. Section 4 describes the research methodology, and Sect. 5 provides details about findings regarding IEQ domain concepts and conceptual models representing these domain concepts. In Sect. 6, the conclusions and future work are given.

2   A Motivating Example

During the COVID-19 pandemic, various restrictions were imposed on the use of public spaces. In many countries, radical measures were temporarily introduced, preventing certain public buildings from being visited, for example, educational institutions were temporarily closed (by closure we mean the absence of in-person classes). Over time, the understanding of how the virus spreads has changed. Researchers and experts in various fields found that in closed spaces, the virus is mainly spread in the form of aerosol droplets [2,30,37]. Already in 2020, researchers raised the alarm and recommended paying attention to the effective ventilation of the premises and controlling situations when there are many people in the premises [24,31].

The authors of this paper were involved in a research project[1] in Latvia in 2020 and 2021 to find ways to reduce the risk of contracting SARS-CoV2 and other respiratory viruses indoors. Within the framework of the project, the possibilities of creating smart rooms, which are monitored with the help of sensors and provide information about the risks of infection, were studied [1,25].

In May 2022, the Ministry of Education and Science of Latvia took an important step in the field of climate control monitoring. The Ministry purchased and installed 14,000 sensors in educational institutions and 1,000 sensors in municipal social care centers [21]. From June 1, sensor data on air quality in classrooms is publicly available[2] not only to the Ministry of Education and Science

---

[1] Supported by the National Research Program of Latvia, Project No. VPP-COVID-2020/1-0025.

[2] Mesh Group SIA, https://co2.mesh.lv/home/dashboard.

and schools, but also to anyone interested. *"Further action already depends on the municipality and the school, looking for the most appropriate solutions to improve the situation. ... The portal shows not only the CO_2 level in the room, but also the air temperature and relative air humidity in the room. These indicators should be evaluated in relation to each other, as they all form the overall air quality in the room."* [21].

Users can select a building, room and see a graph of sensor data (see Fig. 1). Unfortunately, information can be obtained from the chart that sometimes the CO_2 level has been too high, but the exact cause and possible actions to improve the situation are not clear.

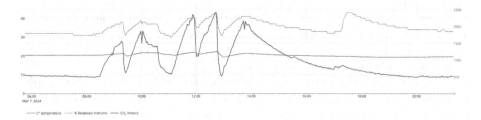

Fig. 1. Sensor data chart in the school room during school hours

Reading such charts is easy on the one hand to see if CO_2, temperature or humidity is within the required range. If any indicator is regularly outside the permissible limits (students' parents are worried if the CO_2 level in the room is too high, as in our example Fig. 1), then someone demands from the responsible persons to improve the situation. On the other hand, such a chart is not enough to find out the exact causes of the undesirable conditions and to carry out the reorganization.

In order to perform a more accurate analysis in the specific room (Fig. 1), information is needed about: what and when happened in the room; how many people were in the room; what is the ventilation of the room; how was the rapid ventilation performed (windows, doors and their air permeability); what is the heating; what is the outside weather; where the sensor equipment is placed, etc. Only by knowing the details of the use of the room, its sources of pollution, cleaning options, managers can plan improvements in the use of the room, for example, changing the business mode, organizing more efficient ventilation, fundamental changes in the rooms (for example, creating additional ventilation).

Additional efforts must be made to obtain the necessary information, for example, the presence of people in the room, the type of activity performed by people, ventilation events (the ventilation system is turned off or off, the specific window or door is open), external environmental conditions can be recorded. These additional data can be obtained manually, semi-automatically or fully automated with the help of additional sensors and data processing systems. Our colleagues, continuing their research on protection against viral infections indoors, have created a model and system that is already able to warn of the risk of infection in real time (the specific model is adapted to the SARS-COV-2 virus) [35]. Data about the room (dimensions, ventilation data, etc.) are entered into this system, temperature, CO_2, relative humidity, concentration of particles in the air, amount of people, human activities (speech, cough, sneeze) are received from the sensors.

In our research [1,25], we placed many sensors in one building (a floor in a hospital or school, several floors in a university). We found that it is very important not to look at an isolated space, but to look at the building as a system consisting of many interconnected systems (spaces / rooms). In addition, the building has a connection with the external environment. Data analysis must also be performed for the whole part of the building under review (data from many sensors located in different places at the same time). It is the only way to discover the exact causes of pollution and get recommendations for improving the situation. During research, we encountered the problem that it is unclear what sensors should be used, what data should be collected, how to process it, what could be achieved with data processing. In the following, the paper mentions things at a conceptual level that could help in the development of complex sensor systems for indoor climate control.

3   Related Work

There exist a number of ontologies that partly cover some aspects of IEQ domain, in some cases the overlapping part has possibly more detailed representation and has other application domains, e.g. building construction or sensors in general.

In [20], Mikołajczyk et.al have presented ontologies for digital twins developed by four EU-funded projects BIMprove, COGITO, ASHVIN and BIM2TWIN that cover data requirements for buildings construction from different aspects.

The one of mentioned above ontologies COGITO is described in more detail in [6]. This ontology has seven modules: facility itself, construction process and resources, the IoT devices for resource location, quality and safety information, and finally the information for digital twins.

Another ontology for construction management purposes presented by Mikołajczyk et.al [20] is developed during BIM2TWIN project. The core ontology describes all concepts regarding construction processes, including working zones, resources, and also the building. The description of building entities is based on BOT ontology.

The building topology ontology (BOT) is provided in detail in [28].

Regarding sensors there have been many efforts to develop ontologies, and the situation is analysed in [8]. According to Haller et al. [8], W3C (World Wide Web Consortium) in cooperation with OGC (Open Geospatial Consortium) have developed a number of ontologies that represent sensors, actuators, samplers, and respective processes: observation, actuation and sampling. Most significant are two ontologies: SOSA (Sensor, Observation, Sampler, and Actuator) and SSN (Semantic Sensor Network).

Despite some overlapping parts can be reused or adapted in case of IEQ, there are also some parts of domain e.g. environment and pollutants, that should be modelled and integrated with already represented and overlapping parts, to get the most precise understanding of the domain.

4   Research Methodology

One of the most recent literature reviews in the field of IAQ [9] was used in our study as an information source as well as a basis for identifying many different studies that could be analyzed to clarify the domain concepts [9], we supplemented these sources by other relevant research papers. Authors of the literature review [9] evaluate papers that use LCS in IAQ measurements, and the aim of their study is to determine whether the reviewed papers describe methods to identify sources of indoor air pollution. The paper [9] reviews 60 different scientific papers. In the study [9], the following parameters were chosen for the evaluation of papers: study location e.g. country, type of micro-environment e.g. school, house, etc., in which the measurement was carried out, pollutants and methods used to determine the source of pollution, sensors used, year of building construction, floor of the building, placement of sensors, details about doors, windows and ventilation, as well as the number of people in the premises during the measurement and their activity logs.

To be mentioned, some terms used and being important for the domain we documented from these paper evaluation parameters in [9] review. It should be noted that mostly these parameters originally come from Air Quality Expert Group guidelines [13] or Chartered Institute of Building Services Engineers document [10]. These both documents also were used as an information source for our domain studies, each of them providing additional details to the previously named. Air Quality Expert Group guidelines [13] points out the impact of outdoor air quality parameters to the IAQ, for example, the level of outdoor pollutants, the rate of air exchange, the indoor airflow. Chartered Institute of Building Services Engineers guidelines [10] mention also the building construction materials, heating or cooling activities as well as cleaning and many other occupant's activities that can cause the pollution.

So all previously mentioned concepts from IAQ domain we used to define the initial evaluation parameters for the papers chosen for in depth studies.

For the in depth studies we have chosen the same papers that we had evaluated in our previous research [25] regarding sensor data visualization. In our previous work we studied the research papers from the review [29] that have implemented a web portal in addition to the mobile application to display the IAQ measurements, because our goal was to understand and develop an IAQ management system that can be used for both the long-term and real-time data analysis with appropriate visualization features.

During the in depth studies the initial list of evaluation parameters were expanded by new concepts that we discovered by reading the research papers. For each research paper the details regarding all applicable evaluation parameters were documented to gain understanding about the meaning of domain concepts used in different studies. Our goal was to form a coherent picture regarding the domain concepts.

5   Domain Concepts and Conceptual Model of Indoor Environmental Quality Management

This chapter describes the conceptual model we have developed for IEQ management. We use UML notation. The created conceptual models are essentially concept maps, which are represented by a UML class diagram in order to more accurately show the relationships between the most important concepts of the domain. Attributes are added to classes if the attribute itself is an important domain/subdomain forming concept.

The indoor climate control system implemented in Latvian schools is relatively simple at the conceptual level. Its conceptual model is given in Fig. 2. Type indicates the type of measurement: CO_2, temperature or relative humidity. For each measurement type, value ranges (Level) are maintained that determine how desirable or undesirable each IEQ measurement is.

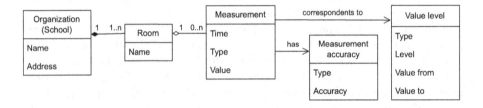

Fig. 2. Conceptual model of sensor data in Latvian schools

We have divided the whole domain of IEQ into several subdomains to make it easier to manage the concepts and to represent their interrelationships. We started by extracting the most important concepts of the IEQ domain and then developed several conceptual models of the IEQ subdomains, which are given in the following subsections. There are inter-linkages between these subdomain models, which are not shown due to the limited scope of the paper. Not all data objects have the most important attributes presented, for example, Measurement is presented without Time, Type and Value attributes, as is done in the model of the system implemented in Latvian schools in Fig. 2.

The indoor environment quality domain is a broader domain than indoor air quality domain, it overlaps partly with domain of building construction and management, as well as includes some concepts from sensor networks, but in this section we will provide the information in following six logical parts of the domain: IEQ measurements, external impact, building characteristics, sensors and measuring process, pollutants, management aspects.

5.1 Indoor Environment Quality Measurements

The IAQ research studies have been conducted in different *microenvironments*. The most common type mentioned is University building [5,17], laboratories [18,19], more specifically chemical engineering research lab [5,17], open computer laboratory [12], office rooms [11,34], university dormitory [11]. However some other places are also investigated: a warehouse workshop [32], indoor places different from buildings, e.g. vehicles [15]. These microenvironments are placed in different *locations* over all world.

The main concept for all studies is *internal pollution* or what is exactly measured during experiments. There are different types of gases that are harmful to human health and the environment that are measured, e.g. carbon dioxide (CO_2) [5,12,15,16,23,26,32,34,38], carbon monoxide (CO) [5,11,16,17,32], sulfur dioxide (SO_2) [5,11], nitrogen dioxide (NO_2) [5,11,17,32], ozone (O_3) [5,11,32]. Also propane (C_3H_8), butane (C_4H_{10}), methane (CH_4), and ethanol (C_2H_5OH) [17], as well as ammonia (NH_3) [17,36] can be mentioned. Some researchers compute *Air Quality Index* [11,18] that is calculated from 6 measurements: $PM_{10}, PM_{2.5}, CO, NO_2, SO_2$ and O_3, where PM stands from Particulate Matter but 10 and 2.5 refers to the size. Examples of PM are dust from roads, construction sites and other sites. Dust particles (PM) are measured quite often, e.g. $PM_{2.5}$ [12,19,32,38], PM_{10} [19,26,32,38]. Some other aspects of measurements are more related to the Indoor Environment Quality than to IAQ, e.g. in case of measurement of environmental parameters such as temperature and relative humidity [3,5,11,12,16,18,23,32,34,36,38], as well as atmospheric pressure [18,34], luminosity (lighting) [16,23,32] and acoustic conditions (noise) [32].

For many particular pollutants *causes of pollution* (or *sources*) are known, the knowledge about them can help detect the exact pollutant source, e.g., source of ammonia (NH_3) can be people and their activities, as well as tobacco smoke, indoor materials and others [17]. Due to one of the pollution sources in buildings are the inhabitants the *room occupancy* is documented [5,11,34], or detected in some cases by a sensor [12]. Closely related to the occupancy estimation is also the *logging of the activities* of inhabitants with different *activity type* and *activity periods*. For example, researchers work from 07:30 to 15:00, 5 days per week [5], laboratory experiments and teaching activities are performed according a schedule [18], or cleaning schedule is once a week [32].

The most important concepts of this subdomain can be seen in Fig. 3. On the left side of the figure is the most important part of the subdomain. There are many Rooms in the part of the building (Microenvironment) located at the address (Location). Rooms can have different Sensors that will get Measurements. The right side shows the most important things about pollution and its sources.

5.2 External Environment Impact

In research studies that we reviewed the least attention has been payed to the out-door environment impact to the indoor environment. This can be explained

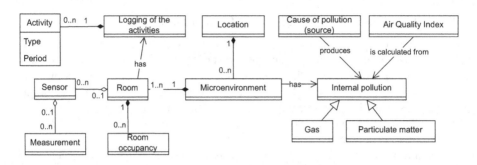

Fig. 3. Conceptual model of subdomain "Indoor environment quality measurements"

by the original focus of our previous work on the IAQ [25], which references we used for more deeper study in this work. Nevertheless, some aspects are mentioned. *Environmental pollution* through butane, dust, benzene, smoke, ammonia and other pollutants is mentioned in [27], but the authors of [12] describe the *pollution level of area* stating that the indoor measurements were performed in the low polluted area, so no outdoor condition monitoring was performed. *Environmental conditions (meteorology)* e.g. temperature, relative humidity, and wind speed are mentioned in [11].

Some additional parameters that should be monitored regarding external environment's impact are mentioned in [9]: the *level of air tightness of the building's facade* and the *distance of building from major pollutants* e.g. distance from major traffic.

The following conceptual model (Fig. 4) contains the concepts related to this subdomain "External environment impact". External conditions have a significant impact on the climate in a room. In the model, the most attention is paid to pollution that can come from the external environment. However, the indoor climate is also influenced by the weather outside (Environmental conditions (meteorology)). For example, outdoor air temperature and relative humidity can both improve and worsen indoor temperature and relative humidity levels. The CO_2 level outside is usually lower and serves as a source of room purification.

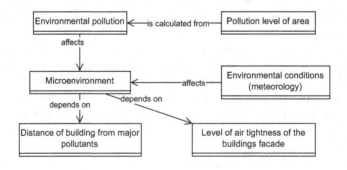

Fig. 4. Conceptual model of subdomain "External environment impact"

5.3 Building Characteristics

The buildings where the IEQ is measured and managed are built from different *building fabric* e.g. concrete and brick walls [5], *details of external doors, windows* can be found in descriptions of studies, e.g. buildings may have large wooden doors [5], single glazing windows [32]. Many information can be concluded about the building knowing its *construction* or *renovation year*, e.g. 1946 [32]. Two important features of the building having impact on IEQ are *ventilation details* and *heating or cooling of the spaces*. Buildings can have central ventilation system [5,32], ventilation in the exhaust fan installed on the wall [26], natural ventilation by opening windows manually [18,19,32]. The heating details also can be found, e.g. the air is heated and recirculated by two air-water fan-coils [18,19], or it can be documented that heating took place or not [32].

Many studies provide details about *floor of the building* where measurements took place, e.g. on different floors out of 23 floors [11], 1st floor [32] or is mentioned that building has 16 floors [38]. Many studies provide *floor plan* (or *room plan*) [5,16,19]. For more precise description also data about *room geometry* is provided in following forms: $3 \times 3 \times 3$ meters [26], total room area 200 (m^2) [32].

Regarding the interior of the room there are also some IEQ influencing aspects: *furniture, surfaces*, and *finishes*, e.g. metal book shelves [5], floor covering: coating [32], and appliances and *other pollutant-generating equipment*, e.g. sol-vent printing machine and computers [32], propane gas stoves [17].

Some *other factors impacting IEQ* can be mentioned regarding rooms, e.g. natural light during the day [23].

The conceptual model for the subdomain "Building characteristics" (Fig. 5) contains the most important mentioned concepts. In reality, there are many more concepts, especially if we are creating a detailed solution for climate control. For example, coding the entire building plan, marking rooms, doors, windows, ventilation alone requires a relatively large data model. If the building is perceived as a complex system, then it should be modeled as a graph with different types of vertices and different types of edges, to which different attributes are attached, for example, the air permeability of windows and doors in open form. Formal notation in the form of a graph facilitates various simulations and modeling to perform process analysis and generate recommendations for improving climate management.

5.4 Sensors and Measuring Process

Sensors can be characterized by *sensor type*, e.g. MOS (Metal Oxide Semiconductor) and NDIR (Near-infrared) [5,16], that means witch particular pollutants can be measured, e.g. NDIR for CO_2 measuring. All studies provide details about used *sensor model*, e.g. in [36] air quality sensor MQ-135 and temperature and humidity sensor DHT-22 were used.

Sensors are characterized by *nominal range*, e.g. 0–5000 (ppm) for CO_2 sensor [5], for temperature sensor from –40 °C to 120 °C [16], or for particulate matters sensors the range is 0–1000 $\mu g/m^3$ [32]. The *measurement accuracy* also is

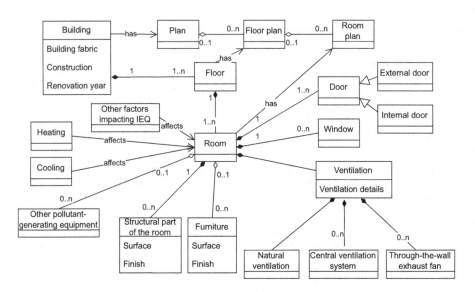

Fig. 5. Conceptual model of subdomain "Building characteristics"

documented, e.g. for the sensor MICS-6814 accuracy is ±15–25% [17], for sensor SHT10 ±0.5 °C (temperature) [16]. Also the *calibration details* of sensors usually are given, e.g. auto-calibration [12], pre-calibration [5], or calibrated range is given: 300–5000 ppm [34], or authors state that used sensors obtained high accuracy without calibration [38]. Sometimes *response time* is also given e.g. less than 30 s [16]. *Sampling intervals* and *sample size* are additional parameters of sensors that sometimes are mentioned e.g. 15 min [5], every 120 s [15], the dust level is observed in every minute [27], whereas the sensor readings have a certain sample size (in bytes) [27].

For the *measurement value* the *unit of measure* can be pointed out, e.g. temperature and humidity in the air is measured in degree Celsius and percentage respectively [36].

The *measurement process* is characterized with *measurement period* e.g. 6 h, 2 weeks [11], 10 days [12], 2 month [19], or exact date from 15 October 2018 to 15 November 2018 are named in [32]. The measurement is performed by sensors that are placed in a certain place of the room, that can be characterized by *placement location*, *height*, and sometimes *distance from equipment*, e.g. sensors of system are placed in around the exhaust fan [26], they are placed far from the equipment [18], or are placed in height of 1.5 m above the ground [32].

The conceptual model "Sensors and measuring process" includes the most important concepts without which data acquisition is not of sufficient quality (Fig. 6). Other embedded or small devices that produce data can also be added to sensors, for example, 1) a video camera, which, together with appropriate software, determines the number of people in a room; 2) a microphone with software that captures and classifies all sound events.

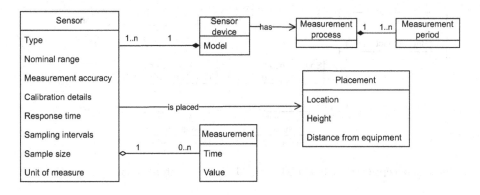

Fig. 6. Conceptual model of subdomain "Sensors and measuring process"

5.5 Pollutants

Some concepts regarding pollutants already were mentioned in previous subsections, for example, *causes of pollution* (or *sources*), *internal pollution*, the *room occupancy, logging of the activities* are described in Subsect. 5.1; *environmental pollution* is discussed in Subsect. 5.2; and *pollutant-generating equipment* is discussed in Subsect. 5.3. Here we will mention some additional concepts found during the scientific paper studies. *Knowledge about sources of pollutants and their impact on IEQ* can help to improve the IEQ, e.g. removing visible damp spots or mould in the room [9,14]. *Known source apportionment methods* e.g. receptor-oriented and source-oriented pollutants source apportionment methods can help identify the pollution sources [9]. *Guidance on improving conditions* [9] represent the actions needed to undertake.

It is important to know the *exposure time* for an individual person [10], e.g. exposure time can be different for some person groups, including children or asthmatics [17], also often exact time, for example, eight hours, for particular pollutant is defined [5,10]. *Exposure limits* also must be respected so as not to harm people's health, e.g. 0.05 ppm for O_3 is set by WHO [5].

The last conceptual model includes at once two subdomains "Pollutants" and "Management aspects", which are explained in Subsects. 5.5 and 5.6, respectively (Fig. 7). The model is small because many concepts regarding pollution are already included in other models. In addition, management issues are not sufficiently described in research papers. A possible reason for the lack of information is the fact that there are not many established climate control systems that utilize the full capabilities of sensors and smart software. One of the goals of this paper is to help approach the creation of such systems.

5.6 Management Aspects

The measurement of pollutants and observation and evaluation of measurement results, as well as preventing the harmful situations in advance, is necessary

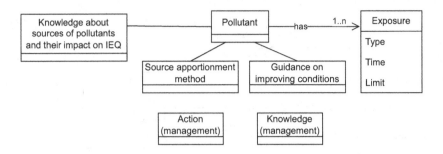

Fig. 7. Conceptual model of subdomain "Pollutants" and "Management aspects"

to ensure IEQ in short and long term. Therefore sometimes *actions*, should be undertaken, according to *Guidance on improving conditions*, e.g. real-time alerts can inform people [18], ventilation can be adjusted [17,34] or deactivation of harmful equipment can be undertaken [17,18], working of exhaust fan can be regulated [26], and air purification systems can be activated [18].

Knowledge about well recognized and newest methods for measurement, modelling, and calculating of different indexes and parameters regarding IEQ should be documented to be sure that the best possible methods are used, e.g. [12] suggest that relative variations of the Volatile Organic Compounds level can be used to evaluate IAQ instead of using the absolute measure. Also knowledge about results in different studies can help to understand the indoor environment taking into account all influencing parameters, e.g. pollution level is higher near to the ground 1–20 m [34] or in [18] is stated that recommendation for laboratory temperature is 23 °C and relative humidity should be less than 70%.

6   Conclusions

We have created small conceptual models for several subdomains or aspects of the large domain of IEQ quality management. These models are connected to each other by additional relations. It is impossible to represent the entire model within the scope of this paper and its perception would be difficult. We have proposed to include in the conceptual model those concepts that were most frequently mentioned in studies of the relevant field. From our experience in prototyping climate control systems, we know that models need to be built much larger and include other less-mentioned concepts.

In our research we tried to start filling the indicated gap of fragmented and diverse research in indoor environment quality research, that is tightly connected and partly overlapping with domains of smart buildings, application of sensors, and epidemic control systems development. We systematized the concepts used in different research studies and developed corresponding data models.

The provided data models reflect the main concepts of IEQ domain, these models can serve as a basis for development of a IEQ management systems, as well as for further development of provided models adding more details to gain a comprehensive understanding of the IEQ domain. Despite the existence of standards and ontologies in some overlapping domains with IEQ domain, e.g. building management and sensors, it is necessary to provide an integrated view specialized for IEQ domain.

Therefore, our future work will be in direction of precise and in-depth comparison of overlapping parts of our models with the ontologies and standards in building management and sensors, to evaluate and possibly extend our models. An experimental evaluation of the models will also be carried out, creating an IEQ monitoring system based on these models.

Disclosure of Interests. The authors have no competing interests to declare that are relevant to the content of this paper.

References

1. Arnicans, G., Niedrite, L., Solodovnikova, D., Virbulis, J., Zemnickis, J.: Towards a system to monitor the virus's aerosol-type spreading. In: Byrski, A., Czachórski, T., Gelenbe, E., Grochla, K., Murayama, Y. (eds.) ANTICOVID 2021. IAICT, vol. 616, pp. 95–106. Springer, Cham (2021). https://doi.org/10.1007/978-3-030-86582-5_9
2. Asadi, S., Bouvier, N., Wexler, A.S., Ristenpart, W.D.: The coronavirus pandemic and aerosols: does covid-19 transmit via expiratory particles? (2020)
3. Azmi, N., et al.: Design and development of multi-transceiver lorafi board consisting lora and esp8266-wifi communication module. In: IOP Conference Series: Materials Science and Engineering, vol. 318, p. 012051. IOP Publishing (2018)
4. Bari, M.A., Kindzierski, W.B., Wheeler, A.J., Héroux, M.È., Wallace, L.A.: Source apportionment of indoor and outdoor volatile organic compounds at homes in Edmonton, Canada. Build. Environ. **90**, 114–124 (2015)
5. Benammar, M., Abdaoui, A., Ahmad, S.H., Touati, F., Kadri, A.: A modular IoT platform for real-time indoor air quality monitoring. Sensors **18**, 581 (2018)
6. Bernardos, S., et al.: D3. 1–survey of existing models, ontologies and associated standardization efforts. Technical report., COGITO (2021)
7. Chamola, V., Hassija, V., Gupta, V., Guizani, M.: A comprehensive review of the covid-19 pandemic and the role of IoT, drones, AI, blockchain, and 5G in managing its impact. IEEE Access **8**, 90225–90265 (2020)
8. Haller, A., et al.: The modular SSN ontology: a joint w3c and OGC standard specifying the semantics of sensors, observations, sampling, and actuation. Semant. Web **10**(1), 9–32 (2019)
9. Higgins, C., Kumar, P., Morawska, L.: Indoor air quality monitoring and source apportionment using low-cost sensors. Environ. Res. Commun. **6**(1), 012001 (2024)
10. Holman, C., Hawkings, C., McHugh, C.: Indoor air quality guidance: Assessment, monitoring, modelling and mitigation. Technical report., Chartered Institute of Building Services Engineers (CIBSE) Institute of Air Quality Management (2021)
11. Idrees, Z., Zou, Z., Zheng, L.: Edge computing based IoT architecture for low cost air pollution monitoring systems: a comprehensive system analysis, design considerations & development. Sensors **18**, 3021 (2018)
12. Karami, M., McMorrow, G.V., Wang, L.: Continuous monitoring of indoor environmental quality using an arduino-based data acquisition system. J. Build. Eng. **19**, 412–419 (2018)

13. Lewis, A.C., et al.: Indoor air quality. Technical report, Air Quality Expert Group (2022). https://doi.org/10.5281/zenodo.6523605
14. Madureira, J., et al.: Source apportionment of co2, pm10 and vocs levels and health risk assessment in naturally ventilated primary schools in Porto, Portugal. Build. Environ. **96**, 198–205 (2016)
15. Marques, G., Miranda, N., Kumar Bhoi, A., Garcia-Zapirain, B., Hamrioui, S., de la Torre Díez, I.: Internet of things and enhanced living environments: measuring and mapping air quality using cyber-physical systems and mobile computing technologies. Sensors **20**, 720 (2020)
16. Marques, G., Pitarma, R.: An indoor monitoring system for ambient assisted living based on internet of things architecture. Int. J. Environ. Res. Public Health **13**, 1152 (2016)
17. Marques, G., Pitarma, R.: A cost-effective air quality supervision solution for enhanced living environments through the internet of things. Electronics **8**, 170 (2019)
18. Marques, G., Pitarma, R.: An internet of things-based environmental quality management system to supervise the indoor laboratory conditions. Appl. Sci. **9**, 438 (2019)
19. Marques, G., Roque Ferreira, C., Pitarma, R.: A system based on the internet of things for real-time particle monitoring in buildings. Int. J. Environ. Res. Public Health **15**, 821 (2018)
20. Mikołajczyk, A., et al.: Ontologies in digital twin: methodology, lessons learned and practical approach. Open Res. Europe **3**(105), 105 (2023)
21. Air quality meters have been installed in all latvian schools (in latvian) (2022). https://www.izm.gov.lv/lv/jaunums/visas-latvijas-skolas-uzstaditi-gaisa-kvalitates-meritaji
22. Minoli, D., Sohraby, K., Occhiogrosso, B.: IoT considerations, requirements, and architectures for smart buildings – energy optimization and next-generation building management systems. IEEE Internet Things J. **4**, 269–283 (2017)
23. Moiş, G.D., Sanislav, T., Folea, S.C., Zeadally, S.: Performance evaluation of energy-autonomous sensors using power-harvesting beacons for environmental monitoring in internet of things (iot). Sensors **18**, 1709 (2018)
24. Morawska, L., Milton, D.K.: It is time to address airborne transmission of coronavirus disease 2019 (covid-19). Clin. Infect. Dis. **71**, 2311–2313 (2020)
25. Niedrite, L., Arnicans, G., Solodovnikova, D.: Visualization of indoor sensor data to reduce the risk of covid-19 infection. In: CEUR Workshop Proceedings, vol. 3158, pp. 101–112 (2022)
26. Pradityo, F., Surantha, N.: Indoor air quality monitoring and controlling system based on IoT and fuzzy logic. In: 2019 7th International Conference on Information and Communication Technology (ICoICT), pp. 1–6. IEEE (2019)
27. Rahman, M., et al.: An adaptive IoT platform on budgeted 3G data plans. J. Syst. Arch. **97**, 65–76 (2019)
28. Rasmussen, M.H., Lefrançois, M., Schneider, G.F., Pauwels, P.: Bot: the building topology ontology of the w3c linked building data group. Semant. Web **12**(1), 143–161 (2021)
29. Saini, J., Dutta, M., Marques, G.: Indoor air quality monitoring systems based on internet of things: a systematic review. Int. J. Environ. Res. Public Health **17**, 4942 (2020)
30. Setti, L., et al.: Airborne transmission route of covid-19: why 2 meters/6 feet of inter-personal distance could not be enough (2020)

31. Somsen, G.A., van Rijn, C., Kooij, S., Bem, R.A., Bonn, D.: Small droplet aerosols in poorly ventilated spaces and SARS-CoV-2 transmission. Lancet Respir. Med. **8**, 658–659 (2020)
32. Sun, S., Zheng, X., Villalba-Díez, J., Ordieres-Meré, J.: Indoor air-quality data-monitoring system: long-term monitoring benefits. Sensors **19**, 4157 (2019)
33. Umair, M., Cheema, M.A., Cheema, O., Li, H., Lu, H.: Impact of covid-19 on adoption of IoT in different sectors. arXiv preprint arXiv:2101.07196 (2021)
34. Velicka, J., Pies, M., Hajovsky, R.: Wireless measurement of carbon dioxide by use of IQRF technology. IFAC-PapersOnLine **51**, 78–83 (2018)
35. Virbulis, J., Telicko, J., Sabanskis, A., Vidulejs, D., Jakovics, A.: Numerical model and system for prediction and reduction of indoor infection risk. Latv. J. Phys. Tech. Sci. **60**(s6), 5–19 (2023)
36. Zakaria, N.A., Abidin, Z.Z., Harum, N., Hau, L.C., Ali, N.S., Jafar, F.A.: Wireless internet of things-based air quality device for smart pollution monitoring. Int. J. Adv. Comput. Sci. Appl. **9**, 65–69 (2018)
37. Zhang, R., Li, Y., Zhang, A.L., Wang, Y., Molina, M.J.: Identifying airborne transmission as the dominant route for the spread of Covid-19. Proc. Nat. Acad. Sci. **117**, 14857–14863 (2020)
38. Zhao, L., Wu, W., Li, S.: Design and implementation of an IoI-based indoor air quality detector with multiple communication interfaces. IEEE Internet Things J. **6**, 9621–9632 (2019)

Using the Concept of Accommodation to Facilitate Problem-Solution Analysis

Anders W. Tell, Erik Perjons[✉], and Martin Henkel[✉]

Department of Computer and Systems Sciences, Stockholm University, Stockholm, Sweden
{anderswt,perjons,martinh}@dsv.su.se

Abstract. Design science often focuses on the problem and solution spaces in artifact creation, yet the alignment between these spaces is seldom explored thoroughly. This paper introduces the concept of "accommodation" to analyse the fit between a problem and its solution. Accommodation highlights the significant semantic and practical implications inherent in the relationship between problem and solution spaces beyond mere knowledge of the two. We define accommodation and demonstrate its utility in evaluating both structural and causal links between solutions and problems. This approach is exemplified through a case study in the healthcare sector.

Keywords: Problem · solution · design science · evaluation · accommodation · effectuation · mechanism · fit · design candidate

1 Introduction

In the field of design science research (DSR), problem and solution spaces are frequently explored and examined [7, 8, 19, 22, 29]. The problem space encompasses the range of challenges, complexities, or issues that need to be addressed within a given domain. Conversely, the solution space is defined by the potential strategies, methods, products, and actions available to tackle the challenges identified in the problem space.

The matching between problems and solutions is a critical process that involves identifying and connecting specific problems with appropriate solutions. This process requires a systematic approach, careful analysis, and often creative thinking. However, the fit between problems and solutions is less often analysed in depth on conceptual and pragmatic levels. In this paper, we introduce the concept of *accommodation* as a means to improve the analysis of how problems "fit together" with solutions.

Without a thorough analysis of problems and solutions, there is a risk that solutions are applied indiscriminately (as in the saying, 'if you have a hammer, everything looks like a nail') and also that solutions do not reach their full potential (akin to using a hammer as a bookend). This issue becomes less obvious yet more problematic in complex environments such as introducing IT systems in the healthcare domain, where the accommodation between problems and solutions in the form of IT systems must consider the dynamics of organisational and individual practices, among other factors.

A. Lupeikienė et al. (Eds.): DB&IS 2024, CCIS 2157, pp. 66–75, 2024.
https://doi.org/10.1007/978-3-031-63543-4_5

Both organisational practitioners and design science researchers need to understand how to align problems and solutions better, especially since non-matched problems and solutions can often coexist simultaneously. However, there is a lack of structured approaches to address such situations. The goal of this paper is to introduce a conceptualisation of the term accommodation as a means to facilitate the analysis of how a problem fits together with a solution and how such a fit could be more formalised. The paper also presents a case from a healthcare project of how the concept of accommodation can be applied to an ongoing DSR project.

2 Related Research

In design science, the relationship between problem and solution has been discussed differently among researchers. In a seminal paper, four different forms of design science contributions are presented [13]. The design science contribution could be *routine design*, that is, known solutions for known problems, or an *improvement*, that is, new solutions for known problems. The contribution could also be an *innovation*, i.e., a solution that addresses a problem that is unexplored and offers a novel and unexpected solution. Finally, an existing solution could be repurposed to a new problem context, called *exaptation*. Based on the idea of exaptation, different research cycles in design science projects are presented in [2]. These cycles aim to help match problems with solutions. However, none of these two papers delves into the issue of fit between problem and solution in a more detailed manner.

Another way to ensure that a problem and solution are well synchronized and efficient in DSR is presented in [7]. The authors suggest a framework for understanding the roles that different types of knowledge play in DSR journeys, including both descriptive (encompassing propositional and explanatory knowledge) and prescriptive design knowledge. By understanding the different knowledge pathways and how they interact, researchers and practitioners can better adapt their solutions to specific problems. Based on the thinking in [11], the authors in [7] also present the concepts of *fitness for use* and *fitness evaluation* as two means for evaluating the relationship between problems and solutions. These two concepts are used in the conceptualization of accommodation we introduce.

In our paper, the focus is on conceptualising the term accommodation. Similarly, [19] discusses the conceptualisation of problem space within DSR. The authors present a framework for understanding and describing the problem space in DSR, which includes four central concepts: stakeholders, needs, goals, and requirements. The authors also emphasise the importance of producing design knowledge: "*describing a means-end relationship between the problem and the solution space.*". Drawing significant inspiration from [20], we emphasize the design knowledge that describes the relationship between the problem and solution spaces.

3 The Accommodation Approach

The accommodation approach presented in this paper offers a structured way to assess a solution's ability to address a problem, highlighting that the space and relationships between a problem and a solution encompass rich semantics and practical implications beyond mere knowledge of problems and solutions. The approach addresses the need to understand better how a problem is solved by a solution and how interventions, with their investments, costs, challenges, effects, and time delays, bring a solution over time into a position where it can solve the problem, that is, the effectuation of a solution.

3.1 Conceptualisation of Problems and Solutions

The accommodation approach is *anchored* in the conceptualisations of the terms problem and solution. The requirements for these conceptualisations are kept minimalistic and open-ended since the terminology, concepts, and methods vary across disciplinary areas in which DSR researchers work, as seen in the discussion in [19].

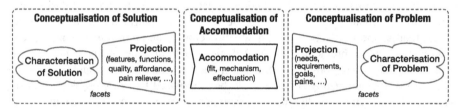

Fig. 1. Illustration of key concepts of the accommodation approach

Conceptualisations of the terms problem and solution can be divided into several facets, characterising the particular ways a problem or a solution can be considered; see the outermost boxes in Fig. 1. The *characterisation facet* represents the intrinsic characterisation of a problem without consideration of any solutions that can address the problem, and the intrinsic characterisation of a solution without consideration of any problems the solution can address.

The *projection facet* (see the "Projection" boxes in Fig. 1) represents an extrinsic set of formulated and selected characteristics, findings, and insights derived from the characterisations directed towards the opposite pole, similar to projecting a movie on a screen. The *problem projection* is directed towards solutions to guide the construction, selection, and evaluation of solutions. The *solution projection* is directed towards problems for the purpose of the selection and evaluation of problems.

A common DSR projection of a problem is to formulate a select set of needs, goals, and/or requirements related to stakeholders, see [19], where the problem formulation leads to the research question [22]. Table 1 illustrates concepts within characterisations and projections of problems and solutions found related to DSR researchers' work.

3.2 Conceptualisation of Accommodation

Accommodation generally represents the way something or someone fits, is suitable or congruous (in agreement, harmony, or correspondence) with each other. Specifically, in DSR, it is a problem and a solution accommodation in focus, or, more often, parts of a problem and parts of a solution that accommodate each other.

Table 1. Commonly occurring concepts used in the field of DSR applications.

Examples of solution projections	Examples of problem projections
"Knowledge Paths in Design Science Research" [8]	
Cause	Effect
Mean	End
Design Feature	Design Requirement
"Positioning And Presenting Design Science Research For Maximum Impact" [13]	
Method, Construct, Model, Instantiation	
"An elaborated action design research process model" [21]	
Instantiation	Application context
Conceptualisation of Problem [19]	
	Need, Goal, Requirement
Value Proposition Design [23]	
Pain Reliever	Pain
Gain creator	Gain
"Principles of marketing"[18]	
Good, Service, Experience, Benefit, Value, Quality, Performance, Feature	Need, Want, Demand
Prescriptive Knowledge in IS Research: Conceptualizing Design Principles in Terms of Materiality, Action, and Boundary Conditions [4]	
Affordance	
"Creative behavior guidebook" [24]	
Formulation of "How might we", or "What if we" questions	
Systems and Enterprise Architecture [17]	
Concern	Concern

In this paper, we focus on three aspects of accommodation: fit, mechanism, and effectuation, which are important to consider in DSR design knowledge creation. These three aspects are described below.

Fit: There is a need to be precise in the specification of design knowledge and principles about what in the problem accommodates what in the solution. More precisely, the concept of "*fit*" provides specificity of what in a problem fits with something specific in the solution. A fit is thus anchored in both a problem's and a solution's characterisations and projections. Examples of fit include "a feature fit with (or satisfied by) a requirement", "a pain reliever fit with (or satisfied by) a pain", and "a cause fits with (or leads to) an effect". A fit can also be absent, represented by a "*misfit*".

In a strict application of the accommodation concept, only projections are used to formulate fit, such as a 'stated feature' 'satisfies' a 'stated requirement'.

Mechanism: There is also a need to represent design knowledge of *how, or* the specific *way,* a problem and a solution are linked. Therefore, the concept of "mechanism" needs to be introduced. The "mechanism" brings to the surface and clarifies theoretical, design, and instantiation knowledge of the specific ways a cause leads to some effect, a means leads to some ends, or how a feature satisfies a requirement [5; 8], as well as how a pain reliever satisfies a pain [23].

The fit and mechanism provide a structure for representing, explaining, and justifying knowledge gaps, including the prescription gap, which is in focus in DSR. That is, means lead to some ends, as specified in [8].

Effectuation: A problem is not automatically solved once a solution is invented or provided; a temporal and dynamic space exists between a problem and a solution. The concept of "*effectuation*" brings to the surface the importance of and clarifies what happens over time, from the emergence of a problem to the solving it, that is, the situation

Table 2. Illustration of Fits, Mechanisms, and Effectuations found in DSR work

Examples in DSR of Accommodations (Fits, Mechanisms, and Effectuations)		
"Knowledge Paths in Design Science Research" [8]		
Cause	Contributes to (mechanism) (casual knowledge gap)	Effect
Mean	Achieves (mechanism) (prescription knowledge gap)	End
Design Feature	Fulfils (mechanism) (performativity knowledge gap)	Design Requirement
Value Proposition Design [23]		
Pain Reliever	Relieves (mechanism)	Pain
Gain Creator	Creates (mechanism)	Gain
"The Anatomy of a Design Principle" [14]		
Instance	Enacts (effectuation)	Context
"Design Science Research in Information Systems: A Critical Realist Approach" [3]		
problem situation (P)	Initiative (I) (effectuation), Mechanisms (M) (mechanism)	Context (C), Outcome (O),
"An elaborated action design research process model" [21]		
Instance	Implementation (effectuation)	Application Context
"Foundations of capability maps – a conceptual comparison" [27]		
Source, Input Factor, Substantiality	Lead-to (mechanism), Possibility, Substantiality	Result, Product, Substantiality
"The core of 'design thinking' and its application"[5]		
What, Thing	How (mechanism), Working Principle (mechanism)	Value, Result

when the solution has an effect. Here, we find concepts such as intervention and implementation [8; 9; 21]. For each problem-solution pair, zero or more possible effectuations exist that are, to a variable degree, desirable, viable, and feasible.

The importance of dynamic aspects is also recognised in domains such as benefits realisation [26], innovation [10], and change management [16].

3.3 Searching for Problems, Solutions, and Accommodations

A DSR process can start by searching for existing or future problems (with their projected needs and/or requirements that solutions should satisfy) to be addressed by existing or future solutions or searching for existing or future solutions (with their projected features, functions, and affordances) that can solve existing or future problems.

A common starting point in DSR is formulating a problem and a research question, although creativity in the design may lead to a co-evolution of problems and solutions.

The accommodation opens up a third search space where alternative fits, mechanisms and effectuations between a problem and a solution are explored. There are potentially many ways to effectuate a solution that can affect the desirability and viability of the solution in relation to the problem.

A common example from the IS domain is where the provisioning of a model [13] is intended to lead to an improved understanding of a complex situation. There are many alternative mechanisms to explore, such as reading the model, which leads to an increasing understanding of the situation, vs. discussing the topic that the model covers, leading to an increased appreciation of the problematic situation. There are also many variants of effectuations to explore, such as the model is sent to the user, or the user is trained to read the model before being sent the model, or/and there are several activities aiming towards the user acceptance [20] of the usage of the model.

The three searches, problem, solution, and accommodation, generate "*design candidates*" in the design triplet form, < problem, accommodation, solution >, where each design candidate carries different characteristics and fitness, which can be used to rank and select design candidates.

Furthermore, the search processes can be directed by the chosen frames [6, 25], used to interpret and evaluate problems, solutions, and accommodations, where *reframing* can lead to new design candidates to consider and evaluate.

3.4 Support for the Development of Design Knowledge

The accommodation concept provides a straightforward construct supporting the formulation and development of design knowledge.

The structural *fit* clarifies the choice of the "set of features, goals, and requirements of the artefact (design and/or instantiation) that are to be subject to evaluation" [28]. The *mechanism* brings to the surface the ways that underpin evaluations of "fitness for use". The *effectuation* enriches evaluations by representing what happens over time until the problem is being solved or is solved.

Moreover, the design triplet provides a basis for evaluating design candidates with respect to the problems and solutions and their inherent qualities, the fitness for use discussed in [11] and [7] and the new concept of fitness for effectuation.

Fitness for use concerns the practical applicability and effectiveness of the solution in real-world scenarios. Essentially, it evaluates whether the solution, when applied in normal circumstances, adequately resolves the problem as intended.

Fitness for effectuation concerns evaluating a solution's readiness and potential to be effectively implemented before and during problem-solving, similar to the feasibility of a project to bring about changes through interventions that incur outcomes, benefits, and costs, aiming at an intended operational situation. It concerns the attributes of a problem and a solution, the resources required for its implementation and alignment with stakeholder values and business, social and environmental objectives.

However, the design triplet does not reach into the time after problem-solving and the evaluations of the *fitness for evolution* [8, 15] and mutability of artefacts [12]. Fitness for evolution addresses the ability of a solution to adapt to changes in the problem space over time, while artefact mutability is the inherent capacity of a design artefact to be changed or adapted over time.

Accommodation supports the argumentation, assurance, and validity of how a solution solves a problem and the formulation of a testable hypothesis. An example of a hypothesis from the healthcare domain could be: "By creating a social media platform where patients with diabetes can meet peers and self-report their medication use (solution), their adherence to treatment plans (problem) is expected to increase by 30% within a year, through the facilitation of peer support where peers remind each other of medication use (accommodation - mechanism)".

4 Showcase

In this section, an ongoing research project is used to briefly illustrate how the conceptualization of accommodation can be used. The project aims to develop a prototype of a digital process management system to support the entire rehabilitation process for patients with cognitive problems after COVID-19. We will use the research projects to apply the concept of accommodation to demonstrate the relationships between problems and solutions, forming the design triplet < problem, accommodation, solution >.

First, we focus on creating a **problem characterisation** - a representation of the problem part of the triplet. One of the more specific problems to be addressed in the project is that the *Patients do not carry out cognitive training as much as they should (P1)*. This observation can be due to several factors, which can be seen as sub-problems, such as a patient being uncertain about the execution of the exercises; the exercises are not sufficiently adapted to a patient's specific needs and progress; and the patient may not see or understand the progress they are making during training. All these factors may decrease a patient´s motivation. In this section, we just focus on one of these sub-problems: *Patients are uncertain about the execution of the exercise (P1.1)*.

The **problem projection:** The problems could also be expressed as needs. A need can be defined as something that is urgently desired, while a problem can be seen as an unmet need. The benefit of including the concept of need is that they are often used before specifying a set of requirements. While a requirement is a statement of a desirable property of a specific solution, a need is independent of any solution. Given the sub-problems specified above, the following need could be derived: *The patient needs to interact with rehabilitation personnel (N1.1)*.

Second, the **solution characterisation** in the design triplet < problem, accommodation, solution > is specified, such as *Rehabilitation personnel acting as personal coaches during ongoing rehabilitation (S1)*. From the characterization, a feature is selected to be **solution projection**: *The system has a chat function (F1)*.

Third, and finally, the **accommodation** part in the design triplet < problem, accommodation, solution > is specified. Examining the accommodation means that we need to examine *fit* (what element of the problem and solution fit each other), the mechanism (argument for the fit), and the effectuation (the way the fit is implemented).

From the solutions and problems identified, we focus on the accommodation of need N1.1 (*The patient needs to interact with rehabilitation personnel*) and the solution feature F1 (*The system has a chat function*). This is the fit < N1.1, F1 > in focus.

For the *mechanism*, we need to find arguments or evidence that explains and/or justifies that the solution addresses the problem, forming a testable hypothesis. In this case, we thus need to argue that N1.1 is solved fully or partially by F1. That is, we could argue that interaction with rehabilitation personnel (N1.1) is a form of communication and may be mediated by a chat (F1) and provide evidence that a chat function is at least partially a good substitute for interaction. We could also question the accommodation by pointing out that an interaction with a chat function is not as inspiring as an interaction with a human, thereby representing a *misfit*.

The next step in the accommodation analysis is to apply the *effectuation* concept by examining how the fit and mechanism can be brought about. We could do this in a number of ways, for example, by providing different effectuation options:

- E1: Rehabilitation personnel send a message to the patient on how to use the chat.
- E2: Rehabilitation personnel share their screen with a patient and explain how to use the chat.
- E3: Rehabilitation personnel meet the patient in a physical meeting and show how the patient should use the chat.

Combining the three effectuation options results in three *design candidates*: < N1.1, E1, F1 >, < N1.1, E2, F1 >, and < N1.1, E3, F1 >.

To select the design candidate that is the best fit, the design candidates should be evaluated, for example, using the following three fitness types: Fitness for use, Fitness for evolution, and Fitness for effectuation. After this evaluation, the design candidates can be ranked before selecting the final candidate for implementation.

To increase the motivation for the patient to perform cognitive training, the design candidate < N1.1, E3, F1 > was selected for prototype implementation after evaluation.

5   Analogy to Production and Consumption of Information

The work on accommodation is part of a design effort to develop a Work-Oriented Approach to Information Products (WOA), supporting the representation, design, use, evolution, and evaluation of information products that solve problems in practices [1].

In WOA, information products can be considered solutions to information needs that agents have as a result of their work as solutions to information needs that an agent has, as a result of the work they do. Similarly, producing an information product, such as a model, which has specific features that address the information needs.

Producers offer and tailor their information product features, like affordances and pain relievers, to meet consumers' specific needs and requirements. These mechanisms ensure consumers effectively utilise products, addressing their information needs and alleviating pains. Additionally, training is provided to enhance consumer proficiency in using these products.

6 Conclusions

In this paper, we introduce the concept of accommodation as a means to link and evaluate the fit between solutions and problems. An accommodation consists of structural fit, elements for examining how a solution addresses a problem (i.e., mechanism) and how the solution should be deployed (i.e., effectuation). This concept can be used as part of design science projects or in other domains where there is a need to systematically examine how solutions relate to and solve problems.

Furthermore, the analogy of the production and consumption of information products will be further explored directly in the larger Work-Oriented Approach (WOA), aiming to improve the representation, design, use, evolution, and evaluation of information products that solve problems in work practices.

References

1. Tell, A.W.: Henkel M: Enriching enterprise architecture stakeholder analysis with relationships. In: 22nd International Conference on Perspective in Business Informatics Research (BIR2023), Springer Nature (2023)
2. Bider, I., Perjons, E., Johannesson, P.: Just finished a cycle of a design science research project: whats next? Complex Systems Informatics and Modeling Quarterly 0(22), (2020)
3. Carlsson, S.A.: Design science research in information systems: a critical realist approach design research in information systems: theory and practice. In: Hevner A, Chatterjee S (eds) Springer US, Boston, MA (2010)
4. Chandra, L., Seidel, S., Gregor, S.: Prescriptive knowledge in is research: conceptualizing design principles in terms of materiality, action, and boundary conditions. In: 2015 48th Hawaii International Conference on System Sciences (2015)
5. Dorst, K.: The core of ‚design thinking' and its application. Design Stud. 32(6), (2011)
6. Dorst, K.: Frame innovation: Create new thinking by design. MIT press (2015)
7. Drechsler, A., Hevner, A.: A Four-Cycle Model of IS Design Science Research: Capturing the Dynamic Nature of IS Artifact Design (2016)
8. Drechsler, A., Hevner, A.: Knowledge Paths in Design Science Research. Found. Trends in Inform. Syst. 6(3), (2022)
9. Drechsler, A., Hevner, A.R.: Utilizing, Producing, and Contributing Design Knowledge in DSR Projects. In: Chatterjee, S., Dutta, K., Sundarraj, R.P. (eds.) DESRIST 2018. LNCS, vol. 10844, pp. 82–97. Springer, Cham (2018). https://doi.org/10.1007/978-3-319-91800-6_6
10. Everett, M.R.: Diffusion of Innovations, 5th Edition. Free Press (2003)
11. Gill, T.G., Hevner, A.R.: A Fitness-Utility Model for Design Science Research (2011)
12. Gregor DJ, Shirley: The Anatomy of a Design Theory. (2007)

13. Gregor, S., Hevner, A.R.: Positioning and presenting design science research for maximum impact. MIS Quart. **37**(2), (2013)
14. Gregor, S., Kruse, L.C., Seidel, S.: The anatomy of a design principle. J. Assoc. Inform. Syst. (2020)
15. Hevner, A., Gregor. S.: Envisioning entrepreneurship and digital innovation through a design science research lens: a matrix approach. Inform. Manage. **59**(3), (2022)
16. Hiatt, J., Creasey, T.J.: Change management: The people side of change. Prosci (2003)
17. ISO/IEC/IEEE: 42010:2022 Architecture description (2022)
18. Kotler, P., Armstrong, G.: Principles of marketing. Pearson education (2010)
19. Maedche, A., Gregor, S., Morana, S., Feine, J.: Conceptualization of the Problem Space in Design Science Research. In: Tulu, B., Djamasbi, S., Leroy, G. (eds.) DESRIST 2019. LNCS, vol. 11491, pp. 18–31. Springer, Cham (2019). https://doi.org/10.1007/978-3-030-19504-5_2
20. Momani, A.M.: The unified theory of acceptance and use of technology: a new approach in technology acceptance. Int. J. Sociotechnol. Knowl. Develop. **12**(3), (2020)
21. Mullarkey, M.T., Hevner, A.R.: An elaborated action design research process model. Europ. J. Inform. Syst. **28**(1), (2018)
22. Nielsen, P.A.: Problematizing in IS design research. designing for digital transformation co-creating services with citizens and industry. In:15th International Conference on Design Science Research in Information Systems and Technology, DESRIST 2020, Kristiansand, Norway, December 2, Äì4, 2020, Proceedings 15, 259–271. Springer, (2020)
23. Osterwalder, A., Pigneur, Y., Bernarda, G., Smith, A.: Value proposition design: How to create products and services customers want. John Wiley Sons (2015)
24. Parnes, S.J.: Creative behavior guidebook. (No Title) (1967)
25. Schon, D.A., DeSanctis, V.: The Reflective Practitioner: How Professionals Think in Action (1986)
26. Serra, C.E.M., Kunc, M.: Benefits realisation management and its influence on project success and on the execution of business strategies. Int. J. Project Manage. **33**(1), (2015)
27. Tell, A.W., Henkel, M.: Foundations of capability maps - a conceptual comparison the practice of enterprise modeling. In: 15th IFIP WG 8.1 Working Conference, PoEM 2022. 101–117. Springer, (2022). https://doi.org/10.1007/978-3-031-21488-2_7
28. Venable, J., Pries-Heje, J., Baskerville, R.: FEDS: a Framework for Evaluation in Design Science Research. Europ. J. Inform. Syst. **25**(1), (2016)
29. vom Brocke, J., Hevner, A., Maedche, A.: Introduction to Design Science Research. In: vom Brocke, J., Hevner, A., Maedche, A. (eds.) Design Science Research. Cases. PI, pp. 1–13. Springer, Cham (2020). https://doi.org/10.1007/978-3-030-46781-4_1

Knowledge and Knowledge Technologies for Digital Business and Intelligent Systems

Toward Federated Learning Through Intent Detection Research

Daiga Deksne[1,2]([✉])[iD], Jurgita Kapočiūtė-Dzikienė[3,4][iD], and Raivis Skadiņš[1,2][iD]

[1] Tilde, Vienības Gatve 75A, Riga, Latvia
{daiga.deksne,raivis.skadins}@tilde.com
[2] Faculty of Computing, University of Latvia, Raiņa bulv. 19, Riga, Latvia
[3] Tilde IT, J. Jasinskio str. 12, Vilnius, Lithuania
jurgita.dzikiene@tilde.lt
[4] Faculty of Informatics, Vytautas Magnus University,
Universiteto str. 10, Kaunas, Lithuania

Abstract. Modern organizational communication heavily relies on virtual assistants, necessitating robust Natural Language Understanding (NLU) models for effective interaction. This research addresses the challenges of developing NLU models across multiple languages, including Estonian, English, German, Spanish, French, Italian, and Latvian. We explore various intent detection methodologies, including memory-based techniques that encompass both vectorization with Language-agnostic BERT Sentence Embedding (LaBSE), Advanced Data Analysis (ADA), or Sentence-level MultimOdal and LaNguage-Agnostic Representations (SONAR) models, and semantic search using cosine similarity or Levenshtein distance-based approaches. Additionally, we investigate supervised text classification methods such as FastText with the Convolutional Neural Network, LaBSE with Feed-Forward Neural Network, or fine-tuning LaBSE, as well as text generation techniques leveraging OpenAI's Davinci large language model. Our findings highlight the efficacy of memory-based approaches, particularly for non-English languages. We showcase the effectiveness of multilingual and cross-lingual LaBSE vectorization and the SONAR large language model. Furthermore, we introduce open-source intent detection software tailored for Federated Learning (FL). Through a prototype, we demonstrate the seamless integration of this framework into RASA-based virtual assistants, offering practical guidance for organizations interested in deploying intelligent and privacy-preserving conversational agents. This research advances virtual assistant development and highlights the potential of FL for seamless integration with NLU models. In the future, we plan to test it with more languages and with real client scenarios.

Keywords: Intent detection · Memory-based · supervised classification and generation approaches · Estonian · English · German · Spanish · French · Italian · and Latvian languages · Federated learning

A. Lupeikienė et al. (Eds.): DB&IS 2024, CCIS 2157, pp. 79–92, 2024.
https://doi.org/10.1007/978-3-031-63543-4_6

1   Introduction

In today's digital era, virtual assistants are essential for facilitating seamless communication, providing support, and enhancing efficiency. However, crafting reliable and adaptable virtual assistants poses significant challenges, particularly in the development of sophisticated NLU models. These models must accurately interpret user questions and deliver appropriate responses, demanding an advanced capability to process diverse linguistic inputs.

There are two types of NLU models in virtual assistants: generative or intent detection-based. Generative models create responses from scratch, which can lead to more versatile interactions but also increase the likelihood of errors or irrelevant answers, especially in complex or nuanced conversations. On the contrary, the intent detection models categorize user inputs into predefined classes (intents), which allows them to respond with highly relevant and accurate answers quickly. This approach is particularly effective for structured tasks like customer support or booking systems where predictable and consistent responses are required.

This project addresses the complexities associated with the intent detection-based NLU model development for virtual assistants and investigates the use of FL to protect data privacy. Our primary goals include:

- Developing accurate decentralized intent detection models for individual organizations and various languages while maintaining the decentralization of their private data.
- Creating a unified, centralized intent detection model that meets the collective needs of all participating entities.
- Enhancing virtual assistant development outcomes by FL frameworks.

This research is motivated by the need for more accurate virtual assistants, particularly for smaller and less explored languages such as Estonian. Additionally, the exploration of FL is driven by the imperative to uphold data privacy in intent detection-based NLU development within decentralized customer models.

However, this research faces several challenges and limitations. To our knowledge, memory-based approaches have not been explored or applied in FL for NLU intent detection-based models. This introduces new complexities, as there is a need to explore how to effectively learn these decentralized memory-based models and how to integrate them into a centralized model in an FL manner. Additionally, the research recognizes limitations with specific languages, such as Estonian, underscoring our reliance on the quality and comprehensiveness of pre-trained vectorization or Large Language Models (LLMs), which we use as the basis for our intent-detection models.

This paper outlines the methodology, experiments, results, and conclusions, emphasizing the potential of FL in enhancing the intent detection-based NLU model development and its future implications for virtual assistants. Furthermore, we introduce open-source software that leverages FL to ensure data privacy and a prototype that demonstrates how this framework can be integrated into RASA-based virtual assistants, including popular platforms like Bürokratt. This prototype validates our approach and provides practical guidance for incorporating FL into existing virtual assistant systems, enabling organizations to deploy more intelligent and privacy-preserving conversational agents.

2   Related Work

FL is becoming increasingly relevant in the field of NLP, offering a versatile approach to training models across a wide range of applications. While it's well-known for enhancing data privacy by allowing model training on decentralized data without the need to centralize sensitive information, its utility extends far beyond this. In NLP, FL is instrumental in facilitating the development of robust models capable of understanding and generating human language with unprecedented accuracy and depth.

One significant application of recent FL in NLP is in the training of LLMs [5,6,10]. These models require extensive datasets to learn effectively and produce state-of-the-art results in tasks like text classification, translation, and generation. FL enables the aggregation of insights from diverse data sources, facilitating the refinement of these models while strictly adhering to privacy concerns.

Beyond training LLMs, FL facilitates a broad spectrum of NLP tasks, including the adaptation of models to downstream tasks such as text classification, question-answering, and more [29,30]. Crucially, FL is especially valuable in applications where protecting client information is the most important, such as the development of virtual assistants [8].

The FL ecosystem today is rich with frameworks and libraries tailored for NLP, each addressing specific challenges of decentralized data processing. TensorFlow Federated (TFF) by Google [1] facilitates FL algorithm exploration and supports NLP tasks by keeping data on local devices, thus prioritizing privacy. PySyft [35] extends PyTorch and TensorFlow to offer secure computation tools essential for privacy in NLP. FATE [23] provides a secure framework enabling privacy-preserving collaborative NLP model training. Flower [2] emphasizes flexibility and performance, suitable for various NLP applications. FLUTE [12] focuses on rapid FL prototyping, offering optimization, privacy, and scalability features, supporting tasks like language modeling and sentiment analysis. FedNLP [22] benchmarks FL methods for NLP, offering a universal interface for transformer models under diverse data scenarios. FedAdapter [4] boosts FedNLP's efficiency with a novel adapter strategy and configuration profiling, hastening model convergence. However, these innovations are primarily tested with major languages like English, highlighting a need for broader linguistic inclusivity.

In the dynamically advancing domain of FL, the formulation and implementation of cutting-edge algorithms such as FedMA [32], FedAvg [26], FedAvgM, FedAdam [28], FedOPT [27], FedProx [21], and AdaPL [7] stand at the forefront of tackling the complex challenges associated with model training across widely distributed networks. Tailored predominantly for neural networks, these sophisticated algorithms employ advanced gradient descent and optimization techniques to effectively address prevalent issues such as non-iid data distributions and the imperative for variable learning rates, thereby enhancing the efficacy and efficiency of learning processes. Notably, the FedMA algorithm distinguishes itself with a novel methodology for the sequential construction of global models, proving to be exceptionally beneficial for network architectures like Convolutional Neural Networks and Long Short-Term Memory networks. This method utilizes an innovative adaptive weighting mechanism that meticulously optimizes model performance over heterogeneous data distributions, demonstrating the algorithm's ability to navigate the nuanced landscapes of data diversity. Concurrently, FedAvg lays the groundwork for aggregating model parameters across the network, a process subsequently refined by FedAvgM through the assimilation of meta-learning concepts. This refinement facilitates bespoke training adjustments, further personalizing the FL experience. In parallel, algorithms such as FedAdam and FedOPT revolutionize the adjustment of learning rates and momentum, significantly enhancing task performance and model convergence, notably within the realm of NLP. Moreover, FedProx tackles the formidable challenges presented by optimization in non-convex settings through the introduction of a proximal term, a strategic addition that fortifies the robustness and stability of the FL paradigm. Complementing these innovations, AdaFL brings to the fore a sophisticated client selection mechanism coupled with dynamic participant engagement strategies aimed at bolstering communication efficiency and stabilizing model performance across diverse and fluctuating network conditions. These algorithms collectively represent a significant stride forward in the FL field, embodying the collaborative spirit and innovative drive of the research community. They not only address critical technical obstacles such as data heterogeneity, model convergence, and operational efficiency but also pave the way for the widespread application of FL in a multitude of domains. Through their contributions, these algorithms enhance our understanding of decentralized learning systems, setting new standards for the development and application of FL technologies.

In the realm of FL experiments, the availability of appropriate datasets is essential. Among the classical datasets frequently employed for FL and NLP endeavors, we find 20 Newsgroup [18], Reuters-21578 [20], AG News [34], IMDb Reviews [24], TREC [31], DBpedia [19], and others, all of which are primarily tailored for English. On the other hand, multilingual datasets such as Amazon Reviews [25] encompass a broader linguistic range, covering English, Japanese, German, French, Chinese, and Spanish. In the context of intent detection, MultiATIS++ [33] stands out by supporting 9 languages, namely, English, Spanish, German, French, Portuguese, Chinese, Japanese, Hindi, and Turkish. Furthermore, the xSID [13] dataset encompasses 13 languages across 6 language families (including very low-resourced languages): Arabic, Chinese, Danish, Dutch, English, German, Indonesian, Italian, Japanese, Kazakh, Serbian, Turkish, and the Austro-Bavarian German dialect of South Tyrolean. While these benchmark datasets offer invaluable resources for conducting intent detection across a diverse linguistic spectrum, it's crucial to recognize their limitations concerning some languages, such as Estonian. However, for FL experiments, the adaptability of virtually any dataset to fit the FL paradigm is a potential solution. This adaptation process involves preparing the data to emulate a distributed, decentralized scenario. Such preparation usually entails data partitioning to reflect the natural distribution across various devices or geographic locales, thereby simulating the operational conditions of FL.

Yet, the exploration of FL extends beyond these gradient-based methods. There is an emerging interest in applying FL to memory-based models, a domain ripe for innovation but still largely unexplored. Memory-based models, essential for tasks requiring the quick recall of specific instances or attributes, pose distinct challenges in an FL context. Our research attempts to meld FL's decentralized, privacy-centric advantages with the detailed, instance-specific strengths of memory-based approaches. Furthermore, we seek to broaden the scope of FL into the domain of intent detection, with a focus on enhancing language models for underrepresented languages, such as Estonian.

3 Solution Architecture

This project aims to develop tailored aggregated bots for multiple organizations, combining independent bot creation to construct a unified bot for a seamless user experience. This unified approach addresses diverse domain and organization-related questions, ensuring users don't distinguish between different bots.

Our solution architecture (Fig. 1) includes remote bot training environments where trainers develop bots independently. These trainers manage private training data and tailor local models to their bot's specific needs.

Additionally, a central training hub employs a federated approach to train an aggregated NLU model, amalgamating parameters from remote locations. This creates a unified NLU model proficient in discerning intents from shared training data, meeting various organizational requirements.

4 Intent Detection

The essence of any virtual assistant lies in its NLU module, which can operate either in intent detection or answer generation mode. However, intent detection usually requires less training data to achieve high accuracy levels, which better aligns with our customer expectations.

Consequently, our problem-solving strategy prioritizes intent detection, particularly through supervised text classification, which necessitates the availability of a training dataset.

4.1 Dataset

Our intent detection research aimed to test the effectiveness of various text classification approaches across multiple languages by exploring the potential for integrating additional languages into the NLU model in the future. These experiments were conducted using two datasets:

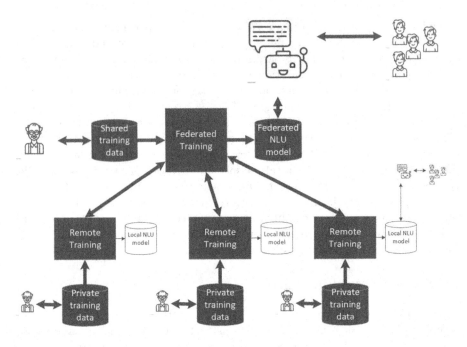

Fig. 1. System overview

- *Multi-language segregated dataset*[1] (for the statistics see Table 1) containing several languages (English, German, French, Italian, Spanish, and Latvian). The dataset contains 37 intents (classes) and is structured to ensure that each text instance is associated with only one class, assuring the nature of single-label classification. All instances were shuffled and split into training (80%) and testing (20%) subsets within the frame of each class and for each language. The dataset is well-balanced resulting in low majority (1) and random baselines (2).
- *Estonian datasets* containing purely Estonian texts. These three datasets (for the statistics see Table 2)[2] were constructed using data provided by RIA from the Bürokratt project. Instances in each dataset were divided using the same methodology as the *Multi-language segregated dataset*. For training and testing, we implemented 5-fold cross-validation. Initially, the entire dataset was shuffled and divided into 5 equal subsets. In each of the 5 iterations of the process, 4 subsets were used for training and the remaining one for testing. This ensured that each subset served as the testing set exactly once. The Sot-

---

[1] The dataset has been created in the StairwAI project (https://stairwai.nws.cs.unibo.it/) funded by the European Union's Horizon 2020 research and innovation programme under grant agreement 101017142.

[2] All Estonian datasets have been made publicly accessible on https://github.com/tilde-nlp/fnlu/tree/main/Other assuring transparency and their usage by others in the future.

siaalkindlustusamet dataset exhibits less balance, leading to a notably high majority baseline that our methods must surpass.

$$majority_{baseline} = max(P_i), \qquad (1)$$

where P_i is the probability of the class.

$$random_{baseline} = \sum (P_i)^2 \qquad (2)$$

Table 1. Statistics about the *Multi-language segregated dataset.*

Language	Instances in training split	Instances in testing split	Majority baseline	Random baseline
English	386	94	0.074	0.033
German	192	47	0.064	0.032
Spanish	193	47	0.064	0.032
French	193	47	0.064	0.032
Italian	193	47	0.064	0.032
Latvian	183	46	0.065	0.031

Table 2. Statistics of the *Estonian datasets.*

Dataset	Number of intents	Number of instances	Majority baseline	Random baseline
Rahvusraamatukogu (National Library)	36	1 104	0.130	0.053
Sotsiaalkindlustusamet (Social Insurance)	7	79	0.418	0.235
Kriisijuhtimine (Crisis Management)	23	287	0.105	0.054

4.2 Approaches

Within the frame of this project, we have used the datasets presented in Sect. 4.1 and tested them with the following text classification methods:

- **FastText+CNN.** This supervised text classification approach combines Fast-Text embeddings [15] with a customized Convolutional Neural Network (CNN) architecture [17]. FastText utilizes subword embedding information, enabling it to construct word vectors even in cases of out-of-vocabulary words or typos. On the other hand, CNN focuses on identifying token n-grams, which is particularly useful for text classification tasks reliant on keywords rather than the entire contextual meaning of the text. For our experiments, we utilized the proprietary FastText embedding model supporting English and Latvian languages in conjunction with the CNN architecture presented in [16]. This method will exclusively serve as the baseline.

- **LaBSE+FFNN.** We utilized the frozen Language Agnostic BERT Sentence Embedding (LaBSE) approach proposed by [11], alongside a two-layer fully connected Feed Forward Neural Network (FFNN) model optimized and fine-tuned for our intent detection tasks. LaBSE differs from traditional BERT embeddings by providing sentence-level representations, capturing the semantics of entire texts simultaneously. It supports 109 languages, including all our target languages, generating fixed-size vectors for texts without retaining word boundaries. LaBSE is not sensitive to word order, therefore it is well-suited for languages with flexible sentence structures, requiring less training data to cover various sentence structures. However, LaBSE's cross-lingual capability may vary across languages.

- **LaBSE-LangChain-k1** (which is the memory-based approach) leverages the LangChain framework, enabling context-aware applications without the need for training. For the *Multi-language segregated dataset*, training instances are vectorized and stored in the Chroma vector database, where cosine similarity and a greedy search algorithm are utilized to locate the nearest training instance to the test instance, subsequently assigning its label. In contrast, for the *Estonian dataset* stored in the Faiss vector database, the method employs the Euclidean distance in conjunction with a greedy search to perform a similar matching and labeling process. LaBSE remains the vectorization model.

- **LaBSE-LangChain-k10-mv.** This method closely resembles LaBSE-LangChain-k1, but instead of searching for a single similar instance, it searches for the 10 closest instances, collects their class labels, and conducts a majority vote to determine the final class.

- **ADA-LangChain-k1.** This approach resembles LaBSE-LangChain-k1, but instead of LaBSE, OpenAI's Advanced Data Analysis (ADA) [14] embeddings, particularly the text-embedding-ada-002 s-generation model, are used to vectorize texts.

- **ADA-LangChain-k10-mv.** This approach is similar to LaBSE-LangChain-k10-mv, but instead of LaBSE, it uses text-embedding-ada-002 model.

- **Davinci-fine-tuning.** For this approach, we utilized OpenAI's davinci-002 large language model [3], a generative transformer model. In our experiments, we fine-tuned the added layers' parameters while keeping the hyperparameter values at their defaults. Additionally, we restricted this model to generate only a single token as the input text's label.

- **SONAR-LangChain-k1** adopts a similar approach to LaBSE-LangChain-k1 but: 1) employs the SONAR vectorization model [9] developed by META research instead of LaBSE; 2) uses the Faiss database instead of Chroma; 3) in case of the semantic search, applies the Euclidean distance measure metric instead of cosine similarity. SONAR is an open-source large language model that supports all our target languages and was chosen to broaden the scope of our experimentation, as it has recently garnered significant attention in numerous text classification tasks across various languages. Faiss, on the other hand, is optimal in scenarios that require the combination of multiple indexes into a single retriever, which can contribute to the easier implementation of the FL paradigm.

4.3   Experiments and Results

The initial experiments utilized a *Multi-language segregated dataset.* For methods involving training, the dataset was shuffled and divided into training (80%) and validation (20%) sets, with accuracy chosen as the primary evaluation metric.

Approaches with randomized parameter initialization were tested 5 times and averaged results along with confidence intervals were calculated. However, this procedure did not apply to methods tested for comparison purposes only, such as FastText+CNN, which serves as a baseline supporting only two languages, or Davinci-fine-tuning, a method that stores models on third-party servers and incurs charges, both of which are unacceptable for our clients. Results obtained with the *Multi-language segregated dataset* are summarized in Fig. 2.

Zooming in on Fig. 2, we can draw the following conclusions. Davinci-fine-tuning, followed by LaBSE-LangChain-k1 and ADA-LangChain-k1, emerged as the most suitable approaches for the English dataset. In contrast, LaBSE-fine-tuning exhibited the highest accuracy for other languages (German, Spanish, French, Italian, and Latvian). Despite its superior performance, LaBSE-fine-tuning proves impractical due to its lengthy training times (up to 1 h on our small dataset) and high hardware demands (exceeding 12 GiB of GPU RAM). Considering the distributed nature of NLU models training across different locations, it's evident that not all participating entities will possess these computational capabilities. Consequently, LaBSE-LangChain-k1 emerges as the next best option, delivering good results for the majority of non-English languages.

For the second set of experiments with the *Estonian datasets*, we narrowed down the list of tested approaches to LaBSE-LangChain-k1 and SONAR-LangChain-k1. The initial experiments served as a pilot to identify effective methods across various languages, where memory-based approaches emerged as the optimal solution. Subsequent experiments focused on the Estonian language, particularly using the promising memory-based approach LaBSE-LangChain-k1. Additionally, for comparison, we included the recently released SONAR model in our tests as another memory-based method. Furthermore, we conducted a more comprehensive investigation, evaluating not only accuracy but also precision, recall, MicroF1, and MacroF1. The results in Table 3 demonstrate the slight superiority of SONAR-LangChain-k1 over LaBSE-LangChain-k1. Both LaBSE and SONAR have their advantages and drawbacks in terms of speed and resource usage. LaBSE is faster, completing requests in 27–30 milliseconds compared to SONAR's 120–130 milliseconds, but SONAR consumes less disk space at 2.85 GiB, while LaBSE requires 5.27 GiB.

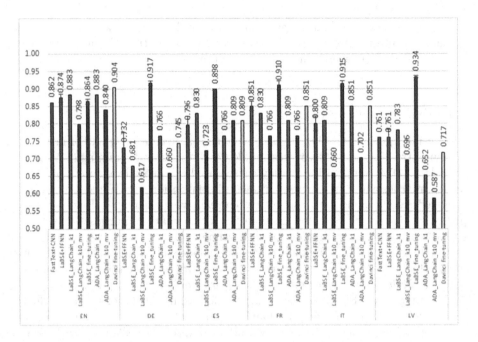

Fig. 2. The accuracy values achieved with different approaches and languages on the *Multi-language segregated dataset* with 37 intents.

4.4 Discussion

The experiments with a *Multi-language segregated dataset* demonstrate that all tested approaches are suitable for our problem-solving needs, as the achieved accuracies significantly outperform random and majority baselines. Davinci-fine-tuning emerges as the most accurate technique for the well-supported English language, while LaBSE-fine-tuning (with unfrozen parameters and additional layers) proves to be the best technique for all other tested non-English languages (German, Spanish, French, Italian, and Latvian). This outcome is unsurprising, considering that this model is not only multilingual (supporting all our target languages) but also cross-lingual (capable of benefiting from the inclusion of other languages in the model). Despite its significantly good performance, LaBSE-fine-tuning is less practical compared to the second-best approach, LaBSE-LangChain-k1, which requires much less training time and GPU computational resources, making it better suited to the needs of the participating entities in the context of FL.

The experiments conducted with the *Estonian datasets* reveal a slight superiority of the SONAR-LangChain-k1 approach over LaBSE-LangChain-k1. This outcome isn't surprising, considering that the SONAR model has demonstrated strong performance across various text classification tasks in different languages. Our research confirms its effectiveness also for the Estonian language. However, it's worth noting that all datasets used in our experiments are rather small, which complicates the evaluation of statistically significant differences in results.

Table 3. Evaluation results on *Estonian datasets.*

Dataset	LaBSE-LangChain-k1	SONAR-LangChain-k1
Rahvusraamatukogu (National Library) 36 intents	accuracy: 0.760	accuracy: 0.763
	precision: 0.760	precision: 0.763
	recall: 0.760	recall: 0.763
	MicroF1: 0.760	MicroF1: 0.763
	MacroF1: 0.726	MacroF1: 0.758
Sotsiaalkindlustusamet (Social Insurance) 7 intents	accuracy: 0.608	accuracy: 0.709
	precision: 0.608	precision: 0.709
	recall: 0608	recall: 0.709
	MicroF1: 0.608	MicroF1: 0.709
	MacroF1: 0.589	MacroF1: 0.638
Kriisijuhtimine (Crisis management) 23 intents	accuracy: 0.5	accuracy: 0.503
	precision: 0.5	precision: 0.503
	recall: 0.5	recall: 0.503
	MicroF1: 0.5	MicroF1: 0.503
	MacroF1: 0.484	MacroF1: 0.479

Despite the small size of the datasets used, they meet our customers' expectations, showing that positive results are achievable even with limited data.

Given that memory-based approaches have demonstrated their effectiveness in accurately addressing our intent detection problems, they are naturally well-suited for integration within the FL framework.

5   Solution Implementation

The intent detection experiments underscored the effectiveness of memory-based approaches, particularly LaBSE-LangChain-k1 and SONAR-LangChain-k1 methods, with the latter showing slight superiority on *Estonian datasets.* In memory-based approaches, training entails storing instances and conducting semantic searches, offering several advantages. It eliminates the need for predefined intents during centralized model training and allows the model to adapt to fluctuations in training data. Furthermore, errors in the data have minimal impact on the model's integrity, as intents are independent across participating entities. Each entity can introduce or modify intents, re-vectorize local models, and update the centralized model autonomously, mitigating common issues in standard FL algorithms.

Our federated intent detection solution with the core of the memory-based NLU model is implemented as open-source software, accessible on GitHub[3] under the Apache 2.0 license. It includes two components: a federated intent detector used for both training and real-time inference, and vectorization services offered

---

[3] https://github.com/tilde-nlp/fnlu

through Docker containers with options for LaBSE and SONAR embedding models. The solution has undergone initial testing with the *Estonian datasets*.

The prototype showcases an example implementation integrating FL into Rasa[4] bot software, with setup instructions for configuring and deploying the federated NLU system in distributed environments. This approach can be adapted for integration into other Rasa-based software products like Bürokratt.

Additionally, there are also setup instructions detailing how to set up the federated NLU system with one central site and multiple remote sites across participating entities. These instructions serve as a comprehensive guide for configuring and deploying the system in a distributed environment.

6   Conclusions

Our project aims to develop customized virtual assistants for diverse organizational needs, utilizing innovative NLU solutions. We explored various intent detection methodologies (memory-based, supervised classification, text generation), highlighting the effectiveness of memory-based techniques (such as vectorization of text and semantical search over them), particularly for non-English languages like Estonian. This aligns with our focus and suggests the potential for seamless implementation in FL frameworks.

Additionally, we introduce open-source intent detection software employing FL, enhancing accuracy while prioritizing data privacy and security. A prototype showcases its integration into RASA-based virtual assistants, including platforms like Bürokratt.

In the future, we plan to conduct extensive testing of the FL system in real-world environments, encompassing diverse languages and client scenarios.

Acknowledgments. This research has been supported by "Eesti keeletehnoloogia 2018-2027" project: EKTB78 Liitõppe rakendamise võimalused dialoogiandmete põhjal.

References

1. Authors, T.T.F.: TensorFlow Federated (2018). https://github.com/tensorflow/federated
2. Beutel, D.J., Topal, T., Mathur, A., Qiu, X., Parcollet, T., Lane, N.D.: Flower: a friendly federated learning research framework. CoRR arxiv:2007.14390 (2020)
3. Brown, T., et al.: Language models are few-shot learners. Adv. Neural. Inf. Process. Syst. **33**, 1877–1901 (2020)
4. Cai, D., Wu, Y., Wang, S., Lin, F.X., Xu, M.: Fedadapter: efficient federated learning for modern nlp. In: Proceedings of the 29th Annual International Conference on Mobile Computing and Networking. ACM MobiCom 2023, Association for Computing Machinery, New York (2023). https://doi.org/10.1145/3570361.3592505

---

[4] https://www.kratid.ee/en/burokratt.

5. Che, T., et al.: Federated learning of large language models with parameter-efficient prompt tuning and adaptive optimization. In: Bouamor, H., Pino, J., Bali, K. (eds.) Proceedings of the 2023 Conference on Empirical Methods in Natural Language Processing, pp. 7871–7888. Association for Computational Linguistics, Singapore (2023). https://doi.org/10.18653/v1/2023.emnlp-main.488. https://aclanthology.org/2023.emnlp-main.488

6. Chen, C., Feng, X., Zhou, J., Yin, J., Zheng, X.: Federated large language model: a position paper (2023)

7. Chen, Z., Chong, K.F.E., Quek, T.Q.S.: Dynamic attention-based communication-efficient federated learning. CoRR arxiv:2108.05765 (2021)

8. Cureton, M., Corradini, A.: Federated learning for intent classification. In: 2023 IEEE 19th International Conference on Intelligent Computer Communication and Processing (ICCP), pp. 315–322 (2023). https://doi.org/10.1109/ICCP60212.2023.10398713

9. Duquenne, P.A., Schwenk, H., Sagot, B.: Sonar: sentence-level multimodal and language-agnostic representations. arXiv e-prints pp. arXiv–2308 (2023)

10. Fan, T., et al.: Fate-llm: a industrial grade federated learning framework for large language models. arXiv preprint arXiv:2310.10049 (2023)

11. Feng, F., Yang, Y., Cer, D., Arivazhagan, N., Wang, W.: Language-agnostic BERT sentence embedding. In: Muresan, S., Nakov, P., Villavicencio, A. (eds.) Proceedings of the 60th Annual Meeting of the Association for Computational Linguistics, vol. 1: Long Papers, pp. 878–891. Association for Computational Linguistics, Dublin (2022).https://doi.org/10.18653/v1/2022.acl-long.62. https://aclanthology.org/2022.acl-long.62

12. Garcia, M.H., Manoel, A., Diaz, D.M., Mireshghallah, F., Sim, R., Dimitriadis, D.: Flute: a scalable, extensible framework for high-performance federated learning simulations. arXiv preprint arXiv:2203.13789 (2022)

13. van der Goot, R., et al.: From masked language modeling to translation: non-english auxiliary tasks improve zero-shot spoken language understanding. In: Toutanova, K., et al. (eds.) Proceedings of the 2021 Conference of the North American Chapter of the Association for Computational Linguistics: Human Language Technologies, pp. 2479–2497. Association for Computational Linguistics (2021). https://doi.org/10.18653/v1/2021.naacl-main.197. https://aclanthology.org/2021.naacl-main.197

14. Greene, R., Sanders, T., Weng, L., Neelakantan, A.: New and improved embedding model(2022). https://openai.com/blog/new-and-improved-embedding-model. Accessed 13 Feb 2024

15. Joulin, A., Grave, E., Bojanowski, P., Mikolov, T.: Bag of tricks for efficient text classification. In: Lapata, M., Blunsom, P., Koller, A. (eds.) Proceedings of the 15th Conference of the European Chapter of the Association for Computational Linguistics, vol. 2, Short Papers, pp. 427–431. Association for Computational Linguistics, Valencia (2017). https://aclanthology.org/E17-2068

16. Kapočiūtė-Dzikienė, J., Balodis, K., Skadiņš, R.: Intent detection problem solving via automatic dnn hyperparameter optimization. Appl. Sci. **10**(21), 7426 (2020)

17. Kim, Y.: Convolutional neural networks for sentence classification. In: Moschitti, A., Pang, B., Daelemans, W. (eds.) Proceedings of the 2014 Conference on Empirical Methods in Natural Language Processing (EMNLP), pp. 1746–1751. Association for Computational Linguistics, Doha (2014). https://doi.org/10.3115/v1/D14-1181. https://aclanthology.org/D14-1181

18. Lang, K.: Newsweeder: learning to filter netnews. In: Machine Learning Proceedings 1995, pp. 331–339. Elsevier (1995)

19. Lehmann, J., et al.: Dbpedia-a large-scale, multilingual knowledge base extracted from wikipedia. Semant. Web **6**(2), 167–195 (2015)

20. Lewis, D.: Reuters-21578 text categorization test collection. Distribution 1.0, AT&T Labs-Research (1997)
21. Li, T., Sahu, A.K., Zaheer, M., Sanjabi, M., Talwalkar, A., Smith, V.: Federated optimization in heterogeneous networks. Proc. Mach. Learn. Syst. **2**, 429–450 (2020)
22. Lin, B.Y., et al.: FedNLP: benchmarking federated learning methods for natural language processing tasks. In: Carpuat, M., de Marneffe, M.C., Meza Ruiz, I.V. (eds.) Findings of the Association for Computational Linguistics: NAACL 2022, pp. 157–175. Association for Computational Linguistics, Seattle (2022). https://doi.org/10.18653/v1/2022.findings-naacl.13. https://aclanthology.org/2022.findings-naacl.13
23. Liu, Y., Fan, T., Chen, T., Xu, Q., Yang, Q.: Fate: an industrial grade platform for collaborative learning with data protection. J. Mach. Learn. Res. **22**(1), 1–6 (2021)
24. Maas, A.L., Daly, R.E., Pham, P.T., Huang, D., Ng, A.Y., Potts, C.: Learning word vectors for sentiment analysis. In: Lin, D., Matsumoto, Y., Mihalcea, R. (eds.) Proceedings of the 49th Annual Meeting of the Association for Computational Linguistics: Human Language Technologies, pp. 142–150. Association for Computational Linguistics, Portland (2011). https://aclanthology.org/P11-1015
25. McAuley, J., Leskovec, J.: Hidden factors and hidden topics: understanding rating dimensions with review text. In: Proceedings of the 7th ACM Conference on Recommender Systems, pp. 165–172 (2013)
26. McMahan, B., Moore, E., Ramage, D., Hampson, S., Arcas, B.A.: Communication-efficient learning of deep networks from decentralized data. In: Artificial Intelligence and Statistics, pp. 1273–1282. PMLR (2017)
27. Reddi, S., et al.: Adaptive federated optimization. arXiv preprint arXiv:2003.00295 (2020)
28. Reddi, S.J., et al.: Adaptive federated optimization. CoRR arxiv:2003.00295 (2020)
29. Roth, H., Xu, Z., Renduchintala, A.: Adapting LLMs to downstream tasks using federated learning on distributed datasets. NVIDIA Technical Blog. (2023). https://developer.nvidia.com/blog/adapting-llms-to-downstream-tasks-using-federated-learning-on-distributed-datasets/. Accessed 13 Feb 2024
30. Schumann, G., Awick, J.P., Gómez, J.M.: Natural language processing using federated learning: a structured literature review. In: 2023 IEEE International Conference on Artificial Intelligence, Blockchain, and Internet of Things (AIBThings), pp. 1–7 (2023). https://doi.org/10.1109/AIBThings58340.2023.10292481
31. Voorhees, E.M., Harman, D.K., et al.: TREC: Experiment and Evaluation in Information Retrieval, vol. 63. MIT press, Cambridge (2005)
32. Wang, H., Yurochkin, M., Sun, Y., Papailiopoulos, D.S., Khazaeni, Y.: Federated learning with matched averaging. CoRR arxiv:2002.06440 (2020)
33. Xu, W., Haider, B., Mansour, S.: End-to-end slot alignment and recognition for cross-lingual NLU. In: Webber, B., Cohn, T., He, Y., Liu, Y. (eds.) Proceedings of the 2020 Conference on Empirical Methods in Natural Language Processing (EMNLP), pp. 5052–5063. Association for Computational Linguistics (2020). https://doi.org/10.18653/v1/2020.emnlp-main.410. https://aclanthology.org/2020.emnlp-main.410
34. Zhang, X., LeCun, Y.: Text understanding from scratch. CoRR arxiv:1502.01710 (2015)
35. Ziller, A., et al.: Pysyft: a library for easy federated learning. In: Federated learning Systems: Towards Next-Generation AI, pp. 111–139 (2021)

Future Directions in Defence NLP: Investigating Research Gaps for Low-Resource Languages

Vitalijs Teze[✉][iD] and Erika Nazaruka[iD]

Riga Technical University, 6A Kipsalas Street, Riga 1048, Latvia
vitalijs.teze@edu.rtu.lv, erika.nazaruka@rtu.lv

Abstract. This paper examines the integration of Natural Language Processing (NLP) technologies within security and defence domains, particularly focusing on the challenges posed by low-resource languages. Recognizing the critical need for sophisticated technological support to process the vast amounts of unstructured linguistic data in multinational operations and peacekeeping missions, we aim to bridge the research gap in military and defence applications for processing such information. Through a literature review, we identify potential advancements in NLP technologies that cater to low-resource settings, thus facilitating improved communication, intelligence sharing, and operational efficiency. Our analysis underscores the pivotal role of NLP in enhancing the operational effectiveness and strategic capabilities of defence and security organizations, especially in linguistically diverse and computationally constrained environments. By systematically examining existing literature, the study not only highlights significant advancements but also reveals critical gaps and opportunities for future research in the application of NLP technologies for defence and security in the context of linguistic diversity and computational limitations.

Keywords: Natural language processing · Low-Resource languages · Defense and security

1 Introduction

The rapidly evolving landscape of security and defence necessitates sophisticated technological support to handle the vast amount of unstructured linguistic data encountered in field operations. In this context, NLP technologies emerge as pivotal tools capable of transforming raw text into actionable intelligence. However, the effectiveness of these technologies is significantly challenged by low-resource languages—a common scenario in multinational operations and peacekeeping missions. Recognizing the critical role of NLP in enhancing the operational effectiveness and strategic capabilities of defence and security organizations, especially in low-resource settings, this paper sets forth to explore the current state and potential advancements in NLP technologies tailored for these applications.

Objective: This study aims to address research gaps in military and defence solutions for processing low-resource linguistic information in its various forms, including spoken and written (handwriting, printed documents, or typed text). Our goal is to recognize, understand, and translate such information, thereby facilitating improved communication, intelligence-sharing, and operational efficiency in multinational and peacekeeping operations.

Research Question: Specifically, we seek to answer the question, "How have recent advancements in NLP and machine learning (ML) technologies been applied to process low-resource linguistic information in military and defence contexts, and what gaps exist in current research regarding the recognition, understanding, and translation of spoken and written forms (including handwriting, printed documents, and typed text) of such information?".

By systematically examining existing literature, this study identifies several potential research gaps that offer opportunities for significant contributions to the fields of Command, Control, Communications, Computers, Intelligence, Surveillance, and Reconnaissance (C4ISR), and joint multinational and/or peacekeeping operations. Among these are the development of NLP models that not only process linguistic information from low-resource languages but also ensure secure, robust, and culturally sensitive applications in defence settings.

As global security dynamics continue to evolve, the role of NLP technologies in defence and security applications becomes increasingly indispensable. This paper aims to contribute to the ongoing discourse on enhancing NLP capabilities in the face of linguistic diversity and computational limitations, ultimately supporting more effective and adaptable security and defence strategies.

2   Establishing the Review Strategy

To explore research gaps and evaluate our topic's effectiveness, a detailed literature review is essential, focusing on optimal methods in Computer Science, Information Technology, and Software Engineering. Utilizing Google Scholar (GS) and Semantic Scholar (SS), we searched for "systematic literature review software engineering" without date restrictions. Initial results were 18,200 on SS and one on GS, which increased to 3,570,000 after query adjustment.

Despite different sorting options, both identified "Systematic literature reviews in software engineering—A systematic literature review" [1]. as the most relevant, cited 3105 on SS and 4892 times on GS, respectively. Further analysis of citing papers, specifically filtered for Computer Science on SS, led to a shortlist of 9 significant papers, detailed in Table 1, based on citation count and relevance.

The detailed analysis of the papers allowed to produce a strategy for further review.

- Planning and Protocol Development: Define the review's purpose, develop a protocol, and establish criteria [2, 3].
- Extensive and Structured Literature Search: Conduct systematic searches using automation and visual text mining tools [4].
- Inclusion of Snowballing Technique: Implement backward and forward snowballing for comprehensive coverage [5].
- Quality Assessment and Selection: Rigorously screen and evaluate studies for quality and relevance [6, 7].

Table 1. The most cited papers applicable for literature review strategy establishment.

Paper title	First author	Year	Citations
Systematic literature reviews in software engineering—a systematic literature review	Kitchenham, B.	2009	3105
Guidelines for snowballing in systematic literature studies and a replication in software engineering	Wohlin, C.	2014	2617
Experimentation in software engineering	Wohlin, C.	2012	1479
A guide to conducting a systematic literature review of information systems research	Okoli, C.	2010	1428
Systematic literature reviews in software engineering—a tertiary study	Kitchenham, B.	2010	900
A guide to conducting a standalone systematic literature review	Okoli, C.	2015	667
A systematic review of systematic review process research in software engineering	Kitchenham, B.	2013	576
Standing on the shoulders of giants: challenges and recommendations of literature search in information systems research	Brocke, J.	2015	475
Automating systematic literature review	Felizardo, K. R.	2020	20

- Data Extraction, Synthesis, and Reporting: Extract data meticulously, synthesize findings, and report with a focus on methodological rigor and diversity [3, 8].
- Continuous Refinement of Process: Address challenges and refine search processes and quality assessment techniques as needed [1, 9].

3 Literature Review Plan

The review is aiming to address research gaps in military and defence solutions to process low-resource linguistic information in its different forms, i.e. spoken and written (handwriting, printed documents, or typed text), to recognise, understand and translate it.

We will try to find out how have recent advancements NLP and machine learning (ML) technologies been applied to process low-resource linguistic information in military and defence contexts, and what gaps exist in current research regarding the recognition, understanding, and translation of spoken and written forms (including handwriting, printed documents, and typed text) of such information?

The review will be conducted over the existing literature related to NLP technologies in low-resource, security, and defence contexts. The studies that are going to be considered need to be published in the last 10 years to ensure relevance and incorporation of recent advancements. We will focus on English language sources, include peer-reviewed journals, conference proceedings, academic theses, books, and reputable industry reports.

We are going to look for various combination of keywords like "NLP", "low-resource language processing", "defence", "security", "confidential data", machine learning in defence", "language technologies in security", etc. Using boolean operators to refine the search is going to be considered. The databases that are going to be utilized are IEEE Xplore, ACM Digital Library, Scopus, Science Direct, GS, and SS.

Studies that focus on NLP technologies in low-resource settings, specific applications in defence and security, and methodologies for handling confidential data are going to be included in the research. Another group of papers that is going to be included is the one that contributes to C4ISR decision making process. The papers that are not directly related to defence or low-resource settings, outdated methodologies, and non-English papers (unless exceptionally relevant and translatable) are going to be excluded from the research.

We are going to summarize study objectives, methodology, key findings, and specific relevance to our research topic and identify research gaps to highlight the directions for future research.

4 Literature Review Execution

The list of the primary keywords used in the search is the following: "Natural Language Processing", "Low-resource Languages", "Defence", "Security", "Machine Learning", "Data Confidentiality", "Linguistic Data Processing", "Speech Recognition", "Text Analysis", "Artificial Intelligence in Defence".

The search conducted with the keywords alone produced the result that is nearly impossible to process. So, it was considered to execute the following boolean combinations as an initial criterion, with a note that in case of insufficient number of papers found, usage of synonyms was considered:

- "Natural Language Processing" AND "Defence": To find studies that specifically address NLP applications in defence. (I)
- "Low-resource Languages" AND "Security": For research on NLP technologies in security settings dealing with less common languages. (II)
- "Machine Learning" AND "Data Confidentiality": To explore ML techniques with a focus on maintaining data privacy. (III)
- "Natural Language Processing" AND "Low-resource": For general studies on NLP in low-resource settings. (IV)
- "Speech Recognition" AND "Military": To find information on speech recognition technologies in military use. (V)
- "Text Analysis" AND "Confidential": For text analysis methods with an emphasis on confidentiality issues. (VI)
- "Artificial Intelligence" AND "Defence Technologies" To explore broader AI applications in defence technologies. (VII)
- "Natural Language Processing" AND "Linguistic Data Processing" AND "Security": For a comprehensive search on linguistic data processing in security contexts. (VIII)
- "Machine Learning" AND "Speech Recognition" AND "Defence": To find studies at the intersection of ML, speech recognition, and defence. (IX)

If the search resulted in more than 100 articles, the query was refined by incorporating additional keywords to reduce the number of results. The keywords, along with their respective mappings, are as follows: "Military" (1), "Defence" (2), "Security" (3), and "Low-resource" (4).

Table 2 presents the number of results obtained from the initial search conducted on the selected databases, covering publications from the years 2014 to 2024, and including "Computer Science" as the field of study where applicable.

Table 2. Initial database search results.

Search criterion	IEEE Xplore	ACM digital library	Scopus	Science direct	Google scholar	Semantic scholar
I	21 (1)	86 (1, 3, 4)	7 (1)	5 (1, 3, 4)	227 (1, 3, 4)	30 (1, 3, 4)
II	10	88	10	69	111 (1, 2)	1 (1, 2)
III	6 (1)	70 (1)	4 (2)	78 (1, 2)	45 (1, 2, 3, 4)	38 (1, 2)
IV	2 (2)	87 (1, 2)	2 (2)	42 (1)	252 (1, 2, 3)	2 (1, 2)
V	19 (2)	65 (2, 4)	7 (2)	4 (2, 3, 4)	135 (2, 3, 4)	1 (2, 3, 4)
VI	7	48 (1, 2, 4)	6	53 (1)	21 (1, 2, 3, 4)	17 (1, 2)
VII	15	38	71	80 (1, 3)	8 (1, 3, 4)	82
VIII	0	0	0	0	20	21 (1)
IX	76	65 (1, 4)	61	100 (1, 3)	113 (1, 3, 4)	81

The refined results were manually analysed by examining the titles and abstracts of the studies. This analysis enabled us to identify a set of challenges and corresponding suggestions for resolution where applicable, contributing to both indicating advancements in the field and the identification of research gaps in the application of NLP within a defence context.

4.1 Challenges in Low-Resource Natural Language Processing

The data released by the U.S. Department of Defense states that between the years 1990 and 2014, there were 266 various kinds of interventions involving the deployment of personnel to countries and regions where 879 different languages are spoken [10]. It is claimed that there are frequently situations where the US military struggles to find either translators or any automated translation capabilities [11, 12].

One of the discussed use-cases where an artificial intelligence (AI) tool might be at hand is a condition when a commanding officer is monitoring a battlefield with a dynamically changing situation. When an AI/ML solution is available in such a situation, it is possible to delegate some of the information processing tasks to the automated process, which can compare rapidly changing inputs to various previously executed wargame exercises and live engagements [13, 14]. The complexity and technical nature of military communication can further complicate the situation for EFL (English as a Foreign Language) troopers, impacting their ability to understand critical technical details effectively [15].

Another suggested application of NLP technologies in military and defence contexts is the utilization of AI solutions at strategic and political levels for producing and publishing massive quantities of misinformation to destabilize opponents. NLP technologies are crucial in both generating such content and defending against it by identifying and countering misinformation [14].

The list of challenges in language processing also includes the military term dictionary quality, which is prone to such drawbacks as discrepancies and inconsistencies, including duplicate entries and alignment errors. This is further complicated by the fact that while word-to-word translation might be straightforward, the multi-word phrases and expressions usually need to be treated as separate logical entities, which might have a translation consisting of a different number of words in another language [12]. In a low-resource setting, it is often the case that words needing translation are not found in existing dictionaries; these are named Out-of-Vocabulary (OOV) words. Such words need to be accounted for in the translated text with as much context preservation as possible, aiming for the highest accuracy possible. The presence of OOV words, combined with the need to sometimes reorder phrases and the words within them, can lead to a degradation in not only accuracy but also in the fluency of the translation, meaning that the translated text may not read naturally [16].

Verbs, being the main source of data about various actions intended by the text, can be not only missing from the dictionary but also, especially in languages rich in morphological variations, provide extended context such as person, number, tense, aspect, and mood, depending on their form. These details need to be accounted for in the translation [17].

Before the translation system can be used, it requires training on a corpus of military and defence-related data. Collecting such data from various sources is a challenge. The knowledge represented in the data needs to be extracted, cleared of ambiguities, mapped to knowledge entities, and purged of semantic noise [18, 19]. The translation model training process can be computationally and time-resource intensive [20], and needs to be performed in advance before any operation can take place.

Military and defence data, given its relation to national security issues, need to be treated as confidential by default. Given that some of the data exchange can happen in rapidly changing battlefield conditions, it is not always possible to ensure such treatment via a manual process [21]. An automated solution such as Data Leak Prevention [22] requires the capability for real-time operation on a device with limited resources, which might be the only device available on the battlefield [21].

In addition to confidentiality issues the need for computational resources is significant when a multilingual model that incorporates large number of languages like No Language Left Behind (NLLB) [23] is used. The number of CPU cores required for NLLB model for one-instance translation with an inference time of 17 s is 48 [24]. Neither such inference time nor the resources required to achieve it do not seem applicable to a rapidly changing battlefield scenario. Models like BERT, while highly accurate, consume significant memory resources and scale poorly with increasing training text length [20].

4.2 From Challenges to Solutions

The military data is multi-source, heterogeneous, and often loosely structured, which complicates its management and application. Traditional methods of data processing are inadequate to handle such complexity efficiently. Knowledge graphs offer a structured and semantic representation of data that is systematic and enhances data retrieval and utilization. They facilitate knowledge cognition and reasoning by visually mapping relationships and entities and can be used as a base for training a translation model. It is possible to construct a military knowledge graph, including knowledge modelling, extraction, fusion, and storage processes. Utilizing Neo4j for visual representation and MongoDB for efficient data management tackles the challenges of handling complex military data effectively [18]. It is suggested that this approach can be built upon to introduce an intelligent query system.

The potential knowledge graph can be enriched by processing openly available information. This process requires the data to be acquired and classified before being added to the graph. Using existing NLP models such as BERT [20] has proven helpful for this task, especially when the presented text needs to be classified as military or defence-related in general. However, it is more challenging to distinguish between texts related to one of two closely related military branches. The accuracy of classification for scraped text processed with NLP models decreases when the training dataset is smaller and the text to classify is shorter [25].

To systematically access military vocabulary from a knowledge graph and improve the precision and recall of document retrieval systems, which can be used as a source for training a military and defence-specific model, a query expansion method called Keyword to Formal Concept Query Expansion is argued to provide a notable improvement. This method enhances access to a broad spectrum of military documents beyond the limitations of keyword-based searches [26].

Several semi-automated methods were implemented to refine the domain-specific term base in existing military dictionaries. This involved removing redundancies, resolving spelling variations, and adjusting tokenization, which helped prepare the term base for computerized processing There two methods suggested to refine and validate existing term base are [12]:

- **Frequency Count Method**: This method was used to refine the domain-specific term list by identifying high-frequency military-specific terms and suggesting non-specific terms for exclusion. This method relies on the principle that domain-specific terminology will occur more frequently within domain-relevant documents.

- **Terminology Extraction Method**: Two approaches were compared to refine and validate the term base. The first approach involved using existing term extraction methodologies without restrictions to identify overlaps with the existing term base. The second was more restrictive, using the term base as a filter to identify new, valid entries. Both methods aimed to establish a refined, validated list of military-specific terms.

Posing a question to a knowledge-based system in a military context often involves complex relations and requires deep semantic analysis to be properly understood and processed, which can hinder effective information retrieval and question answering under limited data scenarios. Using semantic analysis coupled with predefined statement templates significantly enhances the system's ability to interpret and respond to intricate military-related queries accurately. This approach helps in structuring the answer retrieval process effectively, even with limited data [19].

Addressing Out-of-Vocabulary (OOV) words in a low-resource setting for translating from English to Tamil using a pause-based phrase extraction technique, along with the addition of a combination of transliteration and thesaurus intersection techniques, has helped to reduce translation errors. However, it has not eliminated these errors completely. It is suggested to rely on a two-level thesaurus intersection to find the most appropriate synonyms for OOV words [16].

An algorithm specifically designed for low-resource languages, focusing on semantic-based techniques to handle the intricacies of verb forms and their meanings across different contexts, is proposed to facilitate translation between languages with rich morphological variations. It aims to identify root words and use intermediate languages in the translation process when direct translation pairs are inadequate [17].

It is argued that implementing various data augmentation methods, such as semantic augmentation, transformation of existing data, and effective use of monolingual data, can significantly enrich the training dataset and improve translation accuracy. Additionally, it is suggested that developing multilingual translation models capable of handling multiple language pairs simultaneously allows for the sharing of linguistic features across languages. This approach particularly benefits low-resource languages by leveraging higher-resource languages [24, 27–29]. In addition to data augmentation methods another suggested way of enhancing low-resource language processing is using a Cross-Lingual Knowledge Transfer which is a methodology applicable during model's pretraining and finetuning stages. The potential in using English-based pretrained models to support NLP tasks in languages with fewer resources has been demonstrated [28]. It is argued that better results are achieved when high-resource model share its linguistic roots with the low-resource model [24, 29].

Grouping multiple low-resource locales together in a model named Multilingual Transformer Language Models has shown an improvement in model's performance and reduced computational and maintenance costs [30]. Similarly to [24] the approach suggested in [30] argues that grouping languages that belong to the same language group together in one model is more effective than using an individual language model.

To identify confidential information in a text the Depthwise Separable Convolutional Neural Network was proposed. The model utilizes depthwise separable convolutions, which separate the convolution operation into spatial and depth (channel) convolutions, reducing computational complexity significantly. This approach not only speeds up the computation, allowing to be executed on devices with low computational resources, but also reduces the model size without a significant loss in accuracy [21].

To reduce consumption of large amounts of memory and computational power it is suggested that teacher models, that can be large multilingual translation models, can be used to transfer knowledge to a smaller student model. In the process labelled as Knowledge Distillation it was possible to reduce performance and computational costs of translation [24].

The Composition to Augment Language Models is a proposed framework designed to connect otherwise individually trained models by adding a cross-attention mechanism between the models, enabling new capabilities. This approach preserves the weights in the models it aims to connect, thus avoiding threats such as catastrophic forgetting [29]. It is possible to utilize this approach to connect individually trained local models for multinational operation purposes.

5 Identified Research Gaps

Having reviewed a diverse range of papers related to NLP, ML, and their applications in military and defence contexts, there are several potential research gaps that this paper could address, particularly in the realms of C4ISR and joint multinational and/or peace-keeping operations. There were several areas identified where additional research could make a significant contribution:

1. **Multilingual and Cross-Lingual NLP for C4ISR**: Many of the reviewed papers focus on single-language or bilingual NLP applications. In multinational and peace-keeping operations, dealing with various low-resource languages and dialects at the same time is crucial. Additional research could explore developing or improving multilingual or cross-lingual NLP models that can effectively process and interpret data across multiple languages, which is vital for communication and intelligence-sharing in diverse multinational environments.

2. **Resource-Efficient NLP Models for Field Deployment**: In C4ISR scenarios, computational resources can be limited. Many current NLP models, especially deep learning-based ones, require substantial computational power. Current research mostly suggests improvements to existing models, that does not necessarily guarantee overall ability to run on a limited-resource device in battlefield conditions. Research into lightweight, resource-efficient NLP models suitable for deployment in field operations with limited computing infrastructure would fill a significant gap.

3. **Real-Time NLP for Surveillance and Reconnaissance**: The reviewed papers include various applications of NLP, but there is a potential gap in real-time processing and analysis of textual data for surveillance and reconnaissance. This includes real-time sentiment analysis, threat detection, or information extraction from field reports and communications, which are critical in joint operations.

4. **NLP for Improved Situational Awareness in Joint Operations**: There is a need for NLP applications that can enhance situational awareness by aggregating and analysing unstructured data from various sources (like field reports, local news, social media) in multinational operations. The reviewed papers address this at the training stage of

the model, however real-time processing of such data is not covered. Further research could involve designing and developing systems that automatically summarize critical information, detect anomalies, or provide actionable intelligence from large volumes of text data.

5. **Secure and Robust NLP Technologies for defence Applications**: Given the sensitive nature of military operations, research into secure, robust, and adversarial-resistant NLP models is crucial. The reviewed papers cover real-time confidential data identification, however, does cover security and robustness of the model itself. This includes ensuring that the technologies used are resilient against misinformation and cyber threats, which is particularly important in defence settings.

6. **Cultural and Contextual Adaptation in NLP**: In peacekeeping and multinational operations, understanding the cultural and contextual nuances is essential. Additional research could focus on developing NLP models that are not only linguistically accurate but also culturally and contextually sensitive, enhancing communication and intelligence analysis in diverse environments. There were no papers focusing on cultural differences between participants of multinational missions.

6   Discussion

This literature review has systematically explored the utilization of NLP technologies in low-resource settings with a specific focus on security and defence applications. The examination of existing literature highlights research advancements and reveals some gaps that offer avenues for future research.

Our analysis demonstrates an interest from the research community in analysing methods for building a military and defence-related knowledge base and exploring various methods of language translation, including for low-resource languages. However, the focus predominantly remains on bilingual translation, with multilingual capabilities often overlooked. The literature displays attempts of designing and developing resource-efficient NLP models. This highlights the importance of developing lightweight and efficient models that can operate within the computational constraints of field operations. Furthermore, real-time processing and aggregation of textual data appear under-researched, particularly in discussions beyond building knowledge graphs. Additionally, the cultural nuances of potential multinational communications have not been addressed in the reviewed literature, suggesting a gap that needs to be filled.

The practical implications of these findings are substantial. For instance, the development of real-time NLP applications for surveillance and reconnaissance could revolutionize the way textual data is processed on the battlefield, providing immediate insights, and enhancing operational efficiency. Similarly, NLP technologies that improve situational awareness in joint operations could significantly affect decision-making processes, ensuring that critical information is accurately and quickly assimilated.

The gaps identified suggest several directions for future research. First, there are no indicators of research of multilingual and cross-lingual NLP technologies that can seamlessly operate across diverse linguistic landscapes in real-time, which is crucial for international peacekeeping and military collaborations. Additionally, the exploration of lightweight NLP models presents a critical research avenue, offering the potential to bring advanced NLP capabilities to the forefront of field operations with limited resources.

Furthermore, investigating secure and robust NLP technologies for defence applications will be vital in safeguarding these systems against misinformation and cyber threats.

While the potential for NLP in defence and security contexts is vast, there are several challenges and limitations to acknowledge. The sensitive nature of military operations necessitates a heightened focus on the security and robustness of NLP technologies, requiring sophisticated approaches to ensure these systems are resilient against adversarial attacks and misinformation campaigns. Additionally, the cultural and contextual nuances present in multinational operations necessitate the development of NLP systems that are not only linguistically accurate but also culturally and contextually aware.

7   Conclusions

In conclusion, this literature review underscores the critical role of NLP technologies in enhancing the capabilities of security and defence operations, especially in low-resource settings. By addressing the identified gaps, future research can significantly contribute to the advancement of NLP applications, ultimately strengthening the operational effectiveness and strategic capabilities of defence and military organizations worldwide.

In response to the research question, "How have recent advancements in NLP and machine learning (ML) technologies been applied to process low-resource linguistic information in military and defence contexts, and what gaps exist in current research regarding the recognition, understanding, and translation of spoken and written forms (including handwriting, printed documents, and typed text) of such information?"—our findings indicate:

Recent advancements in NLP and ML have primarily focused on enriching knowledge bases and developing frameworks for translating low-resource languages. Nonetheless, there remains a notable absence of a comprehensive, unified approach capable of handling the real-time acquisition, processing, and representation of data across multiple languages simultaneously.

By addressing the six identified research gaps, future studies can significantly enhance the operational effectiveness and strategic capabilities of NLP applications in the defence sector. This enhancement is particularly crucial for supporting low-resource languages and ensuring robust, context-aware communication systems in multinational military operations. Ultimately, such advancements could contribute to the development of a unified defence framework applicable to multinational C4ISR operations at both strategic and tactical levels.

References

1. Kitchenham, B., Pearl Brereton, O., Budgen, D., Turner, M., Bailey, J., Linkman, S.: Systematic Literature Reviews in Software Engineering—A Systematic Literature Review (2009)
2. vom Brocke, J., Simons, A., Riemer, K., Niehaves, B., Plattfaut, R., Cleven, A.: Standing on the shoulders of giants: challenges and recommendations of literature search in information systems research. Commun. Assoc. Inf. Syst. **37**, 205–224 (2015). https://doi.org/10.17705/1cais.03709

3. Okoli, C.: A guide to conducting a standalone systematic literature review. Commun. Assoc. Inf. Syst. **37**, 879–910 (2015). https://doi.org/10.17705/1cais.03743
4. Felizardo, K.R., Carver, J.C.: Automating systematic literature review. In: Contemporary Empirical Methods in Software Engineering, pp. 327–355. Springer International Publishing (2020)
5. Wohlin, C.: Guidelines for snowballing in systematic literature studies and a replication in software engineering. In: ACM International Conference Proceeding Series. Association for Computing Machinery (2014)
6. Kitchenham, B., Pretorius, R., Budgen, D., Brereton, O.P., Turner, M., Niazi, M., Linkman, S.: Systematic literature reviews in software engineering—a tertiary study (2010)
7. Okoli, C., Schabram, K.: Working Papers on Information Systems A Guide to Conducting a Systematic Literature Review of Information Systems Research (2010)
8. Wohlin, C., Runeson, P., Höst, M., Ohlsson, M.C., Regnell, B., Wesslén, A.: Experimentation in Software Engineering. Springer, Berlin Heidelberg, Berlin, Heidelberg (2012)
9. Kitchenham, B., Brereton, P.: A systematic review of systematic review process research in software engineering (2013)
10. Christianson, C., Duncan, J., Onyshkevych, B.: Overview of the DARPA LORELEI program. Mach. Transl. **32**, 3–9 (2018). https://doi.org/10.1007/s10590-017-9212-4
11. Defense Advanced Research Projects Agency: LORELEI Imagines Rapid Automated Language Toolkit. https://www.darpa.mil/news-events/2015-10-08
12. Rose, G., Holland, M., Larocca, S., Winkler, R.: Semi-Automated Methods for Refining a Domain-Specific Terminology Base (2010)
13. Hallaq, B., Somer, T., Osula, A.-M., Ngo, K., Mitchener-Nissen, T.: Artificial Intelligence Within the Military Domain and Cyber Warfare
14. Svenmarck, P., Luotsinen, L., Nilsson, M., Schubert, J.: Possibilities and Challenges for Artificial Intelligence in Military Applications
15. Chen, L.C., Chang, K.H., Yang, S.C.: An integrated corpus-based text mining approach used to process military technical information for facilitating EFL troopers' linguistic comprehension: US anti-tank missile systems field manual as an example. J. Natl. Sci. Found. **49**, 403 (2021). https://doi.org/10.4038/jnsfsr.v49i3.10146
16. Mrinalini, K., Nagarajan, T., Vijayalakshmi, P.: Pause-based phrase extraction and effective OOV handling for low-resource machine translation systems. ACM Trans. Asian Low-Resour. Lang. Inf. Process. **18**, 1–22 (2019). https://doi.org/10.1145/3265751
17. Anik, M.S.H., Islam, M.A., Alim Al Islam, A.B.M.: An approach towards multilingual translation by semantic-based verb identification and root word analysis. In: 2018 5th International Conference on Networking, Systems and Security (NSysS), pp. 1–9. IEEE (2018)
18. He, Y., Zhang, X., Oi, F., Xu, G., Gui, G.: Construction of military knowledge graph based on Neo4j and MongoDB. In: 2022 IEEE 8th International Conference on Computer and Communications (ICCC), pp. 2043–2047. IEEE (2022)
19. Liu, B., Yan, R., Zuo, Y., Tao, Y.: A knowledge-based question-answering method for military critical information under limited corpus. In: 2021 2nd International Conference on Computer Engineering and Intelligent Control (ICCEIC), pp. 86–91. IEEE (2021)
20. Devlin, J., Chang, M.-W., Lee, K., Toutanova, K.: BERT: Pre-training of Deep Bidirectional Transformers for Language Understanding (2018)
21. Lu, Y., Jiang, J., Yu, M., Liu, C., Liu, C., Huang, W., Lv, Z.: Depthwise Separable Convolutional Neural Network for Confidential Information Analysis (2020)
22. Shvartzshnaider, Y., Pavlinovic, Z., Balashankar, A., Wies, T., Subramanian, L., Nissenbaum, H., Mittal, P.: VACCINE: using contextual integrity for data leakage detection. In: The World Wide Web Conference, pp. 1702–1712. ACM, New York, NY, USA (2019)
23. NLLB Team, et al.: No Language Left Behind: Scaling Human-Centered Machine Translation (2022)

24. Song, Y., Ezzini, S., Klein, J., Bissyande, T., Lefebvre, C., Goujon, A.: Letz translate: low-resource machine translation for luxembourgish. In: 2023 5th International Conference on Natural Language Processing (ICNLP), pp. 165–170. IEEE (2023)

25. Gunasekara, C., Carryer, T., Triff, M.: On natural language processing applications for military dialect classification. In: 2021 20th IEEE International Conference on Machine Learning and Applications (ICMLA), pp. 211–218. IEEE (2021)

26. Chen, L.-C., Chao, W.-T., Hsieh, C.-J.: A novel query expansion method for military news retrieval service. In: 2014 International Conference on Asian Language Processing (IALP), pp. 183–186. IEEE (2014)

27. Wang, Z.: Low resource neural machine translation. In: 2022 IEEE 9th International Conference on Cyber Security and Cloud Computing (CSCloud)/2022 IEEE 8th International Conference on Edge Computing and Scalable Cloud (EdgeCom), pp. 166–171. IEEE (2022)

28. Chi, Z., Huang, H., Liu, L., Bai, Y., Gao, X., Mao, X.-L.: Can pretrained English language models benefit Non-English NLP systems in low-resource scenarios? IEEE/ACM Trans. Audio Speech Lang. Process. **32**, 1061–1074 (2024). https://doi.org/10.1109/TASLP.2023.3267618

29. Bansal, R., et al.: LLM Augmented LLMs: Expanding Capabilities through Composition (2024). https://doi.org/10.48550/arXiv.2401.02412

30. Miao, L., Wu, J., Behre, P., Chang, S., Parthasarathy, S.: Multilingual transformer language model for speech recognition in low-resource languages. In: 2022 Ninth International Conference on Social Networks Analysis, Management and Security (SNAMS), pp. 1–5. IEEE (2022)

European Union's Legislative Proposals Clustering Based on Multiple Hidden Layers Representation

Eya Hammami[1,3]([✉]) and Rim Faiz[1,2]

[1] LARODEC Laboratory, University of Tunis, Tunis, Tunisia
[2] IHEC, University of Carthage, Carthage, Tunisia
`rim.faiz@ihec.ucar.tn`
[3] IRIT Laboratory, University of Toulouse 3, Toulouse, France
`eya.hammami@irit.fr`

Abstract. Recently, there are opportunities and challenges for both legal practitioners and AI researchers due to the abundance of legal documents that are available in digital form. This development requires a lot of assistance and work for presenting this content in a helpful and distributed manner, which could have the potential to offer legal professionals many advantages. Therefore, we propose in this work an approach to cluster legislative procedures of the European Parliament based on the topics obtained from Kmeans algorithm using encoders and decoders of Pretrained Large Language Models (PLMs). The main objective of this method is to arrange legislative procedures according to their policy areas.

Keywords: NLP · Clustering · PLMs · SBERT · Sentence Transformers · Legislative Proposals

1 Introduction

The complex language of legislative procedures can make it difficult to navigate the vast array of documents produced. Therefore, Artificial Intelligence (AI), Machine Learning (ML), and Transformers have played a transformative role in revolutionizing how we handle, organize, and extract insights from these complex legal documents. Currently, clustering similar documents together based on content is an important task in handling legislative procedure documents. Where the most important part is the representation phase of those texts. In this step the use of Pretrained Large Language Models (PLMs) has improved the representation phase of legal text documents by providing a powerful technique for producing embeddings that represent the complexities of legal language semantics and context. These models, such as BERT (Bidirectional Encoder Representations from Transformers) and GPT (Generative Pre-trained Transformer), depend on significant pre-training on large corpora to understand the intricate patterns

A. Lupeikienė et al. (Eds.): DB&IS 2024, CCIS 2157, pp. 106–119, 2024.
https://doi.org/10.1007/978-3-031-63543-4_8

and contexts found in texts. The resulting embeddings of these PLMs provide enhanced and rich contextual representations of the original texts, which simplify clustering tasks by allowing document categorization based on their underlying principles of law, concepts, and contextual similarities. In this paper, we propose a method that aims to explore the use of outputs from different intermediate hidden layers of PLMs with different pooling techniques, by considering each time different part of the legislative proposal documents during the embedding representation phase. The idea behind this method is that more accurate and meaningful embedding representations would result from being able to recognize the syntactic and semantic linkages that exist within the document's sentences. The following are a summary of our main contributions:

- Create a legislative proposal dataset using the Legislative Observatory of the European Parliament platform[1].
- Combine intermediate representations from various layers of the pretrained transformer models to help in incorporating more information.

This paper is organized as follows: we present in Sect. 2 a state of the art that examines the different approaches for text clustering. In Sect. 3, we present the architecture of our proposal in detail. Finally, the experimental results of our proposed model are presented in Sect. 4.

2   Related Work

Clustering is an unsupervised task that involves assembling items that are similar into clusters. More specifically, related objects should be clustered together, while dissimilar objects should be separated into different clusters. Along with the development of advanced clustering algorithms, the most important research aspect of clustering is the development of a proper representation of the objects [1,2], including similarity measures that allow the algorithms to figure out how similar or dissimilar two objects are. These Clustering techniques are widely used in the legal field, researchers were able to classify similar legal documents by topic or by case citations and legal citations [3–6]. [3], used both hard and soft clustering on three heterogeneous datasets in order to develop a taxonomy and assist legal firms in their knowledge management activities. [4], demonstrate an effective soft clustering algorithm based on subject segmentation, unlike traditional approaches based on lexical similarity. The researchers in this work use subjects, document citations, and click-stream data from user activity databases to achieve high-quality of categorization. [7], developed a method for categorizing legal judgments from the Kerala High Court of India by employing Latent Dirichlet Allocation (LDA) technique for categorizing texts based on their topics. They compute the cosine similarity between each text in the corpus and topics and assign the document to the cluster to which topic it is closest. Their study demonstrated that the developed topic-based clustering methodology is

---

[1] europarl.europa.eu/portal/en.

capable of effectively classifying judicial judgments into different clusters. [5], used citations and paragraph linkages to cluster Supreme Court of India judicial case rulings in order to construct efficient search engines. Furthermore, they create links between pairs of paragraphs from different judgments that have a cosine similarity exceeds a specific threshold derived on the basis of their TF-IDF representation. Then, an improved clustering algorithm relying on the Jaccard coefficient was presented by picking the legal case judgment with the highest similarity to the other legal case judgments inside the cluster. Similarly, [6], employed case citations when grouping judicial case judgments from the Indian Constitution. The suggested method converts the dataset into a binary matrix, indicating whether or not each example has a citation. Following that, the dataset is partitioned into groups using the traditional k-means algorithm and the Euclidean distance. [8], adopted LDA to extract the key concepts from texts documents of the Supreme Court and State High Court of India. Their study presents an architecture for legal practitioners to reduce the cost of reading entire papers, obtaining key concepts for argument preparation, and determining whether the case is similar to the lawyer's current case. [9], utilized a paragraph vector approach (Doc2Vec) to compare text similarity in order to update the clustering findings of legal documents without re-implementing the clustering method. They used in their work data samples from civil aviation legal provisions. [10], investigated and compared the application of hard clustering approaches like K-means and Affinity Propagation, overlapping hierarchical clustering, and soft clustering like Lingo to sparse numerical vectors which were obtained using the Bag of Words models for airline service failure texts claims. However we noticed that the majority of these previous works were more concentrated on the clustering techniques rather than the representation phase of these legal texts documents. Therefore, we tried to investigate the use of PLMs for legislative proposals documents. In this paper, we suppose that in the PLM, the most transferable contextualized representations of input text tend to occur in the middle layers, while the top layers specialized for language modeling. Therefore, the use of the last layer's output may restrict the power of the PLM representation. For this, we tried to explore the use of the outputs from different layers of the pretrained transformers models aiming to get better representation of our legal legislative proposal documents.

3   Methodology

This section describes in details our suggested approach. The general architecture of our approach is depicted in Fig. 1, where we can see that the approach consists of two major steps. The first phase consists of generating the document representation using dense vectors for each part of the legislative proposals documents (see Sect. 4.1). The second step involves applying the Kmeans and the HDBSCAN algorithms to cluster those embeddings into similar groups that could design a specific policy areas.

3.1 Legislative Proposals Representation Phase

During this step, our main objective is to get useful and significant embedding representations of each part from the legislative proposals documents. For this, we use pretrained transformers language models along with a sliding window technique that tackles the limits of transformers sequence length. This technique would significantly consider any document length, regardless of the pre-trained models that we are going to use. Thus, it first divides the input text into smaller segments via the window size and stride length parameters and generates embeddings for each segment to obtain finer representations of the text. Thereafter, the embeddings of the smaller segments are combined into a single embedding vector by taking the average of all of them as in Eq. (1).

$$E_{d_i} = average(E_{s_1}, ..., E_{s_i}) \tag{1}$$

Where E_{d_i} represents the final embedding of each part from the legislative proposals documents and E_{s_i} represents the embedding of the ith segment within those parts. Alongside this sliding window method, we generate the embedding also from the intermediate hidden layers of the pretrained language model by averaging the output of the last 4 layers as shown in Fig. 2. The Algorithm 1 details all the steps of our document representation phase.

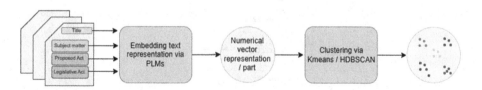

Fig. 1. Architecture overview.

Algorithm 1. Documents Representation

Require: d, WS, S **Output:** E_d
Ensure: $segments \Leftarrow [\emptyset]$ $CP \Leftarrow 0$ $\qquad\qquad\qquad \triangleright CP$ means Current Position
1: **while** CP is within the length of the Text **do**
2: $\quad$ $Segment \Leftarrow d[CP : CP + WS]$
3: $\quad$ $embedding \Leftarrow PLM(Segment)$
4: $\quad$ $segments.append(embedding)$
5: $\quad$ $CP = CP + S$
6: **end while**
7: $E_D \Leftarrow Sum(embedding)/len(segments)$
8: $Final_{E_d} \Leftarrow avg[h_1, h_2, h_3, h_4]$

The input parameters of our algorithm are:

– specific part from the legislative proposals documents (d).

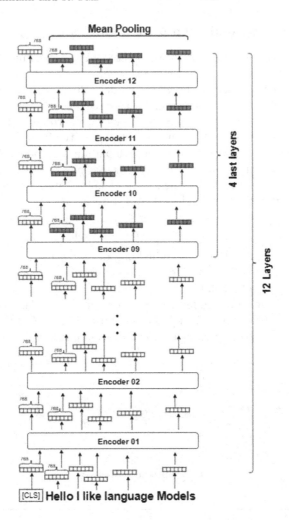

Fig. 2. Document Embedding Representation from 4 last intermediate hidden layers

- the window size (WS) parameter, which refers to the number of elements or tokens in each segment or window. It determines the length or size of the segments into which the input text is divided.
- the stride length (S) parameter which determines the step or distance between the starting points of consecutive windows. It specifies how much the window moves or slides after processing each segment.

Given those input parameters, the algorithm outputs one single vector (E_d) that represents the combined embedding which is a finer representation of the entire input text, where the information from different segments has been aggregated. The steps 1, 2, 3, 4, 5 and 6 shown in the algorithm consists of extracting a segment of text from the current position using the WS parameter. Then, it applies a (PLM) to convert the segment into a fixed-size embedding vector. This step generates an embedding for the current segment. After that, it appends the generated embedding to the segments list. Next, it moves the sliding window forward by the S positions via incrementing the Current Position. After processing all segments, we get a list of embeddings, one for each segment. The subsequent step is to compute the average of all these embeddings element-wise. The resulting vector will be a combined embedding for the entire input text. The final phase entails doing the average for the outputs from the last 4 hidden layers ($h1, h2, h3, h4$) of the PLM that we used.

3.2   Legislative Proposals Categorization Phase

This phase consists of applying unsupervised clustering algorithm in order to cluster the legislative proposals documents based on their underlying concepts and contextual similarities which could represent their policy area using dense embedding vectors that was created during the first phase. We used two different clustering algorithms. The first one is kmeans[2] which is a popular clustering approach for machine learning that divides a dataset into a specified number of clusters. It works by iteratively allocating data points to the nearest cluster centroid, which are then updated based on the mean of the points given to each cluster. The second one is HDBSCAN[3] algorithm which is a density-based clustering technique that excels in identifying clusters with different forms and densities within a dataset. Unlike KMeans, which requires a predetermined number of clusters, HDBSCAN calculates the ideal number of clusters based on data density. It creates a cluster hierarchy based on the local density of points and then selects the most stable clusters from it.

4   Experimental Study

4.1   Experimental Settings

Dataset: The data required for this process is obtained from freely available online legal database "oeil.secure.europarl.europa.eu" website, where those documents represent legislative proposals under European Parliament. Typically a legislative proposal document contains four important parts which are the Title, the Subject Matter, the Proposed Act and the Legislative Act. Where the proposal legislation's title provides a quick and clear description of its objective. It is the proposal's basic identifier. Then, the Subject Matter section looks into the exact topic or issue covered within the proposed legislation. It could provide context and fundamental understanding of the subject. Right after that the Proposed Act section covers the proposed law's language. It incorporates the clauses, and sections which outline the modifications to current laws, rules, or

---

[2] https://scikit-learn.org/stable/modules/generated/sklearn.cluster.KMeans.html.
[3] https://scikit-learn.org/stable/modules/generated/sklearn.cluster.HDBSCAN.html.

policies. It describes also the steps to be taken. Following that the Legislative Act part comes when the proposal turns into law, where it outlines the formal legislative act. It is the legislation's final version after it has gone through all the legislative process. For the purpose of this study we focused only on these four sections within a legislative proposal document. We collected around 5505 documents from year 1990 to 2022 using a scraping tool[4] developed by Michele Scotto di Vettimo which is a researcher in political sciences. After the preprocessing we get 4496 documents, The average length for each section of the preprocessed collected documents are shown in Table 1.

Table 1. Average length for each section of Legislative Proposal documents obtained after the preprocessing.

Legislative Proposal Section	Average Length
Title	8.3598
Subject Matter	15.6214
Proposed Act	247.5538
Legislative Act	231.9132

Evaluation Metrics: The performance of our method to cluster Legislative Proposal documents has been evaluated using four external metrics (Purity, Normalized Mutual Information (NMI), Precision and Recall) based on the true class memberships in a document set which represent the policy area.

Purity: The Purity Score measures the degree of similarity among cluster assignments and true labels. It computes the proportion of correctly assigned samples in a cluster to the cluster's most common class label. It ranges from 0 to 1 where purity score of 1 indicates that each cluster contains only instances of a single class, and if it is close to 0 this indicates that the clusters are totally confused and that there is no consistency among clustering and real class labels [11].

NMI: NMI is a useful metric for clustering because it can show how similar two different sets of cluster assignments are, regardless of how the number of clusters in each set varies. It returns a value ranging from 0 to 1 where 0 represents completely dissimilar clusterings and 1 represents fully identical clusterings [11,12].

Precision & Recall: Precision and recall are frequently utilized in classification problems, but they can also be applied to clustering. Precision indicates the accuracy of the positive predictions among all predicted positives, whereas recall measures the proportion of actual positives that were correctly predicted [13].

---

[4] https://mscottodivettimo.github.io/project/scrapeu/.

Table 2. Pretrained Sentence Transformers models trained and tuned on a large and diverse dataset of over 2 billions training pairs for semantic search and sentence similarity tasks.

PLMs	Base Model	Dimensions	Size (MB)	Max SL *
all-roberta-large-v1	roberta-large	1024	1360	512
all-mpnet-base-v1	mpnet-base	768	420	512
SGPT-2.7B-msmarco-specb-bitfit	gpt-neo-2.7B	2560	10743	2048
SGPT-1.3B-msmarco-specb-bitfit	gpt-neo-1.3B	2048	5300	2048

* Max SL= Maximum Sequence Length.

Hyperparameter Settings: All of the PLMs that we utilized for this paper was imported from Huggingface[5]. More details about them are illustrated in Table 2, where we selected two ecoders pretrained models and two decoders based models [14] for the representation phase of our legislative proposal texts. More specifically, those models are pretrained sentences transformers[6,7] models that have better average performance on encoding sentences over around 14 diverse tasks from different domains. Then, we used HDBSCAN algorithm with its default parameters and we set the parameter K for the Kmeans algorithm to 21 which belongs to the total number of the policy areas that we have in our sample dataset. During this work we consider these policy as our true labels. All the experiments are conducted using pytorch[8].

4.2 Experiment Results and Discussion

The results shown in Tables 3, 4, 5 and 6, present the results that we obtained when we applied our approach on different parts of our European Parliament's Legislative Proposals dataset (such as: Title, Subject Matter, Proposal Act and Legislative Act) especially when we used Kmeans algorithm for the clustering. In Tables 7, 8, 9 and 10, we show also the results that we obtained when we applied our proposed approach on different parts of our dataset but when we used HDBSCAN algorithm for the clustering. During our experiments, we used different pooling strategy for each PLM, and each time we generated the results using first just the last hidden layer for the embedding representation of our texts, then we generated the results using the average output of four last hidden layers for the embeddings representation phase. We adapted the use also a kind of sliding window to tackle the limit of sequence length of the PLMs. Specifically, when the text length within such part of the legislative proposal document exceeds the maximum sequence length within the PLMs. In these tables, the results with star mark "*" represent that the embeddings were generated from the average output of the four last hidden layers of the PLM.

---

[5] https://huggingface.co/.

[6] https://www.sbert.net/.

[7] https://github.com/Muennighoff/sgpt.

[8] https://pytorch.org/.

Table 3. Legislative Title clustering using Kmeans

PLMs	Legislative Title			
	NMI	Purity	P	R
all-roberta-large-v1 $_{cls-pooling}$	0.3549	0.4877	0.2134	**0.3115**
all-roberta-large-v1 $_{cls-pooling}$ *	0.3662*	0.5031*	**0.2623***	0.3000*
all-roberta-large-v1 $_{mean-pooling}$	0.3667	0.5031	0.1771	0.1643
all-roberta-large-v1 $_{mean-pooling}$*	**0.3793***	**0.5253***	0.2235*	0.1843*
all-mpnet-base-v1 $_{cls-pooling}$	0.3088	0.4497	0.1205	0.2151
all-mpnet-base-v1 $_{cls-pooling}$*	0.3244*	0.4817*	0.2565*	0.2262*
all-mpnet-base-v1 $_{mean-pooling}$	0.3417	0.4715	0.2784	0.2631
all-mpnet-base-v1 $_{mean-pooling}$*	**0.3982***	**0.5315***	**0.2882***	**0.2821***
SGPT-2.7B $_{last-token-pooling}$	0.1271	0,2108	0.1004	0.1389
SGPT-2.7B $_{last-token-pooling}$*	0.1906*	0.2853*	0.1646*	0.1791*
SGPT-2.7B $_{mean-pooling}$	0.2122	0.3623	0,2841	0,2421
SGPT-2.7B $_{mean-pooling}$*	**0.3102***	**0.4457***	**0.2953***	**0.2633***
SGPT-1.3B $_{last-token-pooling}$	0.1063	0.2604	0.1473	0.1262
SGPT-1.3B $_{last-token-pooling}$*	0.1888*	0.3409*	0.1794*	0.1542*
SGPT-1.3B $_{mean-pooling}$	0.2994	0.4430	0.1659	0.1582
SGPT-1.3B $_{mean-pooling}$*	**0.3016***	**0.4435***	**0.1827***	**0.1612***

* Embeddings from the average output of the four last hidden layers of PLM.

Table 4. Legislative Subject Matter clustering using Kmeans

PLMs	Legislative Subject Matter			
	NMI	Purity	P	R
all-roberta-large-v1 $_{cls-pooling}$	0.4347	0.5522	0.1210	0.1054
all-roberta-large-v1 $_{cls-pooling}$*	0.4477*	0.5671*	0.2454*	0.1518*
all-roberta-large-v1 $_{mean-pooling}$	0.4367	0.5642	0.1713	0.1164
all-roberta-large-v1 $_{mean-pooling}$*	**0.4885***	**0.6092***	**0.3359***	0.1891*
all-mpnet-base-v1 $_{cls-pooling}$	0.3708	0.4879	0.1124	0.1124
all-mpnet-base-v1 $_{cls-pooling}$*	0.4273*	0.5678*	0.2254*	0.1302*
all-mpnet-base-v1 $_{mean-pooling}$	0.3841	0.5235	0.1252	0.1260
all-mpnet-base-v1 $_{mean-pooling}$*	**0.4672***	**0.5729***	**0.2684***	**0.1905***
SGPT-2.7B $_{last-token-pooling}$	0.2742	0.4257	0.1384	0.1415
SGPT-2.7B $_{last-token-pooling}$*	0.3590*	0.5091*	0.2186*	0.2313*
SGPT-2.7B $_{mean-pooling}$	0.2919	0.4372	0.1771	0.1607
SGPT-2.7B $_{mean-pooling}$*	**0.4030***	**0.5549***	**0.2267***	**0.2883***
SGPT-1.3B $_{last-token-pooling}$	0.1478	0.2878	0.1569	0.1258
SGPT-1.3B $_{last-token-pooling}$*	0.3556*	0.5008*	0.1940*	0.2173*
SGPT-1.3B $_{mean-pooling}$	0.1605	0.2967	0.1599	0.1409
SGPT-1.3B $_{mean-pooling}$*	**0.3981***	**0.5415***	**0.2335***	**0.2340***

* Embeddings from the average output of the four last hidden layers of PLM.

Table 5. Proposal Act clustering using Kmeans

PLMs	Proposal Act			
	NMI	Purity	P	R
all-roberta-large-v1 $_{cls-pooling}$	0.3062	0.4292	0.1461	0.1395
all-roberta-large-v1 $_{cls-pooling}$*	0.3118*	0.4544*	0.1708*	0.1455*
all-roberta-large-v1 $_{mean-pooling}$	0.3096	0.4399	0.1540	0.1433
all-roberta-large-v1 $_{mean-pooling}$*	**0.4234***	**0.5487***	**0.2325***	**0.1449***
all-mpnet-base-v1 $_{cls-pooling}$	0.3037	0.4312	0.1124	0.1195
all-mpnet-base-v1 $_{cls-pooling}$*	0.3310*	0.4432*	0.2198*	0.1382*
all-mpnet-base-v1 $_{mean-pooling}$	0.3099	0.4377	0.1553	0.1313
all-mpnet-base-v1 $_{mean-pooling}$*	**0.3816***	**0.5302***	**0.2733***	**0.1698***
SGPT-2.7B $_{last-token-pooling}$	0.2245	0.3652	0.1400	0.1358
SGPT-2.7B $_{last-token-pooling}$*	0.2661*	0.4074*	0.2699*	0.1676*
SGPT-2.7B $_{mean-pooling}$	0.2639	0.4016	0.1505	0.1491
SGPT-2.7B $_{mean-pooling}$*	**0.2918***	**0.4357***	**0.3116***	**0.1905***
SGPT-1.3B $_{last-token-pooling}$	0.1370	0.2947	0.1277	0.1366
SGPT-1.3B $_{last-token-pooling}$*	0.2662*	0.4059*	0.1709*	0.1622*
SGPT-1.3B $_{mean-pooling}$	0.1674	0.3296	0.1668	0.1578
SGPT-1.3B $_{mean-pooling}$*	**0.2773***	**0.4123***	**0.2483***	**0.2234***

* Embeddings from the average output of the four last hidden layers of PLM.

Table 6. Legislative Act clustering using Kmeans

PLMs	Legislative Act			
	NMI	Purity	P	R
all-roberta-large-v1 $_{cls-pooling}$	0.2695	4060	0.1082	0.1263
all-roberta-large-v1 $_{cls-pooling}$*	0.2789*	0.4199*	0.1417*	0.1707*
all-roberta-large-v1 $_{mean-pooling}$	0.2732	0.4093	0.1142	0.1358
all-roberta-large-v1 $_{mean-pooling}$*	**0.3489***	**0.4924***	**0.3413***	**0.2263***
all-mpnet-base-v1 $_{cls-pooling}$	0.2672	0.4064	0.1062	0.1055
all-mpnet-base-v1 $_{cls-pooling}$*	0.2792*	0.4123*	0.1730*	0.1400*
all-mpnet-base-v1 $_{mean-pooling}$	0.2747	0.4093	0.1390	0.1322
all-mpnet-base-v1 $_{mean-pooling}$*	**0.3712***	**0.5129***	**0.2279***	**0.1583***
SGPT-2.7B $_{last-token-pooling}$	0.2329	0.3758	0.1305	0.1460
SGPT-2.7B $_{last-token-pooling}$*	0.2515*	0.4089*	0.1832*	0.1581*
SGPT-2.7B $_{mean-pooling}$	0.2597	0.3982	0.1497	0.1492
SGPT-2.7B $_{mean-pooling}$*	**0.2773***	**0.4190***	**0.2110***	**0.1780***
SGPT-1.3B $_{last-token-pooling}$	0.1429	0.3120	0.1278	0.1248
SGPT-1.3B $_{last-token-pooling}$*	0.2635*	0.3987*	0.2114*	0.1738*
SGPT-1.3B $_{mean-pooling}$	0.1719	0.3270	0.1414	0.1398
SGPT-1.3B $_{mean-pooling}$*	**0.2805***	**0.4187***	**0.2341***	**0.1838***

* Embeddings from the average output of the four last hidden layers of PLM.

Table 7. Legislative Title clustering using HDBSCAN

PLMs	Legislative Title			
	NMI	Purity	P	R
all-roberta-large-v1 $cls-pooling$	0.3284	0.3754	0.1906	0.2211
all-roberta-large-v1 $cls-pooling$*	0.3619*	0.4237*	**0.2421***	0.3127*
all-roberta-large-v1 $mean-pooling$	0.3443	0.3867	0.1518	0.1684
all-roberta-large-v1 $mean-pooling$*	**0.4238***	**0.4915***	0.2145*	**0.3211***
all-mpnet-base-v1 $cls-pooling$	0.2938	0.4497	0.1585	0.1829
all-mpnet-base-v1 $cls-pooling$*	0.3235*	0.4817*	0.2235*	0.2295*
all-mpnet-base-v1 $mean-pooling$	0.3115	0.4715	0.1734	0.1938
all-mpnet-base-v1 $mean-pooling$*	**0.3903***	**0.5315***	**0.2692****	**0.2622***
SGPT-2.7B $last-token-pooling$	0.1318	0.2028	0.1121	0,1334
SGPT-2.7B $last-token-pooling$*	0.1986*	0,2898*	0.1689*	0.1682*
SGPT-2.7B $mean-pooling$	0.2226	0.2926	0.2243	0.1943
SGPT-2.7B $mean-pooling$*	**0,3255***	**0.4012***	**0.2799***	**0.2398***
SGPT-1.3B $last-token-pooling$	0.1112	0.2834	0.1174	0.1260
SGPT-1.3B $last-token-pooling$*	0.1870*	0.3518*	0.1643*	0.1480*
SGPT-1.3B $mean-pooling$	0.1994	0.3793	0.1242	0.1410
SGPT-1.3B $mean-pooling$*	**0.3174***	**0.4272***	**0.1755***	**0.1509***

* Embeddings from the average output of the four last hidden layers of PLM.

Table 8. Legislative Subject Matter clustering using HDBSCAN

PLMs	Legislative Subject Matter			
	NMI	Purity	P	R
all-roberta-large-v1 $cls-pooling$	0.3882	0.4416	0.1120	0.1102
all-roberta-large-v1 $cls-pooling$*	0.4052*	0.5061*	0.2142*	0.1413*
all-roberta-large-v1 $mean-pooling$	0.4133	0.4515	0.1748	0.1254
all-roberta-large-v1 $mean-pooling$*	**0.4760***	**0.5122***	**0.2377***	**0.1712***
all-mpnet-base-v1 $cls-pooling$	0.3198	0.4100	0.1130	0.1122
all-mpnet-base-v1 $cls-pooling$*	0.4135*	0.4246*	0.2183*	0.1717*
all-mpnet-base-v1 $mean-pooling$	0.3626	0.4102	0.1341	0.1304
all-mpnet-base-v1 $mean-pooling$*	**0.4667***	**0.4607***	**0.2562***	**0.1897***
SGPT-2.7B $last-token-pooling$	0.2626	0.4030	0.1181	0.1298
SGPT-2.7B $last-token-pooling$*	0.3418*	0.4241*	0.1914*	0.2193*
SGPT-2.7B $mean-pooling$	0.2829	0.3990	0.1508	0.1424
SGPT-2.7B $mean-pooling$*	**0.3826***	**0.4697***	**0.2081***	**0.2394***
SGPT-1.3B $last-token-pooling$	0.1517	0.2575	0.1474	0.1377
SGPT-1.3B $last-token-pooling$*	0.3466*	0.3302*	0.1766*	0.2405*
SGPT-1.3B $mean-pooling$	0.1635	0.2639	0.1695	0.1441
SGPT-1.3B $mean-pooling$*	**0.4154***	**0.3821***	**0.2360***	**0.2768***

* Embeddings from the average output of the four last hidden layers of PLM.

Table 9. Proposal Act clustering using HDBSCAN

PLMs	Proposal Act			
	NMI	Purity	P	R
all-roberta-large-v1 $_{cls-pooling}$	0.2945	0.3989	0.1447	0.1432
all-roberta-large-v1 $_{cls-pooling}$*	0.3112*	0.4298*	0.1638*	0.1508*
all-roberta-large-v1 $_{mean-pooling}$	0.3245	0.4013	0.1497	0.1482
all-roberta-large-v1 $_{mean-pooling}$*	**0.4012***	**0.4487***	**0.2092***	**0.1658***
all-mpnet-base-v1 $_{cls-pooling}$	0.2965	0.4234	0.1031	0.1141
all-mpnet-base-v1 $_{cls-pooling}$*	0.3245*	0.4341*	0.1638*	0.1422*
all-mpnet-base-v1 $_{mean-pooling}$	0.3008	0.3962	0.1297	0.1247
all-mpnet-base-v1 $_{mean-pooling}$*	**0.3308***	**0.4825***	**0.2582***	**0.1598***
SGPT-2.7B $_{last-token-pooling}$	0.2180	0.3051	0.1379	0.1272
SGPT-2.7B $_{last-token-pooling}$*	0.2786*	0.3980*	0.2897*	0.1468*
SGPT-2.7B $_{mean-pooling}$	0.2372	0.4117	0.1498	0.1352
SGPT-2.7B $_{mean-pooling}$*	**0.2775***	**0.4764***	**0.3078***	**0.1939***
SGPT-1.3B $_{last-token-pooling}$	0.1388	0.2648	0.1195	0.1251
SGPT-1.3B $_{last-token-pooling}$*	0.2724*	0.3436*	0.1960*	0.1615*
SGPT-1.3B $_{mean-pooling}$	0.1440	0.2813	0.1574	0.1781
SGPT-1.3B $_{mean-pooling}$*	**0.2829***	**0.4117***	**0.2395***	**0.2445***

* Embeddings from the average output of the four last hidden layers of PLM.

Table 10. Legislative Act clustering using HDBSCAN

PLMs	Legislative Act			
	NMI	Purity	P	R
all-roberta-large-v1 $_{cls-pooling}$	0.2787	0.3507	0.1191	0.1298
all-roberta-large-v1 $_{cls-pooling}$*	0.2883*	0.4089*	0.1567*	0.1664*
all-roberta-large-v1 $_{mean-pooling}$	0.2953	0.3948	0.1223	0.1415
all-roberta-large-v1 $_{mean-pooling}$*	**0.3943***	**0.4565***	**0.3085***	**0.2344***
all-mpnet-base-v1 $_{cls-pooling}$	0.2796	0.4090	0.1147	0.1116
all-mpnet-base-v1 $_{cls-pooling}$*	0.2852*	0.4233*	0.1621*	0.1411*
all-mpnet-base-v1 $_{mean-pooling}$	0.2931	0.3981	0.1563	0.1537
all-mpnet-base-v1 $_{mean-pooling}$*	**0.3715***	**0.4923***	**0.2381***	**0.1655***
SGPT-2.7B $_{last-token-pooling}$	0.2395	0.3669	0.1231	0.1458
SGPT-2.7B $_{last-token-pooling}$*	0.2434*	0.3814*	0.1712*	0.1630*
SGPT-2.7B $_{mean-pooling}$	0.2633	0.3982	0.1341	0.1519
SGPT-2.7B $_{mean-pooling}$*	**0.2701***	**0.4280***	**0.2230***	**0.1890***
SGPT-1.3B $_{last-token-pooling}$	0.1494	0.3230	0.1172	0.1230
SGPT-1.3B $_{last-token-pooling}$*	0.2759*	0.3896*	0.2256*	0.1851*
SGPT-1.3B $_{mean-pooling}$	0.1788	0.3560	0.1562	0.1341
SGPT-1.3B $_{mean-pooling}$*	**0.2939***	**0.4062***	**0.2523***	**0.1958***

* Embeddings from the average output of the four last hidden layers of PLM.

Through these tables, we noticed that the best results obtained when we combine the outputs from the 4 last hidden layers of the PLM by taking the average of all of them, along with using classic mean pooling strategy. Therefore, we saw clearly that our proposed approach shows significant results according to the precision and recall metrics compared to the classical use of PLMs (using just the output of the last hidden layer of PLMs) over all the ecoder and decoder pretrained models. It seems that our method could create more internally coherent clusters with higher precision.

5   Conclusion

This paper proposes a strategy, to enhance the representation of legislative proposal documents embeddings in low-resource in order to cluster them based on their policy area. So, we conducted extensive experiments on the collected dataset from the Legislative Observatory European Parliament platform, where we demonstrates the effectiveness of embeddings generated using the sliding window technique associated with the aggregation of different outputs from the intermediate hidden layers of the PLMs that we chosed to use.

Limitations

Although PLMs are trained on large amounts of text from many sources, they may lack domain-specific details. Like in our case, legal or political domains language can be highly complex and context-dependent, which might decrease the performance of clustering when utilizing embeddings from PLMs that are not specifically finetuned for law domain. Also, the quality of the dataset used to train the PLMs can significantly affect the embeddings. So, if the dataset lacks diversity in legal documents or if it's not comprehensive enough, the embeddings might not capture the full semantic of law language, which lead to biased clustering results. Furthermore, law texts can be ambiguous, and certain terms might have multiple meanings (polysemy) based on the context. Therefore, PLMs might have trouble to appropriately disambiguate such terms accurately. In addition to that, clustering algorithms might encounter scalability challenges when dealing with large volumes of law documents. Further, interpreting the clusters and explaining their legal meaning might be highly challenging. For that reason the need of human expert evaluation is highly recommended for unsupervised tasks. Hence, we consider that the lack of expert evaluation in this work is the major limitation.

Acknowledgements. This work was supported and funded by Google PhD Fellowships Program and Google Cloud Platform (GCP).

Ethics Statement. The Legislative Proposals documents of European Union used in this study were sourced from publicly available open-access website. No proprietary or confidential documents were accessed without explicit permission. Also there is no specific consent required for their use. Then, the clustering algorithm applied to categorize the Legislative Proposal documents according to their policies area based on content similarity, ensured objective analysis and did not involve subjective biases. Although, efforts were made to redact these kind of sensitive information, there might exist inherent biases due to the nature of legal and political texts.

References

1. Mikolov, T., Sutskever, I., Chen, K., Corrado, G.S., Dean, J.: Distributed representations of words and phrases and their compositionality. In: Advances in Neural Information Processing Systems, vol. 26 (2013)
2. Le, Q., Mikolov, T.: Distributed representations of sentences and documents. In: International Conference on Machine Learning, pp. 1188–1196. PMLR (2014)
3. Conrad, J.G., Al-Kofahi, K., Zhao, Y., Karypis, G.: Effective document clustering for large heterogeneous law firm collections. In: Proceedings of the 10th International Conference on Artificial Intelligence and Law, pp. 177–187 (2005)
4. Lu, Q., Conrad, J.G., Al-Kofahi, K., Keenan, W.: Legal document clustering with built-in topic segmentation. In: Proceedings of the 20th ACM International Conference on Information and Knowledge Management, pp. 383–392 (2011)
5. Raghav, K., Balakrishna Reddy, P., Balakista Reddy, V., Krishna Reddy, P.: Text and citations based cluster analysis of legal judgments. In: Prasath, R., Vuppala, A.K., Kathirvalavakumar, T. (eds.) MIKE 2015. LNCS (LNAI), vol. 9468, pp. 449–459. Springer, Cham (2015). https://doi.org/10.1007/978-3-319-26832-3_42
6. Kachappilly, D., Wagh, R.: Similarity analysis of court judgments using clustering of case citation data: a study. Int. J. Eng. Technol. **7**, 855 (2018)
7. Raghuveer, K.: Legal documents clustering using latent dirichlet allocation. IAES Int. J. Artif. Intell. **2**(1), 34–37 (2012)
8. Mathai, S., Gupta, D., Radhakrishnan, G.: Iterative concept-based clustering of Indian court judgments. In: Bhateja, V., Tavares, J.M.R.S., Rani, B.P., Prasad, V.K., Raju, K.S. (eds.) Proceedings of the Second International Conference on Computational Intelligence and Informatics. AISC, vol. 712, pp. 91–103. Springer, Singapore (2018). https://doi.org/10.1007/978-981-10-8228-3_10
9. Zhang, H., Zhou, L.: Similarity judgment of civil aviation regulations based on Doc2Vec deep learning algorithm. In: 2019 12th International Congress on Image and Signal Processing, BioMedical Engineering and Informatics (CISP-BMEI), pp. 1–8. IEEE (2019)
10. Sabo, I.C., Dal Pont, T.R., Wilton, P.E.V., Rover, A.J., Hübner, J.F.: Clustering of Brazilian legal judgments about failures in air transport service: an evaluation of different approaches. Artif. Intell. Law **30**(1), 21–57 (2022)
11. Amigó, E., Gonzalo, J., Artiles, J., Verdejo, F.: A comparison of extrinsic clustering evaluation metrics based on formal constraints. Inf. Retrieval **12**, 461–486 (2009)
12. Knops, Z.F., Maintz, J.A., Viergever, M.A., Pluim, J.P.: Normalized mutual information based registration using k-means clustering and shading correction. Med. Image Anal. **10**(3), 432–439 (2006)
13. Lamirel, J.C., Ghribi, M., Cuxac, P.L.: Unsupervised recall and precision measures: a step towards new efficient clustering quality indexes. In: Proceedings of the 19th International Conference on Computational Statistics (COMPSTAT'2010), Paris, France (2010)
14. Muennighoff, N.: SGPT: GPT sentence embeddings for semantic search. arXiv preprint arXiv:2202.08904 (2022)

Emerging Technologies and Innovation
for Digital Business

Blockchain-Driven Secure Auditing of Timber-to-Charcoal Supply Chain

Mubashar Iqbal[1]([⊠]), Muhammad Zubair[1], Sabah Suhail[2], Faiz Ali Shah[1], and Fredrik Milani[1]

[1] Institute of Computer Science, University of Tartu, Tartu, Estonia
{mubashar.iqbal,faiz.ali.shah,milani}@ut.ee
[2] Institute of Electronics, Communications and Information Technology, Queen's University, Belfast, UK
s.suhail@qub.ac.uk

Abstract. Auditing processes must balance the data security of audited entities with vulnerabilities that enable fraud through, e.g., data tampering. As such, auditing processes have shortcomings that hinder effectiveness and expose businesses to financial and operational risks. This paper explores how blockchain can impact auditing through its decentralized and distributed ledger, cryptographic principles, and consensus mechanisms that can provide an immutable and auditable transaction history while ensuring data confidentiality. More specifically, we investigate the auditing of a timber-to-charcoal supply chain and show how blockchain can change the auditing to make it tamper-proof, efficient, and secure. First, we analyze how blockchain can overcome limitations inherent in traditional auditing processes. Then, we propose a decentralized and distributed solution using Hyperledger Fabric (HLF) specifically designed to audit the timber-to-charcoal supply chain. Finally, we implement the proposed solution's proof-of-concept and evaluate its functionality, security, and performance. Our contribution extends existing research on integrating blockchain into auditing practices, promoting trust, transparency, and efficiency throughout the timber-to-charcoal supply chain.

Keywords: Blockchain · Hyperledger Fabric (HLF) · Decentralized Application · Timber-to-Charcoal Auditing · Supply Chain

1 Introduction

The auditing process is a dynamic and iterative cycle, empowering businesses to systematically examine and verify financial and operational information, thereby enhancing the organization's governance processes [2]. Thus, robust audit systems can assist companies in reducing and eliminating a variety of challenges, including falsification of financial statements, theft of assets, fraudulent activities, and the risks associated with insufficient operational knowledge and management practices [16]. Nevertheless, despite best practices for establishing standardized auditing procedures for businesses, workflows can become easily fragmented due to a range of issues such as data tampering, insecure communication,

A. Lupeikienė et al. (Eds.): DB&IS 2024, CCIS 2157, pp. 123–140, 2024.
https://doi.org/10.1007/978-3-031-63543-4_9

insufficient access control, human error, and insider threats [2,16,18]. These challenges can impede the anticipated outcomes of the auditing process. To address such challenges, we investigate blockchain integration to enhance security measures and unlock potential transformative impacts in auditing.

Blockchain is a decentralized and distributed ledger technology that operates over a Peer-to-Peer (P2P) network and records transactions across a network of distributed peers [6]. It employs cryptography to secure and link individual data blocks, forming a continuous chain. The ledger is immutable and append-only, creating a tamper-resistant traceable history due to various consensus mechanisms [6,14]. For example, Pedro et al. explored the use of blockchain in auditing to reduce the workload of the auditors, minimize fraud, and optimize the existing processes [1]. Likewise, Rejeb et al. proposed blockchain to address issues concerning verifying raw material sources and maintaining product visibility across the value chain network [14]. The emergence of blockchain in auditing processes is driven by its inherent security features, which promote trust and accountability across financial transactions and supply chain management.

To study the significance of blockchain in the auditing process, we consider the use case of auditing the timber-to-charcoal supply chain. The transformation from timber to charcoal significantly impacts energy production, sustainable resource use, and environmental protection. Given its substantial contributions, optimizing and enhancing the auditing process for this supply chain is crucial to ensure efficiency, sustainability, and compliance with environmental standards. Therefore, we explore how blockchain can enhance the auditing process. In light of this context, our contribution is threefold: (i) We investigate and discuss the blockchain's role in overcoming the traditional auditing process challenges (Sect. 2.2). (ii) We propose the Hyperledger Fabric (HLF) based decentralized application for the timber-to-charcoal auditing (Sect. 3). (iii) We implement a Proof-of-Concept (PoC) of the proposed solution (Sect. 4) and evaluate it with rigorous functional, security, and performance testing (Sect. 5).

2   Preliminaries

This section explores the timber-to-charcoal supply chain use case (Sect. 2.1), examines the role of blockchain in addressing the challenges of the traditional auditing process (Sect. 2.2), and provides an overview of HLF (Sect. 2.3).

2.1   Use Case: Timber-to-charcoal Process

The traditional timber-to-charcoal process (Fig. 1) starts with owners cutting timber and then sending wood to charcoal processors directly or through brokers [10,19]. The processors process the wood to make charcoal at the conversion rate of 80%, which means only 20% of the entire input remains as output. Following this stage, the processed charcoal undergoes further refinement by secondary processors, who convert the charcoal into packaged forms with a conversion rate of 90%. This implies that 10% of the volume is lost during the packaging process.

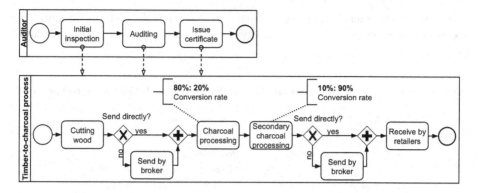

Fig. 1. Illustrating timber-to-charcoal supply chain process.

The packaged charcoal is then distributed to retailers. During this process (e.g., timber-to-charcoal supply chain), external auditors must perform audits and issue certifications, ensuring conformity and adherence to industry standards.

The auditing process starts with contract signing, leading to the commencement of the initial inspection, encompassing checks on environmental conditions, documentation, and supplier certificates. Occasionally, the inspector scrutinizes original invoices for more comprehensive assessments. Subsequently, the audit undergoes scrutiny by another audit officer who makes the final decision. Upon a positive determination, the certificate is issued to the company and logged into the timber certification organization's database.

2.2 Significance of Blockchain in Enhancing Auditing Processes

The traditional auditing process encounters security, operational, technical, and logistic challenges (as Table 1 shows), hindering its ability to yield precise results. To address them, we investigate and discuss blockchain as a solution, aiming to transform the auditing process to be more transparent and secure. For instance, in blockchain, transactions are cryptographically linked, forming an immutable chain of records that cannot be altered or deleted without consensus from the network participants [6,14]. This feature ensures the integrity of audit data, reducing the risks of data tampering and unauthorized modifications [5]. Blockchain operates on a P2P network and uses strong cryptographic techniques, offering a more secure framework for conducting and documenting audit-related interactions [11]. Smart contracts-based decentralized and distributed access controls enforce predefined rules without the need for intermediaries or a designated authority [1,11]. In a P2P network, nodes are distributed worldwide and possess the entire transaction history. If some nodes experience failure or compromise, the remaining nodes stay operational [4]. This distributed and decentralized structure ensures that the system remains operational, maintaining the integrity and continuity of the auditing process. Smart contracts-based self-executing agreements minimize the reliance on manual inputs [8]. At the same time, smart contracts-based decentralized access controls and the immutable recording of every executed action serve as safeguards against insider threats [5,8].

Table 1. Overcoming traditional auditing challenges through blockchain technology.

Type	Challenge	Blockchain role
Security	Data tampering	Immutable and append-only ledger
	Insecure communication	Peer-to-peer network
		Strong cryptographic principles
	Insufficient access control	Decentralized access control
	Single point failure	Peer-to-peer network and distributed nodes
	Human error and insider threats	Smart contracts-based automation
Operational	Lack of real-time information	Distributed ledger and ledger synchronization
	Biased auditing	Decentralized and distributed operations
	Limited stakeholder involvement	Peer-to-peer network and distributed ledger
	Monitoring timber sources	Provenance
Technical	Data quality and accuracy	Consensus and cryptographic principles
	Audit trail challenges	Provenance
Logistical	Resource allocation	Predefined permissioned settings
	Document management	Decentralized document verification

Transactions on the blockchain are immediately accessible (once approved) to all authorized participants, eliminating delays associated with traditional centralized systems [10]. Also, smart contracts can automate data updates, ensuring that information is consistently and instantly recorded [11]. Blockchain leverages distributed and decentralized characteristics to reduce the risk of biased interventions or subjective decision-making by a single entity, promoting objectivity in auditing [10]. A shared and immutable ledger allows stakeholders to access real-time and synchronized information, fostering increased collaboration and engagement. Due to the provenance characteristic of blockchain, each transaction and movement of timber (from sourcing to production) is securely documented, recorded, and verified, reducing the risk of illicit timber sources [9].

Blockchain consensus and cryptographic principles reduce the risk of errors or discrepancies in financial records, ensuring all stakeholders have access to the same unalterable information [4,6,9]. The provenance and traceability of transactions enhance the audit trail by providing a verifiable record of financial activities. Smart contracts can automate resource allocation tasks, streamline processes, and minimize the risk of mismanagement [8]. The distributed nature of blockchain ensures that documents are tamper-proof and resistant to unauthorized alterations. Smart contracts can automate document verification processes, reducing the reliance on manual checks and enhancing efficiency [15].

Thus, the significance of blockchain in auditing extends beyond mere technological innovation. It introduces a new paradigm that addresses longstanding challenges in auditing, offering improved transparency and security. As the technology continues to mature, its integration into auditing practices promises greater trust and reliability in audit outcomes.

2.3 Hyperledger Fabric (HLF)

HLF is a permissioned blockchain platform providing a framework for developing enterprise-level blockchain applications [8]. Smart contracts in HLF are referred to as chaincode. Chaincode is the executable logic that encapsulates the business rules and processes within the blockchain network. Chaincode is deployed and invoked by network participants to interact with the ledger, which is an immutable, decentralized, and transparent record of transactions.

The choice of a permissioned blockchain is guided by diverse business requirements. For instance, the transaction state needs to be stored, and writers (i.e., organizations) are known but not necessarily trusted. According to the Wüst and Gervais [17] model, these requirements align with the characteristics of a permissioned blockchain, making HLF a suitable choice. This decision is also driven by the need for a controlled and secure environment where known participants have defined roles and permissions in the network [8], making HLF an optimal solution for our use case. In contrast, permissionless blockchains (e.g., Ethereum) encounter various challenges due to the public accessibility of transactions, concerns related to regulatory compliance, the need for data confidentiality, and the absence of a structured governance model [6], all of which are pivotal considerations in the context of auditing procedures.

3   HLF-Based Timber-to-Charcoal Auditing

This section proposes the HLF-based timber-to-charcoal supply chain auditing process (see Fig. 2). The process begins with the registration of invoices. Upon receiving invoice data, the system verifies the supplier's certificate. Subsequently, the buyer's certificate also undergoes validation. If the supplier's and buyer's certificates are valid, the invoice data is uploaded to the HLF ledger; otherwise, the registration process is canceled. Only certified companies can initiate a request to change their conversion rate. These companies submit the conversion rate change request to the certifier. The certifier has the option to either approve or decline the submitted request. If the certifier declines the request, the chaincode will solely update the notification status to decline. Alternatively, if the certifier approves the request, the specified conversion rate supersedes the previous one, changing the certified company's conversion rate.

The auditing process includes three phases: (i) compare conversion rates, (ii) calculate aggregated volumes, and (iii) compare results. In the compare conversion rates phase, the process examines the implicit conversion rate of the seller by calculating the volume bought and sold. Following this, the system determines the seller's historic conversion rate. If the implicit conversion rate deviates beyond a specific threshold compared to the historical conversion rate, it is

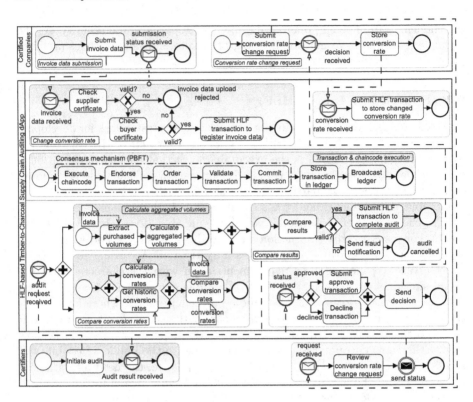

Fig. 2. HLF-based auditing in the timber-to-charcoal supply chain: Blue for invoice uploads, yellow for conversion rate adjustments, green for audit executions, and orange for the consensus mechanism, covering transaction and chaincode execution.

identified as a case of non-compliance. In calculating aggregated volumes phase, the process involves extracting invoice data, examining the volume purchased by the seller, and calculating the volume sold. Subsequently, this conversion rate is compared with the buyer's standard rate. If the volume sold surpasses the volume purchased and exceeds a specific threshold compared to the seller's standard conversion rate, it is identified as non-compliance. The compare results phase compares both results. Any indication of non-compliance in either process is construed as potentially fraudulent behavior by the seller, prompting the notification of the relevant certifier regarding the observed non-compliance.

HLF employs a Practical Byzantine Fault Tolerance (PBFT) based consensus to validate and record transactions [8]. The key participants in this process include peers, endorsers, and orderers. For example, when a participant initiates a transaction, the proposal is submitted to the network, specifying the intended operation as a chaincode invocation. Endorsers endorse the proposal, and the peers validate and agree on the proposed transaction. Once endorsed, the transaction is ordered by a designated ordering service, creating a block of transactions. The block is then distributed to all peers, and each peer independently validates and commits the block to its copy of the ledger.

4 Implementation

This section presents a PoC as an implementation of the proposed HLF-based auditing solution, starting with setting up the HLF network (Sect. 4.1), deploying chaincodes (Sect. 4.2), and performing the auditing process (Sect. 4.3).

4.1 HLF Network Architecture and Configuration

In our PoC, the HLF[1] network constitutes multiple interconnected components (as Fig. 3 shows). For instance, N denotes a Network encompassing peers, a channel, and associated configurations. Org denotes an Orderer organization responsible for enforcing the network's policy rules as outlined in the NC (Network Configuration) and deployed on the Orderer peer node O. Note that the Orderer does not maintain a ledger but ensures the seamless transfer of each transaction to other nodes within the network. There are two additional organizations: $Org1$, representing Certified Companies, and $Org2$, representing certifiers.

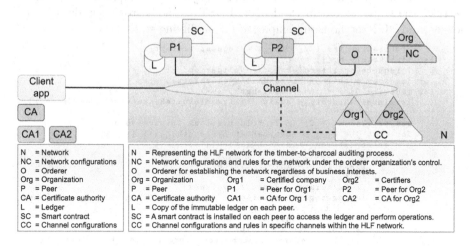

Fig. 3. The network architecture of HLF for the timber-to-charcoal auditing process.

The organizations participate in a unified channel, necessitating collaboration for business transactions. Each endorser node, such as $P1$ for $Org1$ and $P2$ for $Org2$, is a physical node connected to the network. These endorser peers maintain a local copy of the ledger and share a common chaincode, denoted as a Smart Contract (SC). When a new organization joins the network, it acquires a copy of the ledger and installs the same SC on other nodes within the channel. Each

---

[1] For our PoC, we use HLF v2.3.1 and CouchDB v3.1.1.

organization possesses a Certificate Authority (CA) responsible for managing access control for authorized users. Once established, clients interact with the HLF network using a client application to execute user requests.

The outlined HLF network requires specific configurations, e.g., we prepare `crypto-config.yaml` file to set up the security infrastructure, cryptographic keys, certificates, and other essential security-related artifacts. These configurations also outline the organizational structure, the number of peers within each organization, and the entities for whom certificates and keys must be generated. Additionally, we compile `configtx.yaml` file for the ordering service, channel creation, and the characterization of participating organizations by specifying their names and cryptographic materials. Furthermore, it specifies orderers, peers, channels, and policies that regulate interactions within the network.

4.2 Developing RESTful APIs for HLF-Based Auditing Interactions and Chaincode Logic

We develop Restful Application Programming Interfaces (APIs) using `express.js` to facilitate interaction with the HLF-based auditing process (see Appendix A Table 3). The logic for connecting with the HLF network is encapsulated in the `fabricNetwork.js` file, while the API endpoints, categorized by request methods, are contained in `server.js`. For example, GET methods retrieve the states stored in the ledger, POST methods store new data in the ledger, and PUT methods are employed for modifying state data.

```
async PerformAudit(ctx) { // ctx is a request context
    let finalResult = [];
    this._requireCertifiers(ctx); // Validation
    let invoices = await this.readAllInvoices(ctx);
    for (let i = 0; i < invoices.length; i++) {
        let invoiceHistory = await this.readInvoiceHistory(ctx, Invoices[i].
            invoiceId);
        let prevVolume = 0; // To hold previous invoice volume
        for (let j = 0; j < invoiceHistory.length; j++) {
            const invoice = invoiceHistory[j];
            if (j === 0) {
                prevVolume = invoice.volume;
            } else {
                // Calculate aggregated volumes
                let aggregateComparison = await this.CompareAggregateVolumes
                    (ctx, prevVolume, invoice);
                // Compare conversion rates
                let conversionRateComparison = await this.
                    CompareConversionRate(ctx, prevVolume, invoice);
                // Compare results
                let result = await this.ProcessComparisonResults(ctx,
                    aggregateComparison, conversionRateComparison);
                if (result) {
                    finalResult.push(invoice);
                }
                prevVolume = invoice.volume;
            }
        }
    }
    return finalResult;
}
```

Listing 1.1. Excerpt of chaincode implementing auditing process functionality.

We present an excerpt of the chaincode (Listing 1.1) implementing auditing functionality, executed via the `/api/performAudit` API endpoint. To facilitate understanding of the chaincode, we outline the transaction flow based on the chaincode execution for the auditing process (Fig. 4). For instance, the certifier initiates the audit request. The chaincode retrieves the uploaded invoices from the ledger and iterates through each invoice. This process comprises three components: *CompareAggregateVolumes*, *CompareConversionRate*, and *Process-ComparisonResults* as discussed in Sect. 4.3. CompareAggregateVolumes method accepts two parameters: "prevVolume" (purchased volume by the seller) and the "invoice" object, producing a boolean value as its output. The method computes the aggregated volume by considering the seller's conversion rate. If the purchasedVolume exceeds the calculated aggregatedVolume, the method returns false; otherwise, true. A false output indicates non-compliance in the invoice, signifying that the seller sells more volume than initially purchased.

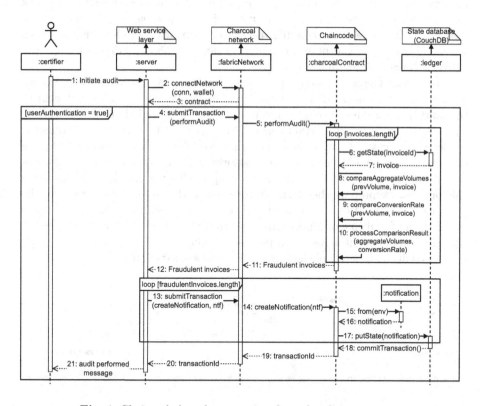

Fig. 4. Chaincode-based transaction flow of auditing process.

The CompareConversionRate method calculates the seller's implicit and historical conversion rates by averaging the conversion rates across all invoices. It then evaluates their difference, identifying non-compliance if the deviation

exceeds a predefined threshold. Specifically, deviations beyond 5% are flagged
if the seller's conversion rate surpasses 50, and 2% for rates equal to or below
50. ProcessComparisonResults method checks non-compliance (e.g., fraudulent
invoices) and prompts the certifier to notify the observed non-compliance (e.g.,
$createNotifcation(ntf)$). Once the auditing process concludes, the system commits the transaction and assigns a unique transaction ID. The transaction flow
diagrams related to other processes are accessible on GitHub (Appendix A).

4.3   Starting HLF-Based Auditing Process

The auditing application leverages a virtual environment implemented through
VMWare to facilitate testing and development processes. Node.js is used for
writing chaincodes, and express.js for developing Restful APIs. We use docker
for containerization, ensuring consistency across various environments and simplifying deployment. We prepare shell scripts to automate the HLF network
and application initiation and execute various tasks (as Fig. 5 shows). For
instance, a network.sh script file installs dependencies [sudo ./network.sh
install], launches the network [sudo ./network.sh start], and stops the
network [sudo ./network.sh stop].

The generate-ccp.sh script produces cryptographic certificates and keys for
each organization using HLF's cryptogen binary. Moreover, this script utilizes
the configtxgen binary to generate the genesis block and channel description.
These settings play an important role in forming the HLF network. Subsequently,
we devise the createChannel.sh script that establishes the channel by assigning
it a distinct name and enlisting the first organization. The certifier's organization must also integrate into the network upon channel creation. To facilitate
this process, we prepare the join-peer.sh script that dynamically receives the
parameters, eliminating the need for code redundancy and enabling the seamless
installation of multiple organizations. The install-peer.sh script executes the
chaincode deployment across each peer node. The next step involves instantiating the chaincode, accomplished using the instanciate.sh script.

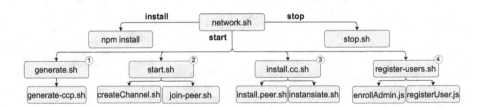

Fig. 5. Call hierarchy of shell scripts.

To interact with the HLF network, the participant must undergo a registration process. Each organization must have at least one administrator responsible
for granting permissions and managing access for others. The logic for enrolling

the administrator is encapsulated in the `enrollAdmin.js`. This establishes a connection to the organization, generating the CA client, and creating a wallet for storing the administrator's certificates alongside the associated username and password. The next phase registers users for transactional activities. The process outlined in `registerUser.js` involves establishing a connection to the organization, linking to the CA through the gateway utilized by the admin's identity, creating the user, and persisting its identity within the wallet.

5 Testing and Evaluation

This section discusses the preparation of the dataset (Sect. 5.1), functional testing (Sect. 5.2), security testing (Sect. 5.3), and performance evaluation (Sect. 5.4) to ensure the efficacy of the proposed approach.

5.1 Setting up Certifiers, Companies, and Testing Dataset for Audit

We register two certifiers (C01 and C02), who are responsible for certifying the companies in the auditing process. We compile a list of 20 certified companies, designated as CC001 through CC020, encompassing wood producers, charcoal processors, secondary charcoal processors, brokers, and retailers. These companies perform transactions involving activities such as uploading invoices and requesting changes to their conversion rates. Some companies hold suspended status (e.g., CC004 wood producer and CC007 charcoal processor), representing test cases where transactions are restricted only to active companies. In HLF, data is stored as key-value pairs in the state ledger [13]. The key serves as an identifier, and the value, containing data and its structure. The ledger keeps track of the state and its version history. For instance, the records added to the ledger for the same key update the state and increment the version.

We compile the invoice data and intentionally include specific non-compliant records (marked as red in Table 4 in Appendix A) to address test cases aimed at identifying fraudulent behavior among sellers and buyers. For instance, INV07 exposes fraudulent behavior as the conversion rate should be 80%, but it is selling 110% of the charcoal volume. INV09 and INV10 should be excluded from being uploaded. In INV09, the seller and buyer certificates are suspended, whereas in INV10, only the buyer's certificate is suspended. The detailed list of certified companies and the invoice data can be accessed on GitHub (Appendix A).

5.2 Functional Testing: Ensuring System Integrity Through Scenario-Based Evaluation

We developed and executed functional test cases to ensure that the solution's expected behavior conforms to the functional requirements (as Table 2 shows). The testing process encompasses various scenarios, such as uploading invoices, initiating the auditing process, verifying compliance, and addressing fraudulent behavior. The test plan briefly describes the test scenario, the steps to execute the test, specific test data, the expected output, and the test result (pass or fail) obtained after conducting the test. These tests yielded a "pass" result, confirming the solution's capability and effectiveness in meeting the specified functional requirements. This rigorous functional testing helps us identify and rectify potential issues in the built solution, ensuring it performs as intended.

Table 2. Overview of functional testing scenarios and outcomes.

Test scenario	Test data	Expected output	Test result
Upload invoice data with buyer and seller status active. **API:** /api/addInvoice	invoiceID: INV11 productID: Timber-Wood volume: 1000 buyer: CC005 seller: CC001	Transaction ID	Pass
Upload invoice data with buyer and seller status suspended. **API:** /api/addInvoice	invoiceID: INV09 productID: Timber-Wood volume: 2000 buyer: CC007 seller: CC004	Error message	Pass
Upload invoice data with buyer status suspended and seller status active. **API:** /api/addInvoice	invoiceID: INV10 productID: Timber-Wood volume: 2000 buyer: CC007 seller: CC003	Error message	Pass
Upload invoice data with missing parameters. **API:** /api/addInvoice	productID: Timber-Wood volume: 2000 seller: CC003	Error message	Pass
Perform the Audit. **API:** /api/performAudit	Invoice data compiled in Table 4	Non-compliance invoices	Pass

5.3 Security Testing: Evaluating Data Integrity Through Endorsement Policy Analysis

We examine the built solution's resilience against unauthorized modification and data tampering by considering the implications of various endorsement policies. This evaluation ensures that the implemented security measures and endorsement policies effectively safeguard the integrity of the data. To conduct security testing, we configure three organizations, CertifiedCompany, Certifier, and

TestOrg, each containing a single peer and CouchDB to manage the world state. The fraudulent company accesses one of the peer's CouchDB for specific record modification identified by the company ID (e.g., CC020). By doing so, the status of CC020 is manipulated from "SUSPENDED" to "ACTIVE" for the peer node "peer0.certifiedCompanies" (see Fig. 6), simulating a fraudulent company CC020 that wants to attempt data tampering. For example, consider a scenario where CC020 seeks to modify its conversion rates. The process is as follows: (i) instantiating the chaincode, (ii) invoking the chaincode to initialize the ledger with default values, (iii) tampering with data in the world state of one of the peer nodes, and (iv) attempting to make a transaction with tampered data.

Fig. 6. Identifying tampered nodes by querying records across peers.

To overcome the aforementioned fraudulent scenario, we implement a strong endorsement policy during the instantiation of the chaincode; a transaction is deemed valid only if it receives endorsement from all nodes [3,8,12]. Any node failing to endorse the transaction is rejected, ensuring a stringent validation process. So, after submitting tampered data from CC020, the data stored in the world state must match across all participating nodes, providing a synchronized view of the ledger. The nodes initiate queries to retrieve the status of each company involved in a transaction. If the status across nodes does not align, the transaction fails to garner endorsement and is consequently declined (as Fig. 7 shows). This practice guarantees data consistency and upholds data integrity within HLF-based applications. Conversely, a lenient endorsement policy allows any participating node to endorse and process a transaction [3]. Therefore, the CC020 could tamper with data without strict validation.

It is observed that if a node has been tampered with in the network, transactions cannot proceed until the integrity of the compromised node is restored. To fix the node, first, we must kill the tampered node docker container and its CouchDB instance (e.g., `docker kill peer0.certified Companies.example.com && docker kill CouchDB`). Second, we redeploy the node with CouchDB and initialize it with an untampered ledger copy.

Fig. 7. Fraudulent transaction failure response during endorsement.

5.4   Performance Evaluation

The performance evaluation takes place on a computing system running Kali Linux version 2021.1, Kernel 5.10.0, and Xfce 4.16.1 desktop environment. The system specifications include an Intel(R) Core(TM) i5-8265U CPU @ 1.60GHz and 16 GB of RAM. We employ Calipher, a widely used tool for analyzing the performance of HLF-based applications [7]. Using Calipher, we simulate network configurations, workload scenarios, and operational conditions to examine how the system behaves under different circumstances. For example, we evaluate the performance in two distinct scenarios, as illustrated in Fig. 8.

In the first scenario, we evaluate throughput measured in transactions per second (TPS) and latency in seconds while incrementing the number of nodes (see Fig. 8a). Throughout this evaluation, we maintain two endorsers, enforcing strong endorsement policies. We found that as the number of nodes increases, the throughput decreases due to additional overhead and resource contention in the network. Latency refers to the time taken for a transaction to be processed from initiation to finalization. The growing network size leads to overhead in reaching consensus among the nodes, resulting in longer transaction processing times. These results highlight the importance of carefully managing the network configuration and resource allocation. As the network size grows, it is recommended that strategies be adopted to mitigate the impact of increased latency and preserve throughput to maintain satisfactory levels of performance.

In the second scenario, we analyze the throughput across varying workloads, considering the data size and the number of blocks generated with an increasing

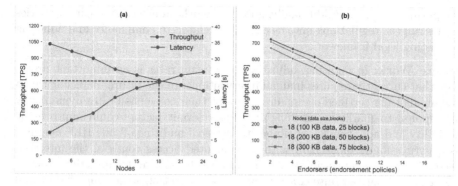

Fig. 8. (a) Illustrating throughput and latency with an increasing number of nodes. (b) Illustrating throughput across varying workloads and endorsers.

number of endorsers executing strong endorsement policies (see Fig. 8b). For this evaluation, we consistently utilize 18 nodes (a threshold determined in the first evaluation, indicated by blue dashed lines) to isolate the impact of changing the workload parameters and endorsers. Our findings reveal a significant decrease in throughput as the number of endorsers increased, resulting in transaction processing overhead while executing endorsement policies. Additionally, we observe how changes in workload parameters affect the throughput. The results highlight the importance of optimizing the HLF-based applications considering specific workload requirements to achieve optimal performance.

6   Concluding Remarks

This work addresses challenges inherent in traditional auditing processes, such as security, operational, technical, and logistical issues. Incorporating HLF is seen as transformative, providing a decentralized, transparent, and secure platform for auditing processes. Through chaincode, the developed solution performs auditing, starting from registering invoices, checking certification statuses, and validating transactions on the blockchain. To ensure the reliability and correctness of the proposed solution, we carried out functional testing, security testing, and performance evaluation. Our findings confirm the viability of the HLF-based solution for secure and transparent timber-to-charcoal auditing.

Limitations: As the network expands, incorporating more nodes and handling an increasing volume of transactions, the proposed blockchain-based solution could encounter scalability issues, potentially impacting its performance and operational efficiency (as Sect. 5.4 shows). The throughput and latency measurements may vary, and optimizing the system for larger-scale applications could be challenging. For instance, the resource requirements for running a HLF network, including memory, processing power, and storage, can be substantial. This might pose challenges, especially for smaller organizations or those with limited computing resources. Additionally, adopting blockchain technology in industries with stringent regulations may face hurdles related to compliance and adhering to existing legal frameworks.

Future Work: In auditing, adjusting conversion rates is an important procedure that currently requires manual interventions. In the future, implementing a system allowing certified companies to adapt their conversion rates dynamically in response to market conditions or other relevant factors could improve the flexibility and adaptability of timber-to-charcoal auditing. While HLF operates as a permissioned blockchain with implemented access controls, the interconnected business organizations share data for verification and transaction processing. This sharing can raise concerns among organizations regarding privacy and confidentiality. Thus, implementing advanced cryptographic techniques, such as Zero-Knowledge Proofs (ZKPs) and homomorphic encryption, can address sensitive business data exposure concerns while maintaining transparency.

A   Appendix: GitHub Repository, Chaincodes-Based API Endpoints, and Sample Invoices List and Data

The GitHub repository (https://github.com/cybercommando/TimberTo Charcoal-HyperledgerFabric) contains a source code, step-by-step procedure to setup the HLF network, relevant chaincodes for the auditing process, sample datasets for audit testing, and video demonstrations.

Table 3. List of API endpoints for the blockchain-based auditing process.

Method	URI	Description
POST	/api/initData	To initialize sample data in the ledger.
GET	/api/performAudit	To Initiate an auditing process.
POST	/api/registerCompany	To register a new company.
GET	/api/getAllCompanies	To get a list of the companies.
GET	/api/getCompany	To get a specific company by the ID.
GET	/api/historicConversionRate	To get the company's historical conversion rates.
PUT	/api/changeCompanyStatus	This request changes the company status.
POST	/api/registerCertifier	This request registers a new certifier.
GET	/api/getAllCertifiers	To get a list of certifiers.
GET	/api/getCertifier	To get the certifier by the certifier ID.
PUT	/api/changeCertifierStatus	This request changes the certifier status.
POST	/api/addInvoice	To upload invoice data to the ledger.
GET	/api/getInvoice	To get the invoice by the invoice ID.
GET	/api/getInvoiceHistory	To get versions of a specific invoice by an invoice ID.
GET	/api/getAllInvoices	To get a list of all invoices.
POST	/api/createNotification	To create a notification to change the conversion rate.
PUT	/api/resolveNotification	To resolve a notification having notification ID

Table 4. Tracking invoice data in the timber-to-charcoal supply chain.

Invoice ID	Product ID	Volume	Seller	Buyer
INV01	Timber Wood	1000	CC001	CC005
INV01	Charcoal Package 1	190	CC005	CC008
INV01	Charcoal Package 2	152	CC008	CC014
INV01	Charcoal Package 2	152	CC014	CC015
INV02	Timber Wood	1000	CC001	CC005
INV02	Charcoal Package 1	200	CC005	CC008
INV02	Charcoal Package 2	158	CC008	CC015
INV07	Timber Wood	500	CC003	CC006
INV07	Charcoal Package 1	100	CC006	CC009
INV07	Charcoal Package 2	110	CC009	CC015
INV09	Timber Wood	2000	CC004	CC007
INV10	Timber Wood	2000	CC003	CC007

References

1. Abreu, P.W., Aparicio, M., Costa, C.J.: Blockchain technology in the auditing environment. In: 2018 13th Iberian Conference on Information Systems and Technologies (CISTI), pp. 1–6 (2018). https://doi.org/10.23919/CISTI.2018.8399460
2. Castka, P., Searcy, C., Mohr, J.: Technology-enhanced auditing: improving veracity and timeliness in social and environmental audits of supply chains. J. Clean. Prod. **258**, 120773 (2020)
3. HLF: Endorsement policies. https://hyperledger-fabric.readthedocs.io/en/release-2.2/endorsement-policies.html. Accessed July 2023
4. Iqbal, M., Matulevičius, R.: Blockchain-based application security risks: a systematic literature review. In: Proper, H., Stirna, J. (eds.) CAiSE 2019. LNBIP, vol. 349, pp. 176–188. Springer, Cham (2019). https://doi.org/10.1007/978-3-030-20948-3_16
5. Iqbal, M., Matulevičius, R.: Comparison of blockchain-based solutions to mitigate data tampering security risk. In: Di Ciccio, C., et al. (eds.) BPM 2019. LNBIP, vol. 361, pp. 13–28. Springer, Cham (2019). https://doi.org/10.1007/978-3-030-30429-4_2
6. Iqbal, M., Matulevičius, R.: Exploring sybil and double-spending risks in blockchain systems. IEEE Access **9**, 76153–76177 (2021)
7. Kuhrt, T.: Hyperledger Caliper (2022). https://wiki.hyperledger.org/display/caliper/Hyperledger+Caliper. Accessed July 2023
8. Lu, N., Zhang, Y., Shi, W., Kumari, S., Choo, K.K.R.: A secure and scalable data integrity auditing scheme based on hyperledger fabric. Comput. Secur. **92**, 101741 (2020). https://doi.org/10.1016/j.cose.2020.101741
9. López-Pimentel, J.C., Rojas, O., Monroy, R.: Blockchain and off-chain: a solution for audit issues in supply chain systems. In: 2020 IEEE International Conference on Blockchain (Blockchain), pp. 126–133 (2020). https://doi.org/10.1109/Blockchain50366.2020.00023

10. Milani, F., García-Bañuelos, L., Reijers, H.A., Stepanyan, L.: Business process redesign heuristics for blockchain solutions. In: 2020 IEEE 24th International Enterprise Distributed Object Computing Conference (EDOC), pp. 209–216 (2020)
11. Mylrea, M., Gourisetti, S.N.G.: Blockchain for supply chain cybersecurity, optimization and compliance. In: 2018 Resilience Week (RWS), pp. 70–76 (2018). https://doi.org/10.1109/RWEEK.2018.8473517
12. Nijssen, S., Bollen, P.: The lifecycle of a user transaction in a hyperledger fabric blockchain network part 1: propose and endorse. In: Debruyne, C., Panetto, H., Guédria, W., Bollen, P., Ciuciu, I., Meersman, R. (eds.) OTM 2018. LNCS, vol. 11231, pp. 107–116. Springer, Cham (2019). https://doi.org/10.1007/978-3-030-11683-5_11
13. Papadopoulos, P., Pitropakis, N., Buchanan, W.J.: Decentralized privacy: a distributed ledger approach. In: Hussain, C.M., Di Sia, P. (eds.) Handbook of Smart Materials, Technologies, and Devices, pp. 1805–1830. Springer, Cham (2022). https://doi.org/10.1007/978-3-030-84205-5_58
14. Rejeb, A., Keogh, J.G., Treiblmaier, H.: Leveraging the internet of things and blockchain technology in supply chain management. Future Internet 11(7), 161 (2019). https://doi.org/10.3390/fi11070161
15. Schmitz, J., Leoni, G.: Accounting and auditing at the time of blockchain technology: a research agenda. Aust. Account. Rev. 29(2), 331–342 (2019). https://doi.org/10.1111/auar.12286
16. Stephens, K., Roszak, M.: A study of the role and benefits of third party auditing in quality management systems. J. Achiev. Mater. Manuf. Eng. 43(2), 774–781 (2010)
17. Wüst, K., Gervais, A.: Do you need a blockchain? In: 2018 Crypto Valley Conference on Blockchain Technology, pp. 45–54 (2018). https://doi.org/10.1109/CVCBT.2018.00011
18. Zarei, H., Rasti-Barzoki, M., Moon, I.: A mechanism design approach to a buyer's optimal auditing policy to induce responsible sourcing in a supply chain. J. Environ. Manage. 254, 109721 (2020). https://doi.org/10.1016/j.jenvman.2019.109721
19. Zubair, M.: A Blockchain Solution for Auditing of Timber-to-Charcoal Process. Master thesis (2021). https://comserv.cs.ut.ee/ati_thesis/datasheet.php?id=73720&language=en

Evaluation of Methods for User Needs Extraction in Digital–Physical Product Ecosystems Using ChatGPT Text Categorization

Alberts Pumpurs[✉] and Jānis Grabis

Riga Technical University, Zunda Krastmala 10, Riga, Latvia
alberts.pumpurs@rtu.com, grabis@rtu.lv

Abstract. The identification and categorization of user needs in digital–physical product ecosystems are key starting point for developing user-centered products and improving user experiences in complex, interconnected environments. Utilizing ChatGPT for text categorization offers a new automated approach to simplify user need elicitation of a user generated content that can be applied to a traditional user needs elicitation method. The Kano model, user personas, the jobs to be done framework, and user journey mapping methods were used in this study to identify user needs in digital–physical product ecosystems. ChatGPT was used in this study to automate the process of identifying and analyzing consumer experiences using the selected methods. The findings of this study offer insights into product ecosystem user needs research and practical guidance in the use of ChatGPT to identify and categorize user needs.

Keywords: Digital–physical product ecosystems · User need extraction · ChatGPT

1 Introduction

1.1 Background and Objectives

In the dynamically changing digital-physical product world, product ecosystems have become complex, and it is important to consider this in further product development and innovation. Traditional methods like the use of the Kano model, user personas, and the jobs to be done framework have been valuable in user experience research when working with user feedback on single products. However, proposed methods haven't yet been tested for user needs assessment for complex connected product structures, such as product ecosystems that consist of many interconnected products. Structuring and making use of large amounts of information is especially complex when working with large amounts of qualitative text. LLM tools like ChatGPT offer a new approach for analyzing user-generated text and summarizing it into consumer preferences and behaviors. This study is relevant to systematically evaluate and compare traditional methods of user need elicitation in the context of product ecosystems. The use of ChatGPT in this process proposes a simplification of how user feedback is categorized and analyzed.

A. Lupeikienė et al. (Eds.): DB&IS 2024, CCIS 2157, pp. 141–157, 2024.
https://doi.org/10.1007/978-3-031-63543-4_10

The aim of the study is to bridge the gap between traditional user need extraction techniques and ChatGPT-empowered capabilities, setting up the stage for a new approach to user-centered design and research.

There are two research questions:

- RQ1: How do traditional methods for identifying user needs, such as the Kano model, user personas, the jobs to be done framework, and user journey mapping, perform in the context of digital-physical product ecosystems?
- RQ2: What is the role and impact of ChatGPT in enhancing the process of identifying and categorizing user needs from user-generated content in digital-physical product ecosystems?

1.2 Overview of Digital–Physical Product Ecosystem

The digital–physical product ecosystem is a complex and interconnected network that integrates digital technology with physical products, creating opportunities for value generation within interconnected networks [1]. This integration allows for the development of novel products and services, as well as the establishment of complex business scenarios in various industries such as the automotive, aviation, and industrial manufacturing industries [2]. The augmentation of physical products with digital technology characterizes the digital–physical product ecosystem, leading to the emergence of smart service ecosystems and the creation of joint value in ecosystems [1, 2].

Digital–physical product ecosystems combine devices, networks, services, protocols, and digital content in complex, modular structures. This structure extends beyond traditional physical products thanks to software integrations and interconnectedness between modular structures and other products and services [3]. From a business standpoint, these ecosystems represent a network of companies united by their interest in expansion of digital technology. These companies expand their business by integrating their products and services into various ecosystems [4]. In conclusion, the digital–physical product ecosystem represents a dynamic and interconnected network that integrates digital technology with physical products, fostering innovation, value creation, and the development of novel products and services across various industries.

1.3 Overview of Methods Considered

Understanding user needs is crucial to the successful development of useful products and services. Several methods have been used to identify user needs, including the Kano model, user personas, the jobs to be done framework, and user journey mapping methods. The Kano model is utilized to categorize customer preferences into essential, performance, and excitement attributes, providing insights into the product features that are most valued by users [5]. User personas, conversely, are fictional characters (generally based on real user data) created to represent different user types, enabling designers to empathize with and understand users and their behaviors and motivations [6, 7]. The jobs to be done framework involves focusing on understanding the "jobs" that customers are trying to accomplish, shedding light on the functional, social, and emotional dimensions of user needs [8]. User journey mapping involves visualizing user experiences and interactions with products or services and identifying pain points and opportunities to enhance the user experience [9]. The identification of user needs through the Kano model, user personas, the jobs to be done framework, and user journey mapping methods provides a holistic understanding of user preferences, motivations, and pain points, ultimately guiding the development of user-centered products and services.

2 Related Work

2.1 Users Need Elicitation in the Ecosystems

The identification of user needs within product ecosystems is a multistep process that involves various methods and frameworks, often in combination with other methods. This background overview explores the use of the Kano model, user personas, the jobs to be done framework, and user journey mapping methods in the context of user need extraction within ecosystems. Ayoub et al. [10] presented a machine learning approach for customer need analysis (elicitation) within product ecosystems, categorizing customer needs related to different topics using an analytic Kano model based on sentiment analysis. Using LDA (Latent Dirichlet allocation) for topic modeling and VADER (Valence Aware Dictionary and sEntiment Reasoner) for sentiment analysis, research demonstrated that it is possible to dynamically classify customer needs using an analytical Kano model.

Although there has been no attempt to use user journey mapping in combination with digital–physical product ecosystems, there is published ecosystem research that involves journey mapping. Specifically, the U.S. Department of Veterans Affairs Office of Mental Health and Suicide Prevention and the Veterans Health Administration Office of Health Informatics Human Factors Engineering Group utilized journey mapping to understand patients' psychotherapy experiences [11]. The study filled a knowledge gap by mapping social innovation initiatives and ecosystems in smart, healthy, and age-friendly areas in Europe. Mickelsson et al. [12] focused on identifying product ecosystems from the user's perspective, emphasizing the value-creating function of ecosystems for users. This user-centric approach provides a foundation for understanding user needs within ecosystems, aligning with the principles of user personas and the jobs to be done framework for understanding complex user perspectives and needs.

2.2 Kano Model Overview

The Kano model is created by Noriaki Kano in the 1980s. The proposed model categorizes user preferences related to the product (features) into five aspects—Must-be Quality, One-dimensional Quality, Attractive Quality, Indifferent Quality and Reverse Quality (Fig. 1a). This model helps business and in particular product developers to better understand customer needs and preferences to create products, that better meet customer expectations [13]. When product developers classify product features based on their impact on customer satisfaction, then though Kano model companies can make aided decision on what product features to focus, to create significant impact in user satisfaction [14]. The process of creating Kano model involves gathering, identifying user feedback and requirements assigning them Kano categories, then analyzing and prioritizing these categories, so they can later be integrated into product development process

[15]. While Kano model most of the times is used to identify and prioritize features that improves user satisfaction for a single product, it could be used for a digital-physical product ecosystem, to tailor lager product offerings and drive engagement while meeting user expectations [14].

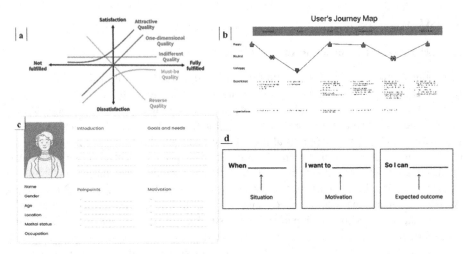

Fig. 1. Proposed models.

2.3   User Journey Map Overview

User Journey Map is an informative visualization tool that shows steps user takes when interacting with a product of service (Fig. 1b). A typical User Journey Map captures user experiences in each defined touchpoint throughout the journey [16]. The purpose of the User Journey Map is to show users interactions with the product or service to better understand user behavior, painpoints, and opportunities for improvement [16]. By identifying user requirements and mapping them with each touchpoint with representative user experiences, challenges and preferences, product developers can elicitate user needs during a particular user-product or service interaction [16, 17]. Suggested steps to create User Journey Map include identifying touchpoints, mapping the user's actions and motions, analyzing painpoints and opportunities for improving them, to then use the gained knowledge to enhance the user experience.

2.4   User Personas Overview

User personas (Fig. 1c) are imagined characters that are based on research data. While these are semi-fictional characters that use a certain product or a service they are based in real data and represent key characteristics, behaviors, goals of a target group [18, 19]. The Objective of user personas is to gain overall understanding of user's needs, preferences, behaviors, painpoints, that can later be used by product developers to develop products and services that better meet user expectations [19]. For the user need elicitation, such an approach helps to establish archetypal targeted user groups mirroring their needs thus product designers can empathize with the with users, prioritize features, and make well-informed design choices that address user requirements. The process of creating user personas involves conducting thorough user research, identifying common patterns among users in terms of product and service usage, crafting detailed personas portraits, completed with names, photos, and narratives [20].

2.5   Jobs to be Done Framework Overview

The Jobs to be Done framework focuses on understanding the motivations, circumstances and goals that make users want to—"hire" a product or a service to accomplish a specific job [21]. The aim of the framework is to extract functional, social, and emotional user needs by examining the context in which they operate with the product. The framework is used to identify unmet user needs by identifying existing reasons why and for what products are used, and user research is performed to identify additional jobs, that the users would want to do with the product but can't [22]. The general steps to create the Jobs to be Done framework are to define the job or task that customers are trying to accomplish, identify circumstances surrounding the job and understanding the desired outcomes [23]. A typical Jobs to be done statement consists of a situation description, motivation and expected outcome (Fig. 1d).

2.6   Impact of ChatGPT in User-Generated Content Analysis

The use of ChatGPT in user-generated content analysis and qualitative data analysis is a growing area of interest in academic research [24]. The authors of recent studies have explored various aspects of this topic, demonstrating the versatility and impact of ChatGPT in these domains [25]. ChatGPT already has a significant impact on user-generated content analysis and qualitative data analysis. For example, Mesec [26] found that ChatGPT is a useful tool for qualitative analysis because it can be used to identify basic themes, concepts, typologies, and evaluations.

ChatGPT has already been used for text coding in studies. Sen et al. [27] conducted a comparative analysis of AI and traditional coding methods, highlighting the strengths and limitations of the use of ChatGPT in qualitative research. Their results suggest that although AI can assist researchers in data analysis, it may not fully capture the nuanced themes that manual text coding can. Morgan [28] presents an optimistic view of ChatGPT's capabilities, suggesting that it can be effectively used across a range of qualitative analysis tasks, including the interpretation of datasets. Both studies, however, contribute to the growing interest in research on the use of AI in qualitative research, each offering unique insights into the potential roles and limitations of the use of tools like ChatGPT in qualitative data analysis.

3 Methodology

3.1 Users' Needs Extraction in Product Ecosystems

This research uses ChatGPT's text analysis, and summarization capability to categorize user feedback of Apple's headphone product ecosystem. Initially, the study gathered a dataset comprising 300 user-generated product reviews from the Amazon user review section. To understand the commonalities within Apple's ecosystem, three distinct products were selected: Apple AirPods, Apple AirPods Pro, and Apple AirPods Max, with each having 100 user-generated reviews to the dataset. Data set was chosen due to large and diverse available user feedback on the particular products as well as is one of the most used headphone ecosystems of consumers.

Further, the research focused on evaluating ChatGPT's ability to extract feedback that is specifically based on the product ecosystem from the overall user feedback. For this purpose, ChatGPT was provided with a predefined concept of a digital-product ecosystem (Fig. 2). Using the definition of ecosystem, and ChatGPT text categorization capabilities—the study successfully extracted 185 user-generated responses (from total 300 reviews), each ranging from 1 to 3 sentences, that explicitly articulated user perspectives on Apple's headphone ecosystem.

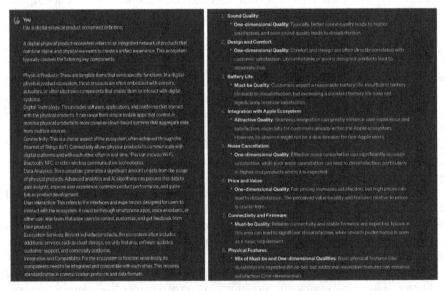

Fig. 2. Ecosystem definition and Kano model ChatGPT output

To test and compare each of the user need elicitation methods within the digital-physical product ecosystems using prompt engineering the following approach is used (Fig. 3). First 185 user-generated responses regarding Apple's headphone ecosystem are selected to be fed into the prompt. Then the selected method is introduced to the Chat-GPT, by retrieving its definition from ChatGPT's knowledge base. Further by prompt engineering in step-by-step sequence attempt is made to reach desirable output where given user feedback is converted to a viable completed method. If prompt is not returning resultative answer that helps the goal, then prompt is improved until it does. If a similar prompt structure with varying variables is failing, then a new prompt approach is selected, and a new prompt approach iteration takes place.

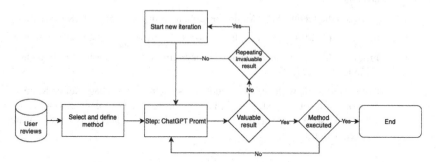

Fig. 3. User need elicitation method test using prompt engineering

3.2 User Need Elicitation Using Kano Model

At first, ChatGPT was tasked to define the Kano model. The AI model successfully identified all components of the Kano model, demonstrating a complete understanding of the model and its purpose. This outcome was subsequently compared to similar results in the existing related literature [29] confirming that no further information was necessary to enhance ChatGPT's clarity on the Kano model. ChatGPT accurately recognized the key aspects of the Kano model: basic features (must be quality), performance features (one-dimensional quality), and excitement features (attractive quality).

Following this, user-generated feedback related to Apple's AirPod ecosystem was integrated into ChatGPT for analysis. The AI was instructed to examine each piece of feedback and categorize it in accordance with the identified Kano model aspects. This process involved the consideration of the possibility of a single feedback entry referencing multiple features. Therefore, such entries were allowed to appear in different categories with corresponding features. The analysis conducted by ChatGPT yielded a total of 273 categorized features related to Apple's ecosystem as per the Kano model's classification. The result is depicted in Fig. 2, along with the commands given to access the result provided in Table 1.

3.3 User Job, Intention and Expectation Extrapolation Using Jobs to be Done Framework

Similar to the previous example with the Kano model, ChatGPT defined the JTBD framework, and its comprehension of the framework was evaluated with the strategy and innovation process developed by Ulwick [23]. ChatGPT had no issues describing the framework and all its aspects.

Table 1. Kano model's classification.

Step	Iter.	ChatGPT input
1	1	Define the Kano model
2	1	Generate a Kano model based on customer feedback on products in Apple's headphone ecosystem
3	2	Based on the feedback on Apples headphone ecosystem generate Kano model
4	3	From this file of Apples headphone ecosystem extract key customer preferences
5	4	From this file of Apples headphone ecosystem extract key customer preferences using feature analysis
6	4	Based on this file with Apples product ecosystem user feedback define Kano categories for sound quality, design and comfort, battery life, integration with apple ecosystem, noise cancellation, price and value, connectivity and firmware, physical features

When tasked with creating JTBD statements, which are typical outputs of the framework, ChatGPT responded that it was a complex task. It decided to simplify the task by consolidating commonalities and recurring user feedback. As a result, it provided correct, but generic, JTBD statements for each identified area within Apple's headphone ecosystem.

Although the results obtained were accurate, they lacked specificity and did not provide much information for in-depth analysis. It was necessary to conduct additional iterations to extract additional detailed insights. In the second iteration, ChatGPT was assigned the task of identifying all jobs generated from the JTBD statements and saving them to an Excel file. Due to the large amount of text output, it decided to summarize the text into manageable chunks. However, it was later determined that exporting the data to an Excel file was the most effective approach. During this process, ChatGPT encountered difficulties creating JTBD statements. In subsequent iterations, it either exported the original 7 JTBD statements or provided Excel user feedback categorized by jobs, which were the seven previously identified categories (Fig. 4).

Based on research into ChatGPT querying approaches, it was decided to break down the JTBD framework tasks into smaller chunks to generate multiple statements in a JTBD format, following the pattern of "When., I want..., so I can...." The same original file was used to identify situations from dataset of the user feedback, as well as user actions with and towards the ecosystem, and the outcomes or goals of their actions. This approach was intended to teach ChatGPT what constitutes jobs, user groups, and goals.

By employing advanced querying methods involving variables, ChatGPT finally managed to provide a list of 541 JTBD statements. However, handling such a large volume of data (over 500 user generated sentences) proved to be more challenging than the original 183 user-generated feedback entries. Consequently, ChatGPT was tasked with splitting the statements into logical sections, calculating sentiments, and providing grouping for filtering purposes. Operator commands for Jobs to be done are given in Table 2).

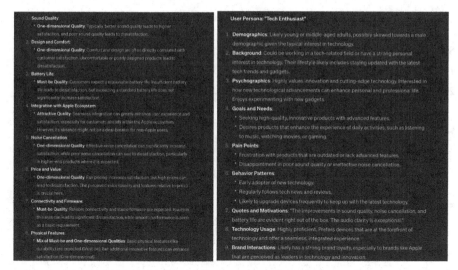

Fig. 4. Excel excerpt JTBD result and user personas

3.4 User Profile Extrapolation Using User Personas

In this instance, ChatGPT was tasked with defining user personas and then comparing that definition with the extracted user persona definitions and descriptions. User personas are archetypal representations of users created through data gathered from multimethod inquiries involving actual target users. Their use serves as a canonical user-centered design method, and they are increasingly utilized in various fields, the field of including health informatics research. Personas are designed to represent a group of users and comprehend the characteristics, goals, and skills of a particular user group [18].

ChatGPT was initially instructed to create user personas based on the provided definition. However, it immediately expressed that this task was complex and sought clarification regarding the task's complexity and interpretation. Despite being given the command to create user personas, ChatGPT generated only one user persona. Subsequent attempts to query for additional personas based on the file also resulted in just one user persona output. When asked whether there were any other personas, ChatGPT listed two personas that had been previously extracted: "tech-savvy audio enthusiast" and "discerning audio user." Just like with the JTBD task, it became evident that this task had to be broken down into segments due to ChatGPT's limitations.

Therefore, the approach was adjusted. Initially, ChatGPT was tasked with scanning the entire file to identify user personas and provide descriptions for these personas. This information would later be used to guide the search for specific details. Instead, a separate query was executed for each persona identified to obtain the previously defined missing information, including demographics, background, psychographics, goals and needs, pain points, behavior patterns, quotations and motivations, technology usage, and brand interactions as seen in Table 3. Running separate queries for each category yielded the necessary outcomes (Fig. 4).

Table 2. JTBD ChatGPT queries.

Step	Iter.	ChatGPT queries
1	1	Define the JTBD framework
2	1	In this excel document with apple headphone product ecosystem user-generated feedback. Create ecosystem oriented JTBD statements from it
3	2	Extract all identified jobs from the original Excel file. Generate all possible JTBD statements and save them in external Excel file. Do not output interim results here
4	3	Using the original file, extract Apple headphone ecosystem related JTBD statements in excel file. Do not generalize. Extract ALL possible statements. No interim result output is needed
5	4	From given user feedback, identify all target unique situations, users are in when using the product. Give their descriptions and list them all here
6	4	From the same file extract all unique actions users are trying to do or goals they are trying to achieve
7	4	From the same original file extract all unique desired outcome and benefits of the users and ensure they are do not duplicates from the actions list
8	4	Using customer or user roles and their description examples and user actions examples and desired goals, benefit description examples and file that describes Apple headphone product ecosystem, please extract as many possible JTBD statements, stated as: as a [target customer or user, or user role], I want to [action or goal], so that I can [desired outcome or benefit]. In place of brackets place corresponding extraction but using previously defined groups, goals, and desired outcomes. Import the full list into excel and add the source from which JTBD statement was extracted
9	4	Keeping all existing data, categorize JTBD statements in logical or contextual groups or topics. Add them to a separate column
10	4	Keeping all existing data, give users satisfaction level per each category using sentiment analysis and add that to excel

3.5 User Experience Process Extraction Using User Journey Map

User journey mapping is a method used to understand and visualize the experiences of product and service users. It is a powerful tool that is used to identify the interactions and touchpoints of customers with an enterprise [30, 31]. When asked for ChatGPT's definition and understanding of the UJM method, it successfully identified the key aspects: scenarios and goals, actions and emotions, touchpoints, pain points, and opportunities. Like previously, ChatGPT was given an ecosystem feedback file and queried to provide a UJM. It took classical UJM stages, such as awareness, considerations, purchase, use, and loyalty, and placed corresponding user feedback in particular stages (Fig. 5).

Although the result was correct and valuable, this approach failed to provide touchpoints and other previously defined UJM attributes. ChatGPT was tasked with extracting missing information and categorizing it under the identified UJM stages. This task was not entirely fulfilled, and there was missing information. For that reason, a task chunking

Table 3. ChatGPT queries.

Step	Iter.	ChatGPT queries
1	1	Define user personas
2	1	Extract typical user personas from the given file. Then for each extracted user persona, provide a key element (e.g., demographics, background, psychographics, goals and needs, pain points, behavior patterns, quotations and motivations, technology usage, and brand interactions) content corresponding to these user personas from the same file. Extract as many goals and needs, pain points, behavior patterns, and user scenarios as possible for each persona
3	1	Create user personas from the information in this file based on the user persona definition
4	2	List all potential user personas with their descriptions from user-generated feedback on Apple's headphone ecosystem
5	2	Fill in the missing information for each tech enthusiast in the file, such as demographics, background, psychographics, goals and needs, pain points, behavior patterns, quotations and motivations, technology usage, and brand interactions
6	2	Go through the file and based on user persona definition, for user persona: "busy professional" fill in the missing information such as demographics, background, psychographics, goals and needs, pain points, behavior patterns, quotations and motivations, technology usage, and brand interactions
7	2	Go through the file and based on user persona definition, for user persona: "audiophile" fills in the missing information such as demographics, background, psychographics, goals and needs, pain points, behavior patterns, quotations and motivations, technology usage, and brand interactions
8	2	Go through the file and based on user persona definition, for user persona: "casual user" fill in the missing information such as demographics, background, psychographics, goals and needs, pain points, behavior patterns, quotations and motivations, technology usage, and brand interactions
9	2	Go through the file and based on user persona definition, for user persona: "value-conscious consumer" fill in the missing information such as demographics, background, psychographics, goals and needs, pain points, behavior patterns, quotations and motivations, technology usage, and brand interactions
10	2	Go through the file and based on user persona definition, for user persona: "home entertainment enthusiast:" fill in the missing information such as demographics, background, psychographics, goals and needs, pain points, behavior patterns, quotations and motivations, technology usage, and brand interactions
11	2	Find matching user feedback for tech enthusiasts, busy professionals, audiophiles, casual users, value-conscious consumers, multi-device users, and home entertainment enthusiasts within the file. Measure user satisfaction levels using qualitative sediments analysis. Export the results to excel

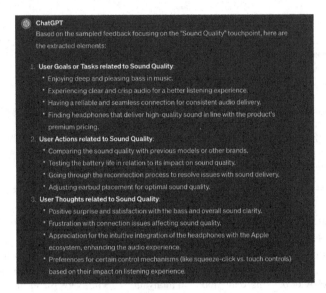

Fig. 5. Excel excerpt of user persona results

approach was selected again and a UJM was created by extracting touchpoints, and then other attributes for each touchpoint were extracted separately (Table 4).

Table 4. ChatGPT queries.

Step	Iter.	ChatGPT queries
1.	1	Define UJM
2.	1	Create a UJM from the file that contains user feedback on Apple's headphone product ecosystem
3.		Extract touchpoints from the given file, and for each touchpoint, extract related user goals or tasks, user actions, user thoughts, user pain points, and opportunities for improvement. Place the extracted information under UJM phase where it fits logically
4.	2	Based on the file, that contains user-generated feedback on Apples headphone ecosystem extract touchpoints users have within the product ecosystem where they interact with the ecosystem
5.	3	For touchpoint: "sound quality" from the user given feedback extract: user goals or tasks related to touchpoint, user actions related to touchpoint and user thoughts related to touchpoint
6.	2	For touchpoint: "sound quality" from the user given feedback extract: user pain points related to touchpoint, opportunities for improvement related to touchpoint
7.	2	Step 6 and 7 repeated for rest of the touchpoints reaching 12 more steps. Totaling 19 steps

4 Data Interpretation and Results

4.1 Comparing the Methods

This study evaluated four traditional user needs extraction methods used within digital–physical product ecosystems for text categorization and analysis using ChatGPT: the Kano model, user personas, JTBD, and UJM. Through a product designer's expert evaluation of user-generated content about Apple's headphone ecosystem, this research offers novel insights into the applicability and effectiveness of these methodologies when augmented by ChatGPT's former capabilities.

While this study used established methodologies such as the Kano model, user personas, JTBD framework, and user journey mapping to analyze Apple's headphone ecosystem, it uniquely leveraged the automated capabilities of ChatGPT to fasten user feedback categorization. Unlike usual-manual methods, ChatGPT's ability to quickly interpret, summarize, and categorize large datasets provided faster insight into user needs and behaviors. Its categorization within the Kano model revealed significant patterns in user expectations and satisfaction across different product types, highlighting distinctions that might be overlooked. Iterative and adaptive prompt-engineering process enabled fine-tuning that reflected the nuances of the product ecosystem. This research demonstrated how AI tools like ChatGPT could rapidly process and organize complex qualitative data, streamlining user needs elicitation and offering scalable solutions for product ecosystem design. The study presents novel insights into AI's potential for improving user experience research, providing a foundational framework for further exploration and practical application.

ChatGPT's analysis using the Kano model yielded a classification of 273 user feedback features into basic performance and excitement categories. This categorization revealed a predominant emphasis on performance and excitement features within the ecosystem, indicating a user preference for innovation and advanced functionality. Extracting information using the Kano approach through ChatGPT took the least number of steps to achieve the desired outcome among the methods and showed potential for scalability for processing the method, as well as post-information analysis.

While the Kano model output 273 results, the JTBD framework extrapolated 541 distinct JTBD statements, highlighting a diverse range of user needs and objectives within the ecosystem withing 10 steps. The JTBD analysis pointed toward a user inclination toward products that meet consumers' basic functional requirements and contribute to a user experience improvement. Reason for that many outputs from 183 user-generated feedback is that each feedback consisted of up to 3 sentences and ChatGPT was tasked to extract all possible results from each user feedback—particularly, that one user feedback may consist of multiple valuable feedback, that fits the criteria.

Getting the desired JTBD statement was not as complicated as dealing with the results analysis and evaluation of 541 unique jobs to be done statements. Each statement provides valuable information, but going through all of them is not a viable option because those statements are long and often complex. Clustering them into groups provides an overall perspective of collective problems and opportunities, but that does not really eliminate the problem of work being required after information extraction, and if the JTBD framework was scaled up to process additional user feedback, then the result analysis would become complicated.

4.2   ChatGPT Integration and Strategic User Experience Insights

ChatGPT's text analysis capabilities played a crucial role in the methodology of this study. The research found that the Kano model and JTBD methodologies aligned well with ChatGPT's functionalities, facilitating a seamless process of user feedback extraction from text. This shows the importance of selecting analytical methods that are compatible with advanced AI tools to enhance efficiency and accuracy. These findings underscore the significant impact that one's choice of methodology can have on UX strategy. Particularly, methods that excel at providing deep insights and actionable outcomes, such as the Kano model, are indispensable for driving meaningful design and strategic initiatives within the Apple ecosystem. These methods enable UX professionals to delve into consumer needs and preferences, forming a robust foundation for informed decision-making. Moreover, the results of this study shed light on the importance of efficiency and scalability in UX research methodologies. The observed positive correlation between the number of steps and iterations of a Kano method and its effectiveness suggests that high complexity does not necessarily lead to superior insights. This has practical implications for resource allocation within UX research, for a potential shift toward streamlined methods overelaborate ones like UJM, which may not provide proportional value in relation to their complexity.

4.3   The Effectiveness of ChatGPT in the Categorization of User Feedback

Thanks to ChatGPT's ability to holistically understand written text and comprehend and execute complex queries, this tool has generated interest among researchers for qualitative text analysis [32]. ChatGPT's knowledge retrieval capabilities were tested for using popular UX method approaches for extracting knowledge on user wants and needs, along with its ability to retrieve necessary content such as user action, goal, tasks, for these methods following the definition of a given methods.

Although the natural tendency is to write bulk task queries, due to content display limitations, the ability to comprehend and provide all datasets with necessary information is limited, most likely by the service provider. Thus, a chunking approach is employed whereby each step is executed in series to get the desired result. However, in this case, the operator must not lose ChatGPT's contextual understanding of the core executable task especially for if/then commands, but due to command limitations, each function needs to be run manually, and this is where ChatGPT sometimes forgets the overall context and needs to be reminded by repeatedly establishing key definitions and explanations of key variables.

ChatGPT has potential for use in qualitative data analysis and knowledge extraction using methods and frameworks. It is not capable of performing text analysis using a method in one query. That means the use of chunking and chaining queries is necessary to achieve results. It is also important for the researcher to be familiar with the UX methods and how they were manually created so they can evaluate the results of each output and iteration. The same is true for user feedback dataset—to effectively extract most of the knowledge, the researcher must be familiar with the topic and dataset.

5   Conclusion

This research has explored the ChatGPT use for the identifying and categorizing user needs in digital-physical product ecosystems in combination with the traditional methods typically used for the same process but for single entity products or services. Proposed and reviewed methods were Kano model, user personas, the jobs to be done framework, and user journey mapping. Results of this research show that there is potential use of large language models such as ChatGPT to improve efficiency of user needs elicitation and analysis in complex product ecosystems.

Findings of this study show that adaptability and positive use of ChatGPT automating and simplifying text of a user-generated content. Using prompt engineering ChatGPT with the help of operator was able to successfully extract and classify user-generated content to meet method requirements. This research demonstrates that ChatGPT, when used with traditional user needs elicitation methods, can significantly streamline the analysis process, reduce the manual effort required in data categorization.

The study also acknowledges the limitations associated with the use of ChatGPT. One of the main challenges encountered when querying ChatGPT is the lack of repeatability in its results. Even minor changes in variables, which may not necessarily be key attributes of the query, can lead to varying results. Additionally, ChatGPT's tendency to remember previous conversations can both aid and hinder the process. Although this feature can be valuable when breaking down tasks into smaller chunks, it can pose difficulties when trying to start new iterations from scratch. To address this issue, the "forget all" command was frequently used to reset ChatGPT's memory. Another significant challenge regarding repeatability arose from ChatGPT's upcoming updates. Significant differences were observed when the results between versions V3.5 and V4 were compared with V4 demonstrating a superior ability to extract content compared to V3.5. This suggests that future versions of ChatGPT are likely to yield improved results when information is extracted from user-generated content. The current results have been evaluated from an expert's perspective, by comparing the quality and valuable information that can be used to deepen the understanding of user-centered problems, opportunities, and positive aspects of Apple's headphone product ecosystem. Future research could benefit from formal analysis and the involvement of multiple UX experts to evaluate the user needs and wants identified by ChatGPT.

References

1. Herterich, M.M., Dremel, C., Wulf, J., vom Brocke, J.: The emergence of smart service eco-systems—the role of socio-technical antecedents and affordances. Inf. Syst. J. **33**(3), 524–566 (2023)
2. Beverungen, D., Matzner, M., Janiesch, C.: Information systems for smart services. IseB **15**(4), 781–787 (2017)

3. Yoo, Y., Henfridsson, O., Lyytinen, K.: Research commentary—the new organizing logic of digital innovation: an agenda for information systems research. Inf. Syst. Res. **21**(4), 724–735 (2010)
4. Selander, L., Henfridsson, O., Svahn, F.: Capability search and redeem across digital ecosystems. J. Inf. Technol. **28**(3), 183–197 (2013)
5. Lee, S., Park, S., Kwak, M.: Revealing the dual importance and Kano type of attributes through customer review analytics. Adv. Eng. Inform. **51**, 101533 (2022)
6. Lemon, K.N., Verhoef, P.C.: Understanding customer experience throughout the customer journey. J. Mark. **80**(6), 69–96 (2016)
7. Zagallo, P., et al.: Through the eyes of faculty: using personas as a tool for learner-centered professional development. CBE Life Sci. Educ. **18**(4), ar62 (2019)
8. Leavy, B.: Customer-centered innovation: improving the odds for success. Strat. Leadersh. **45**(2), 3–11 (2017)
9. Endmann, A., Keßner, D.: User journey mapping—a method in user experience design. i-com **15**(1), 105–110 (2016)
10. Ayoub, J., Zhou, F., Xu, Q., Yang, J.: Analyzing customer needs of product ecosystems using online product reviews. In: Proceedings of the ASME 2019 International Design Engineering Technical Conferences and Computers and Information in Engineering Conference, V02AT03A002. ASME (2019)
11. Dantas, C., Louceiro, J., Vieira, J., van Staalduinen, W., Zanutto, O., Mackiewicz, K.: SHAFE mapping on social innovation ecosystems. Int. J. Environ. Res. Public Health **20**(1), 118 (2023)
12. Mickelsson, J., Särkikangas, U., Strandvik, T., Heinonen, K.: User-defined ecosystems in health and social care. J. Serv. Mark. **36**(9), 41–56 (2022)
13. Wang, T., Ji, P.: Understanding customer needs through quantitative analysis of Kano's model. Int. J. Qual. Reliab. Manage. **27**(2), 173–184 (2010)
14. Mote, S., Kulkarni, V., Narkhede, B.: Kano Model application in new service development and customer satisfaction. IOSR J. Bus. Manag. **18**(1), 10–14 (2016)
15. Shahin, A., Pourhamidi, M., Antony, J., Hyun Park, S.: Typology of Kano models: a critical review of literature and proposition of a revised model. Int. J. Qual. Reliab. Manage. **30**(3), 341–358 (2013)
16. Moon, H., Han, S.H., Chun, J., Hong, S.W.: A design process for a customer journey map: a case study on mobile services. Human Fact. Ergon. Manufact. Service Industr. **26**(4), 501–514 (2016)
17. Rosenbaum, M.S., Kelleher, C., Friman, M., Kristensson, P., Scherer, A.: Replacing place in marketing: a resource-exchange place perspective. J. Bus. Res. **79**, 281–289 (2017)
18. Humphrey, A.: User personas and social media profiles. Persona Stud. **3**(2), 13–20 (2017)
19. Miaskiewicz, T., Kozar, K.A.: Personas and user-centered design: how can personas benefit product design processes? Des. Stud. **32**(5), 417–430 (2011)
20. Djamarullah, A.R., Kusuma, W.A.: Elicitation of needs using user personas to improve software user experience. Ultimatics: Jurnal Teknik Informatika **14**(1), 28–35 (2022)
21. Hankammer, S., Brenk, S., Fabry, H., Nordemann, A., Piller, F.T.: Towards circular business models: identifying consumer needs based on the jobs-to-be-done theory. J. Clean. Prod. **231**, 341–358 (2019)
22. Ribeiro, Á.H.P., Monteiro, P.R.R., Luttembarck, L.: The use of the 'job to be done' methodology to identify value co-creation opportunities in the context of the service dominant logic. BBR Br. Bus. Rev. **16**, 32–45 (2019)
23. Ulwick, A.W., Osterwalder, A.: Jobs to be Done: Theory to Practice. Idea Bite Press (2016)
24. De Paoli, S.: Improved prompting and process for writing user personas with LLMs, using qualitative interviews: capturing behaviour and personality traits of users. arXiv:231006391 (2023)

25. Belal, M., She, J., Wong, S.: Leveraging ChatGPT as text annotation tool for sentiment analysis. arXiv preprint arXiv:230617177 (2023)
26. Mesec, B.: The language model of artificial intelligence ChatGPT—a tool of qualitative analysis of texts. Authorea Preprints (2023)
27. Sen, M., Sen, S.N., Sahin, T.G.: A new era for data analysis in qualitative research: ChatGPT! Shanlax Int. J. Educ. **11**, 1–15 (2023)
28. Morgan, D.L.: Exploring the use of artificial intelligence for qualitative data analysis: the case of ChatGPT. Int J Qual Methods **22**, 16094069231211248 (2023)
29. Aslamiyah, S.: Model Implementasi Strategi Sebagai Determinan Kinerja Bisnis Ketika Pandemi Covid-19. Jurnal Riset Entrepreneurship **5**(1), 17–22 (2022)
30. Maddox, K., Masalonis, A., Motiwala, A., Adams, K., Eugene, N., Speir, R.: Using journey mapping to visualize patient experiences for quality improvement initiatives. Proc. Int. Symp. Human Fact. Ergon. Health Care **11**(1), 56–60 (2022)
31. Godoy, M.P., Rusu, C., Ugalde, J.: Information consumer eXperience: a chilean case study. In: Social Computing and Social Media: Applications in Education and Commerce, pp. 248–267. Springer International Publishing (2022)
32. Young, H.: Deriving desirable artistic generative distributions from individual identity statements. In: Soto, A., Zangerle, E. (eds.) Joint Proceedings of the ACM IUI 2024 Workshops co-located with the 29th Annual ACM Conference on Intelligent User Interfaces (IUI 2024), Greenville, South Carolina, USA, 18 Mar 2024. CEUR Workshop Proceedings, vol 3660 (2024)

Approaches and IT for Digitalization

Network Topology Based Identification and Analysis of Security Threats in Data Centres

Jānis Kampars[ID], Guntis Mosāns[(✉)][ID], and Jānis Grabis[ID]

Riga Technical University, Zunda Krastmala 10, Riga 1048, Latvia
{janis.kampars,guntis.mosans,grabis}@rtu.lv

Abstract. Various physical and virtual devices are interconnected and mutually dependent on each other in modern large-scale data centres. Security threats if analysed without considering these relationships can go undetected or their severity is underestimated. This paper proposes a network topology based on the identification and analysis of security threats. The overall threat detection and prevention approach extracts data from various sources to evaluate component level threats. Component level threats are combined, taking into account the network topology to evaluate their propagation risk. The application of the method is demonstrated using an example of the data centre operating the CloudStack cloud platform.

Keywords: Security threats · Data centre · Topology

1 Introduction

Today, information and communication technologies (ICT) are an essential part of almost any business sector. These technologies are used to automate business processes, to store and process data, which can also include sensitive information. Therefore, when data are accessed by unauthorised third parties or the system is under attack, it can cause a disruption of the business process or even cause permanent damage to the system itself [14]. With the growing dependence on ICT technologies, there is a growing potential for significant damage to public administration IS and electronic communications networks, neutralisation of national politics, economics, and military decision-making centres, misinformation of the public, and the emergence of man-made technogenic accidents, leading to a growing risk of non-military threats with severe consequences [7].

Data centres are typically used as a host for various ICT systems and, therefore, are typical targets of cybercriminals and security threats. According to [12], threats such as viruses, malware, ransomware, spyware, spam, phishing, DDoS, and other related threats are frequent in data centres, which shows the importance of real-time network monitoring and threat prevention. Accidental human error threats are also often threats that indicate the importance of automated real-time network monitoring and threat prevention [13].

According to the NIST cybersecurity framework, cybersecurity includes 5 phases: Identification (raising awareness of potential cyber risks), protection (implementation of risk mitigation measures to protect critical resources), threat identification (use of tools

© The Author(s), under exclusive license to Springer Nature Switzerland AG 2024
A. Lupeikienė et al. (Eds.): DB&IS 2024, CCIS 2157, pp. 161–176, 2024.
https://doi.org/10.1007/978-3-031-63543-4_11

for the detection of a cybersecurity incident), active response in the event of a threat (taking action to mitigate the effects of a cybersecurity incident), and post-incident recovery (a set of measures to ensure the operation of the service after the incident). The biggest challenges for companies and institutions are the identification of threats and the active response phases. Implementing these phases requires full and continuous monitoring of the operation of the internal network and systems, as well as understanding how a cybersecurity incident can be identified.

Modern data centres consist of a large number of interrelated physical and virtual nodes. To detect and evaluate threats, it is not sufficient to analyse individual nodes. Analysis of relationships between nodes and the overall network topology provides a means for a more comprehensive evaluation. An example of topology-driven anomaly detection is the framework for identifying anomalies in software services of the OpenStack cloud computing platform [8]. Topology-based root cause analysis of an IT infrastructure failure is also addressed in [11], where a Markov logic network and an abductive reasoning-based solution are elaborated. The security threats caused by cloud platform misconfiguration or insider attacks are investigated in [3]. A developed security system proactively analyses the intended cloud infrastructure configuration changes and risks associated with them and then either approves or rejects them. Large-scale real-time causality graphs are used to identify incidents in microservices based systems [15]. The variety of data sources and domain knowledge support the analysis. This research argues that comprehensive threat detection and prevention requires the integration of network monitoring data sources, and the network topology-based approach allows the aggregation of threats to understand the general security status at data centres. The objective of this paper is to introduce the overall threat detection and prevention approach referred to as BICTSeMS and to elaborate the topology modelling method. The method also relies on threat identification at the level of individual components of the network, which is beyond the scope of this paper. The method is implemented as part of the overall network monitoring information system.

The rest of the paper is organised as follows. Section 2 describes the BICTSeMS approach. The topology modelling method is elaborated and demonstrated in Sect. 3. Section 4 concludes.

2 Overall Approach

The overall approach to BICTSeMS threat detection and prevention is illustrated in Fig. 1. Initial data refer to certain ICT components through their anonymised IP addresses. All data sets and streams have a temporal dimension (including the network topology itself), therefore versioning, windowing, and aggregations are needed to make data suitable for machine learning [16].

Data integration and aggregation use the knowledge acquired in machine learning model functionality engineering to ensure that all necessary data are available for the training and prediction of machine learning models in the necessary format. Certain features such as the number of inbound and outbound connections are derived from the NetFlow connection graph [9]. Several machine learning models, together with threat identification rules expressed as part of patterns (e.g., an open port), are used to identify

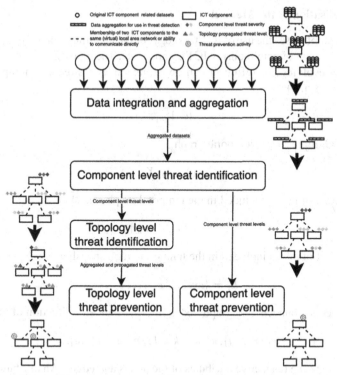

Fig. 1. The general approach of threat detection and prevention

potential threats [1]. Certain threats, such as exposed vulnerable services or incorrect web configuration, can be acted upon immediately and do not require threat aggregation for threat prevention action selection. For this purpose, component-level threat prevention is initiated. As for other threats (e.g. anomalies in NetFlow data [4]), the severity of the detected threat by individual threat detection methods can vary; therefore, threat severity levels need to be aggregated so that the final and more accurate level of threat severity can be determined. This is done as part of the topology-level threat identification, and ensemble learning is used for this purpose. The risk of propagation of the threat is also determined based on the topology of the ICT component network, the severity of the threat, and the propagation coefficient. Finally, the most suitable threat prevention activities [6] and their scope of application are chosen based on threat severity, topology level propagated threats, and information available in the pattern repository.

3 Topology Modelling Method

This section presents the topology modelling method used to aggregate detected threats and estimate the threat propagation risk based on network topology. Method formalisation using set theory and application example is provided.

3.1 Formalisation of the Method

BICTSeMS emphasises the use of ICT topology for the identification of threats of threats and risk assessment of neighbouring ICT components. The topology of the environment is constantly evolving; therefore, it can be expressed as a stream of temporal graph snapshots (see Eq. 1)

$$\{G_t\}_{t=1}^T, \tag{1}$$

where each G_t represents a temporal graph

$$G_t = (N_t, E_t, X_t, Y_t), \tag{2}$$

N_t is the set of nodes included in the temporal graph snapshot.

$$N_t = \{n_1, \ldots n_m\}, \tag{3}$$

E_t is the set of edges included in the temporal graph snapshot

$$E_t = \{e_1, \ldots, e_i, \ldots, e_z\}, \tag{4}$$

so that each edge connects two graph nodes (if order indicates direction of the edge).

$$e_i = \{k, j\}, k! = j, k \in [1, m], j \in [1, m], \tag{5}$$

X_t and Y_t are the respective attributes of the nodes and edges. An attribute set x_k for a specific node n_k can be expressed as follows:

$$x_k = \{Q, h\}, \tag{6}$$

$$h = \{0,1\},$$

$$Q = \{q_1, \ldots, q_p\}$$

where h indicates whether the node is internal (1) or external (0) from the data centre view, Q contains p threat levels of p determined by machine learning models and other BICTSeMS components (such as port scanning, IP blacklist checks).

Certain threats do not require aggregation before prevention actions A can be initialised (e.g., exposed vulnerable services exposed). For this purpose, best practices for ICT security governance PAT are used. A general pattern can be formulated as follows:

$$pat = \{PRE, sev, prop, ACT\}, \tag{7}$$

where PRE contains preconditions context, sev is threat severity index, $prop$ is threat propagation index and ACT are the applicable actions for threat prevention.

Component-level threat prevention actions $ACT_{component}$ are determined using $F^A_{component}$ (see Eq. 8).

$$F^A_{component} : (X, PAT) \rightarrow ACT_{component} \tag{8}$$

Edge attribute set Y_t shows allowed communication protocols and ports (see Eq. 9).

$$Y_t = \{PP_1, .., PP_i, \ldots, PP_z\} \tag{9}$$

PP_i describes the allowed communication protocols, ports and is formalized in Eq. 10.

$$
\begin{aligned}
PP_i &= \{\{pr_1, \{po_1, \ldots, po_u\}\}, \ldots\}, \\
pr_1 &\in PR, \\
po_1 &\in PO, \\
po_u &\in PO,
\end{aligned} \tag{10}
$$

where pr_1 is the allowed communication protocol, po_1, po_u are its allowed port numbers, PR is universal set of all communication protocols, PO is a universal set of all port numbers. Equation 11 shows an example where the network settings do not impose restrictions on the possible communication patterns for edge e_z, its attributes can be expressed as follows:

$$PP_z = \{\{PR, PO\}\} \tag{11}$$

The topology modelling method uses function F^Q (see Eq. 12) to aggregate a set of node-related threats into a single threat value that is used to determine the appropriate threat prevention actions.

$$F^Q : \{q_1, \ldots, q_p\} \to q^{aggr} \tag{12}$$

As a result of this function, a transformed node attribute set $X\prime$ is retrieved with individual node attribute $x_k\prime$ shown in Eq. 13.

$$x_k' = \{q^{aggr}, \text{h}\} \tag{13}$$

The topological modelling method uses function F^R, which determines the risk of threat propagation for all internal graph nodes R. For this purpose, the communication types included in the edge attribute set Yt and transformed attributes are used (see Eq. 14).

$$F^R : (Y_t, X') \to R \tag{14}$$

$$R = \{r_1, \ldots r_z\}, z <= m$$

Based on the aggregated threat level of the ICT component, the propagated risk, and best practices for ICT security governance PAT the method uses function F^A to determine the set of required preventive actions ACT_{topo} to restore the level of security (see Eq. 15).

$$F^A_{topology} : (R, X', PAT) \to ACT_{topo} \tag{15}$$

Actions can be performed on both internal and external nodes. The most appropriate actions are chosen by matching threats with information available in the pattern repository.

3.2 Method Usage Example

As part of this project an adapter for the CloudStack cloud computing platform was developed, allowing us to retrieve data about virtual servers and their corresponding networks. This data is used to construct a directed attributed graph (N_t, E_t, X_t, Y_t). The proposed approach is shown in an example case given in Fig. 2.

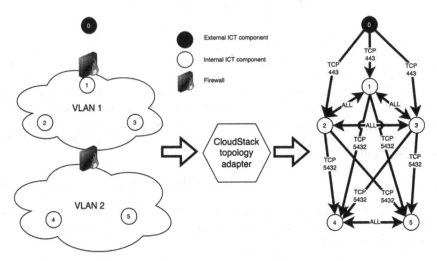

Fig. 2. CloudStack topology adapter

VLAN 1 contains a cluster of three web servers, while VLAN 2 contains a cluster of two database management systems. Web servers can be accessed from outside via a TCP connection, port number 443. The servers of the database management system can be accessed only by the web servers via a TCP connection, port number 5432. External ICT components cannot access database management system servers directly and database management system servers cannot initialise a connection with the web servers themselves. Connections within the web server cluster and database management system servers are not limited since no firewalls are used. A CloudStack topology adapter retrieves the corresponding information from the configuration database and transforms it into a directed attributed graph, as can be seen on the right side of Fig. 2. The edges are directional and have attribute information describing the permitted communication mechanisms. The resulting graph is also temporal, since the topology can evolve over time, which is why it is necessary to persist multiple snapshots.

The node N set at a certain moment of time h is expressed in Eq. 16.

$$N_h = \{n_0, n_1, n_2, n_3, n_4, n_5\} \tag{16}$$

Initially, the node attributes only indicate whether a node is internal or external, since no threats have been detected yet (see Eq. 17).

$$X_h = \{\{\varnothing, 0\}, \{\varnothing, 1\}, \{\varnothing, 1\}, \{\varnothing, 1\}, \{\varnothing, 1\}, \{\varnothing, 1\}\} \tag{17}$$

A fragment of the corresponding edge set E at a certain moment of time h is expressed in Eq. 18.

$$E_h = \{\{0,1\}, \{0,2\}, \ldots, \{4,5\}, \{5,4\}\} \tag{18}$$

A fragment of the edge attribute set is given in Eq. 19.

$$Y_h = \left\{ \begin{array}{c} \{\{\text{"tcp"}, \{\text{"443"}\}\}, \{\{\text{"tcp"}, \{\text{"443"}\}\}, \ldots, \\ \{\{\text{PR}, PP\}\}, \{\{\text{PR}, PP\}\} \end{array} \right\} \tag{19}$$

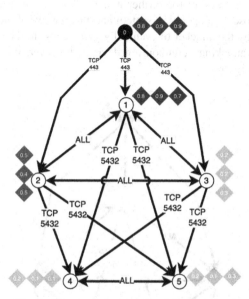

Fig. 3. Threats detected at the component level

During threat identification, both internal and external ICT components are marked with their corresponding detected threat levels (see Fig. 3).

Initially, multiple threat values are provided for each node and stored in the node attribute set. A fragment of the resulting attribute set X_h is given in Eq. 20.

$$X_h = \{\{\{0.8,0.9,0.9\}, 0\}, \{0.8,0.9,0.7\}, 1\},$$
$$\ldots, \{0.2,0.1,0.1\}, 1\}, \{0.2,0.1,0.3\}, 1\}\} \tag{20}$$

Let's assume that all web servers (n_1, n_2, n_3) expose their versions to the outside and that they have been determined by the Server Head Request preprocessor service. This is a threat that can be immediately acted upon.

$$F^A_{component} : (X_h, PAT) \rightarrow \{\varnothing, \{alert\}, \{alert\}, \{alert\}, \varnothing, \varnothing\}, \tag{21}$$

where alert is a preventive action that sends a corresponding email about the detected threat to the responsible administrator. No actions are performed for the remaining nodes

(n_0, n_4, n_5). Using function F^Q the individual threat values are merged into a single threat value for each component (Fig. 4) resulting in a transformation of the original attribute set X'_h (see Eq. 22).

$$X'_h = \{\{\{0.9\}, 0\}, \{0.8\}, 1\}, \ldots, \{0.1\}, 1\}, \{0.2\}, 1\}\} \tag{22}$$

For internal ICT components, it is also necessary to assess how threat risks are further propagated to neighbouring ICT components. For example, a compromised email account on an e-mail server does not contribute to an increased threat risk to neighbouring ICT components, since such a threat does not allow the attacker to control the e-mail server and use it as a gateway for further attacks. Threats such as a misconfigured web server that exposes the operating system and the version of the web server could potentially be used by the attacker to eventually gain access to the server and thus use it as a gateway for attacking neighbouring devices; however, the threat propagation coefficient is relatively low.

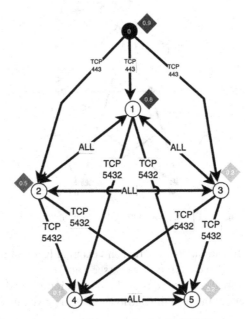

Fig. 4. Aggregated threats at the level of ICT components

Threats such as botnet infections indicate a clear sign of a compromised device and a high value of risk propagation coefficient since botnets can start their attacks by first targeting the nearest neighbours. A classic example is the Morris worm [10], which used heuristic knowledge of network topology to spread and targeted only the victim's closest neighbours. This approach proved to be very efficient and is expected to become increasingly dominant as IPv6, which has much wider address space [5].

The propagation of the threat is also affected by the allowed connections between ICT components. For example, the threat propagation from the potentially infected web server to another web server is higher if compared to the threat propagation coefficient to database management servers, since connections between web servers are not limited, while only TCP connections to port 5432 are enabled for database management system servers.

The threat propagation coefficients for edges and internal nodes are shown in Fig. 5. The edge-level threat propagation coefficient is 1 for edges connecting n_1 and n_2 since both web servers belong to the same network and communication between them is not limited. The propagation coefficient between n_1 and n_4 is 0.3 since only TCP traffic on port 5432 is enabled. Additionally, threat risks can propagate in both directions between n_1 and n_2, while threat risk from n_1 is propagated to n_4 and not vice versa. The threat propagation matrix is shown in Table 1 while the aggregated propagated threats are shown in Fig. 6. Finally, the aggregated detected threat levels and aggregated propagated threat levels are used to select the most appropriate threat prevention activities from the pattern repository ACT_{topo}.

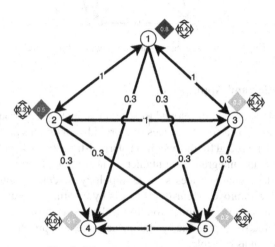

Fig. 5. Threat propagation coefficients

Table 1. Threat-risk propagation matrix

		Threat propagation source				
		1	2	3	4	5
Threat propagation target	1		0.15	0.08		
	2	0.32		0.08		
	3	0.32	0.15			
	4	0.096	0.045	0.024		0
	5	0.096	0.045	0.024	0	

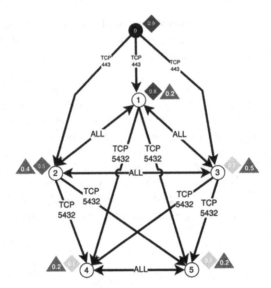

Fig. 6. Final aggregated and propagated threat levels

3.3 Implementation and Application

The BICTSeMS platform was developed to test and validate the approach (Fig. 7). The main element of design is a set of services that provide continuous and automated data management, which is crucial for the operation of a real-time threat detection system. The BICTSeMS architecture integrates a container orchestration platform, which improves the efficiency of deploying services such as topology modelling and threat analysis [2]. The architecture improves security protocols by creating separate workspaces for different roles, from system administrators to legal representatives. Each workspace is designed to be as effective as possible by making activities and processes that are specific to that role as efficient as possible.

This architecture also incorporates a collection of technologies specifically designed to improve the platform's performance and capacity to handle scalability. Apache Kafka is used for constructing real-time data streaming capabilities, while JanusGraph is used for managing complex graphs. Apache Spark provides fast processing speed for real-time analytics, while Apache Cassandra serves as a distributed database that supports the storage requirements of the platform. Keycloak is responsible for security management, offering a solution for Identity and Access Management (IAM). This solution guarantees the protection of sensitive data and system operations by implementing authentication and authorisation procedures. Finally, the platform employs Nginx, a web server known for its performance, to effectively handle web traffic and improve the platform's responsiveness and load balancing capabilities. The development of the main platform involved the creation of a back-end system that can integrate and analyse various types of data streams.

The method of identifying threats involves the processing of data. It starts by retrieving information from various external sources. This includes utilising public blacklists to

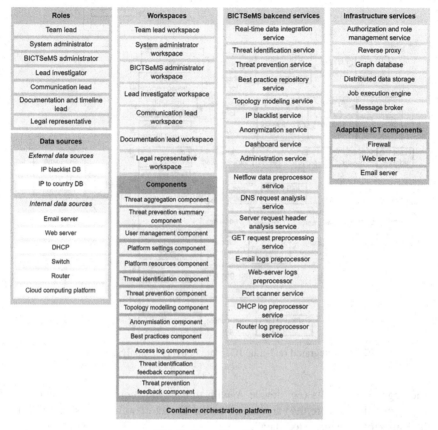

Fig. 7. Overall architecture

check external IP addresses. In addition, extensive logs of emails, Web, DHCP, NetFlow, and HTTP requests are also collected and analysed. Subsequently, the data is filtered and combined to create a unified dataset, anonymised to maintain privacy, and stored to facilitate continuous improvement and analysis of machine learning models at the component level. Real-time data integration relies on Apache Kafka, which allows to run multiple instances of data producers and consumers as well as scale the Kafka cluster as necessary. The real-time data originating from custom adapters, its transformation, and delivery to the analysis service are shown in Fig. 8. Finally, the data are written to Kafka topic device measures and is used for threat identification purposes.

The components of the topology-level threat identification system are illustrated in Fig. 9. They have the following interactions:

1. The process starts with ICT data analysis performed by the services shown in Fig. 8. Threat scores are passed to the Realtime threat integration service and aggregated using a weighted average by threat type (e.g., device A with threat type "compromised device" and threat score 0.6, device A with threat type "compromised device" and threat score 0.5).

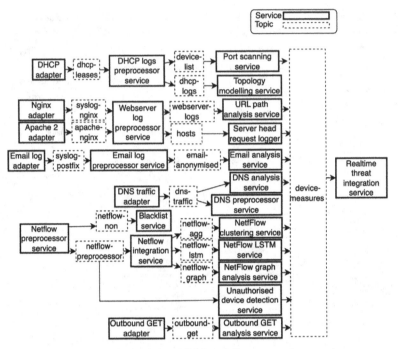

Fig. 8. Integrated real-time ICT data delivery to analyse services

2. The aggregated results (eg, device A with threat type "compromised device" and aggregated threat score 0.6) are passed to the Threat identification service through the Kafka topic "aggregated-data".

3. The Threat identification service queries the pattern repository to determine if the threat score and context correspond to known threat patterns and solutions.

4. If there is a match, the returned threat object also contains a threat propagation coefficient.

5. If a threat matches, prevention actions are immediately triggered.

6. If the threat propagation coefficient is larger than 0, the Threat identification service contacts the Topology modelling service to determine the direct neighbours of the ICT component (for example, we need to determine the topology of device A).

7. The Topology modelling service returns the corresponding topology to the Threat identification service (e.g., the direct neighbours of A are ICT components B and C).

8. The Threat identification service passes individual derived propagated threat values for the components affected by the threat (e.g., component B receives a threat record with score 0.24, threat type propagated-threat, component C receives a threat record with score 0.24.

Finally, topology threats are processed following the same logic as component-level threats. The Real-time threat integration service performs component-level aggregation of threats with type propagated-threat. The Threat identification service queries the pattern repository service if any patterns match the current propagated threat and triggers

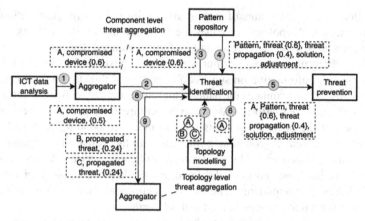

Fig. 9. Identification of the threat at the component and topology level

threat prevention if results are returned. A sample message from Kafka topic device measures with a propagated threat to be aggregated is shown in Fig. 10, and an example of aggregated threat is given in Fig. 11.

```
{
    "domain": "13",
    "nic": "2509",
    "device": "79a39a7255d28f8c53455d8c79755da2",
    "type": "propagation-threat",
    "window": {
        "start": "2023-04-24T14:15:00.000Z",
        "end": "2023-04-24T14:20:00.000Z"
    },
    "data": [
        {
            "model": "threat-identification",
            "model_avg": 0.2001,
            "model_avg_adjusted": 0.30015000000000003,
            "extra_info": []
        }
    ],
    "avg_score": 0.30015000000000003
}
```

Fig. 10. A sample message of an aggregated propagated threat on Kafka topic

NAME	TYPE	LEVEL	TOTAL SCORE	STATUS	ACTIONS
Medium Potential Threat at Device with id: c59d17020ac69736616b4b91b33fec37	misconfigured-device	Medium	0.3716417849063873	active	
High Potential Threat at Device with id: c59d17020ac69736616b4b91b33fec37	potential-attack	High	0.78913044929504	active	
Negligible Potential Threat at Device with id: c59d17020ac69736616b4b91b33fec37	compromised-device	Negligible	0.079120881855487	active	
Low Potential Threat at Device with id: c59d17020ac69736616b4b91b33fec37	compromised-device	Low	0.101404511795578	active	

Fig. 11. Threats identified in the BICTSeMS UI

The list of identified threats is visible in the BICTSeMS UI (see Fig. 12). It is possible to filter threats by status, level, date and perform a free-text search. The platform also provides a range of navigation choices to the platform. The "Dashboard" page is a central hub that offers a complete picture of the system's health and security notifications of the system. The section "Topology" provides the structural layout of a network topology, providing users with a visual representation of the associated devices and the infected devices. The "Prevented threats" layout serves as a repository for historical data and threats, containing information on successfully prevented threats. The last page is the "Pattern repository" that contains the patterns and behaviours of recognised threats. This repository enhances the platform's ability to detect threats by performing comparative analysis. Each of the page components talks to the corresponding back-end service. For example, the Threat UI component interacts with the Threat identification service API to show the threats detected by the Threat identification service. All services which provide API are implemented in NodeJS and provide REST endpoints for integration with BICTSeMS UI components. The Threat Identification Service also provides the feedback endpoints that are used in the feedback form.

Alternatively, threats can be rated on the Telegram messaging platform (see Fig. 12). The functionality is provided by the Threat prevention service, which contains an integrated Telegram bot. This allows to trigger automatic threat preventions near real time in case of valid threats. If the threat is marked as invalid, the message is updated and no further actions are taken. The feedback provided via Telegram is written to the Kafka topic. The threat identification service subscribes to the topic and updates the threat ratings in the Cassandra table accordingly.

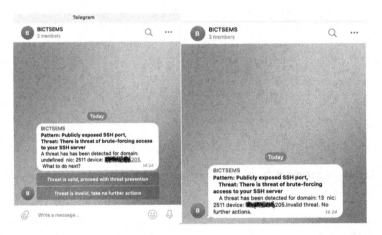

Fig. 12. Threat validation via Telegram

If threat prevention actions are accepted, the adjustment for the specific ICT device is added to the database with status pending = true. This information is intended for ICT device agents that query the BICTSeMS threat prevention service API to detect if any adjustments need to be made.

4   Conclusions

The topology model defines the approach to identifying security threats at the ICT component level, aggregating the level of threats provided by separate threat detection models and components, propagating threat risks based on the network topology data, and finally choosing the most appropriate threat prevention actions based on best practices for ICT security governance stored in the pattern repository. The approach is formalised using set theory, and an application example is also provided. The proposed approach has the following benefits: the ability to rely on several threat detection models and the possibility of expanding BICTSeMS with additional models in the future, the ability to benefit from the best practices for ICT governance expressed in the form of patterns, and the possibility of improving BICTSeMS or adapting it to other environments with the addition of new more specialised patterns, the ability to propagate and aggregate components to ICT component threats to neighbouring components based on the network topology information, thus identifying risks that would not be visible on the level of individual components.

Acknowledgments. This research is funded by European Regional Development Fund Project Nr. 1.1.1.1/20/A/020 "Development of Big-data-driven Information and Communication Technology Security Management Solution (BICTSeMS)" Specific Objective 1.1.1 "Improve research and innovation capacity and the ability of Latvian research institutions to attract external funding, by investing in human capital and infrastructure" 1.1.1.1. Measure "Support for applied research" (round No.4).

References

1. Asif, M., Abbas, S., Khan, M.A., et al.: MapReduce based intelligent model for intrusion detection using machine learning technique. J. King Saud Univ. Comput. Inf. Sci. **34** (2022). https://doi.org/10.1016/j.jksuci.2021.12.008
2. Aurangzaib, R., Iqbal, W., Abdullah, M. et al.: Scalable containerized pipeline for real-time big data analytics. In: Proceedings of the International Conference on Cloud Computing Technology and Science, CloudCom (2022)
3. Bleikertz, S., Vogel, C., Gross, T., Mödersheim, S.: Proactive security analysis of changes in virtualized infrastructures. In: ACM International Conference Proceeding Series (2015)
4. Campazas-Vega, A., Crespo-Martínez, I.S., Guerrero-Higueras, Á.M., et al.: Analysis of NetFlow Features' Importance in Malicious Network Traffic Detection (2022)
5. Chen, Z., Ji, C.: Spatial-temporal modeling of malware propagation in networks. IEEE Trans. Neural Netw. **16**, 1291–1303 (2005). https://doi.org/10.1109/TNN.2005.853425
6. Kapiton, A.M., Skakalina, O.V., Tyshchenko, D.O., Franchuk, T.M.: Automated setup system security configuration of network equipment. Èlektronnoe modelirovanie **45**, 28–42 (2023). https://doi.org/10.15407/emodel.45.03.028
7. Kavan, S., Dusek, J.: Violation of electronic communication systems security as a potential crisis. In: 2022 11th Mediterranean Conference on Embedded Computing, MECO (2022)
8. Niwa, T., Kasuya, Y., Kitahara, T.: Anomaly detection for openstack services with process-related topological analysis. In: 2017 13th International Conference on Network and Service Management, CNSM (2017)

9. Noble, J., Adams, N.: Real-time dynamic network anomaly detection. IEEE Intell. Syst. **33**, 5–18 (2018). https://doi.org/10.1109/MIS.2018.022441346

10. Orman, H.: The Morris worm: a fifteen-year perspective. IEEE Secur. Priv. **1**, 35–43 (2003). https://doi.org/10.1109/MSECP.2003.1236233

11. Schoenfisch, J., Meilicke, C., von Stülpnagel, J., et al.: Root cause analysis in IT infrastructures using ontologies and abduction in Markov logic networks. Inf. Syst. **74** (2018). https://doi.org/10.1016/j.is.2017.11.003

12. Shammugam, I., Samy, G.N., Magalingam, P., et al.: Information security threats encountered by Malaysian public sector data centers. Indonesian J. Electr. Eng. Comput. Sci. **21**, 1820–1829 (2021). https://doi.org/10.11591/ijeecs.v21.i3.pp1820-1829

13. Sharma, G., Vidalis, S., Menon, C., et al.: Analysis and implementation of threat agents profiles in semi-automated manner for a network traffic in real-time information environment. Electronics **10** (2021). https://doi.org/10.3390/electronics10151849

14. Tari, Z., Sohrabi, N., Samadi, Y., Suaboot, J.: Data security threats. In: Data Exfiltration Threats and Prevention Techniques (2023)

15. Wang, H., Wu, Z., Jiang, H., et al.: Groot: an event-graph-based approach for root cause analysis in industrial settings. In: Proceedings—2021 36th IEEE/ACM International Conference on Automated Software Engineering. ASE (2021)

16. Xin, Y., Kong, L., Liu, Z., et al.: Machine learning and deep learning methods for cybersecurity. IEEE Access **6** (2018). https://doi.org/10.1109/ACCESS.2018.2836950

Teaching Rapid Application Development Skills for Digitalisation Challenges

Tarmo Robal(✉)📷, Uljana Reinsalu📷, Janika Leoste📷, Lembit Jürimägi📷, and Risto Heinsar📷

Tallinn University of Technology, 12618 Tallinn, Estonia
{tarmo.robal,uljana.reinsalu,janika.leoste,lembit.jurimagi,
risto.heinsar}@taltech.ee

Abstract. We are on a challenging path for digital transformation. Yet, this process proposes a challenge for availability of skilled experts as the success of digitalisation depends heavily on such workforce. Currently, we are in a shortage of skilled ICT specialists, which holds back the development of digital economy and society. To meet the rapidly changing business needs, a solution to the scarce workforce is seen in low-code development tools. These tools allow to develop software using graphical user interfaces with little or no coding skills, thus expanding the number of potential developers, and enabling fast delivery of business applications. Yet, to deal with the shortage of skilled ICT specialists, we need to educate future generations in the area of rapid application development (RAD). This paper focuses on teaching RAD skills to alleviate digitalisation challenges. We discuss newly developed courses for teaching rapid application development on the Oracle Application Express platform, and preparing young with skills for their future job market using self-regulated learning strategy. We investigate the suitability of this approach and learning gain, and show that self-regulated learning can be efficiently used to teach emerging technologies such as low-code development platforms.

Keywords: Rapid application development · Digitalisation · Engineering education

1 Introduction

Europe and the rest of the world are on a challenging path of digitalisation, where digital technologies are seen to deliver an enormous growth potential for businesses. Digital solutions in various life domains (e.g., education, public administration, healthcare) are expected to open up new opportunities both for people and businesses. In recent years, the term *digital transformation* has emerged to describe the changes the adoption and implementation of digital technologies has on society, industry and business. In its nature, digital transformation is a process that aims to improve an entity by triggering significant changes to its properties through combinations of information, computing, communication, and connectivity technologies [27], going beyond digitization and digitalisation by including

© The Author(s), under exclusive license to Springer Nature Switzerland AG 2024
A. Lupeikienė et al. (Eds.): DB&IS 2024, CCIS 2157, pp. 177–192, 2024.
https://doi.org/10.1007/978-3-031-63543-4_12

the whole organization and changes bureaucratic and organizational culture and relationships to stakeholders [12]. While digital transformation focuses on the future, digitization is allowing to address the past and encode analog information into digital format [29], and digitalisation coins the manifold sociotechnical phenomena and processes of adopting and using these technologies in broader individual, organizational, and societal contexts [9], beyond mere digitizing of existing processes and forms [12] with a focus on the present digital technologies.

The success of digitalisation, however, depends heavily on skilled workforce and available tooling towards digital transformation. One way to solve this problem is to develop digital readiness, resilience and capacity of the society. The EU Digital Education Action Plan (2021–2027)[1] sets out as one of its priorities to enhance digital skills and competencies for the digital transformation, providing opportunities and support for the digitalisation of teaching methods and learning processes, and infrastructure for inclusive and resilient remote learning. Still, there is a shortage of skilled information and communication technologies (ICT) specialists as European education and training systems currently do not prepare enough young people for the digital economy and society. One of the solutions to address this challenge could be to invest in training future generations of workers and to up-skill and re-skill the workforce in the area of rapid application development (RAD).

Low-code platforms (LCDP) fill the gap between business and IT by enabling RAD and allowing to involve non-technical experts into application development. This greatly alleviates the shortage of IT-experts [7]. LCDPs are easy-to-use visual environments that permit everyone, even people without IT and coding skills (also referred to as citizen developers [7]), to develop and deploy fully functional software applications using advanced graphical user interfaces, visual abstractions, pre-built components, and setting configurations requiring minimal or no procedural code [23, 28]. Thereby, LCDPs enable quick generation and delivery of business applications with minimum coding effort. Typically these platforms are provided as a Platform-as-a-Service (PaaS) on cloud infrastructures.

At the end of 2022 Gartner forecasted the market of low-code development technologies to grow 20% in 2023 worldwide, and by 2026, developers outside formal IT departments will account for at least 80% of the user base for low-code development tools, up from 60% in 2021 [1]. This means that already in the nearest future, the majority of technology products and services will be built by those who are not technology professionals. The need for low-code platforms and skilled developers is also driven by DevOps skills shortage, expected to continue to grow.

The high and rapidly growing demand for software developers to support digital transformations, and the shortage of such developers for application building and business automation, has created a fruitful ground for low- or no-code platforms, directly addressing this gap for businesses in achieving their objectives through fast delivery of software solutions. A variety of platforms from many

---

[1] https://education.ec.europa.eu/focus-topics/digital-education/action-plan.

vendors for rapid application development on the concept of low-code exists. To name a few out of these many options, for example, Microsoft Power Apps, Google App Maker (now succeeded with no-code Google AppSheet), Siemens Mendix, Amazon Honeycode, Zoho Creator, and Oracle APEX[2] allow everyone, even without coding knowledge, to build software applications.

To tackle the shortage of skilled ICT specialists for the digital economy and society, we need to educate and train future generations in the area of advanced digital skills and rapid application development, which replaces the traditional methods and off-the-shelf products and allows businesses and IT to collaborate effectively, acting as a catalyst in innovation and streamlining workflows. Knowing RAD platforms, future engineers, i.e., today's students, will be able to effortlessly and in a short time build applications with essentially no or little knowledge of coding. For example, web applications using Oracle APEX.

The current paper addresses teaching RAD skills in higher education (HE) to alleviate digitalisation challenges. In particular, we focus on the implementation of the EU Erasmus+ project *"Embracing rapid application development (RAD) skills opportunity as a catalyst for employability and innovation"* (RAD-Skills) at Tallinn University of Technology (TalTech) through 2022–2024. The aim of the project is to stimulate innovative learning and teaching practices, support digital and green capabilities of the HE sector, and to improve digital readiness, resilience and capacity of future generations for emerging advanced digital technologies, such as LCDPs and RAD. The actions of the project directly address high-quality education and training of ICT professionals to respond to the challenges posed by the constantly evolving market of digital technologies.

In this paper, we study how the newly developed courses for teaching RAD skills and rapid web application development on Oracle APEX low-code platform are perceived by students of TalTech School of Information Technologies. These students are typically already working. We are interested to see whether the self-regulated learning (SRL) strategy applied to teach these new concepts and practical know-how, is sufficient and acceptable by students, contributes to learning gains, and how well do they perform. We address these issues through the following research questions (RQ):

RQ1: *How suitable is self-regulated learning for teaching rapid application development foundational skills for ICT students based on software-vendor provided programs and hosted platforms?* To answer this question, we collect anonymous feedback through a special questionnaire from course participants.

RQ2: *How do self-regulated learners reflect their learning gain for the foundational topics of RAD skills?* To answer this question, we collect student-provided feedback for each topic they cover.

RQ3: *What is the effect of the foundational course delivered on self-regulated learning strategy on students' RAD skills knowledge?* To answer this question, we use the knowledge survey results collected before and after students performed Module 1 of the RAD skills course.

---

[2] https://apex.oracle.com.

The results indicate that self-regulated learning is sufficient and preferred by students to obtain knowledge on emerging technologies such as RAD.

The rest of the paper is organized as follows. Section 2 is dedicated to related work, while Sect. 3 discusses the developed RAD courses used in the study. Section 4 answers the research questions, and in Sect. 5 we draw conclusions.

2   Related Work

Low-code development platforms are products with high-level programming abstraction which end-users can use to develop software through graphical interfaces rather than writing source code. LCDPs have shown considerably higher productivity (a 3–10 times increase) than code-based technology [26], resulting in faster software delivery, and thereby low-code platforms are seen as enablers of digital transformation [24], for example in conjunction with Enterprise Resource Planning (ERP) systems [17]. Therefore, it is essential that LCDPs are also taught at the HE level to prepare students for the future and guarantee the success of digitalisation.

The low-code concept has been around for more than a decade but still, the vast amount of publications are addressing either its technical side or exploitation for industry cases. There are only a few papers addressing Oracle APEX technology for HE, for example, the latest paper by Pastierik and Kvet [15], which explores teaching of web software development for technical and non-technical students using APEX LCDP. It was found that Oracle APEX is a suitable solution for teaching web application development. This paper is the closest to our contribution, with a distinction that for their implementation the courses were organised as on-site weekly lectures and practices, whereas in our research we have chosen a self-regulated learning strategy in totally online form.

Metrolho et al. [13] investigated how to improve students' preparedness for the job market in terms of software engineering practices by including IT professionals as external entities into students' projects to reduce the gap between academic education and industry needs. The projects were carried out based on Scrum methodology and using the OutSystems LCDP. Their study showed that this kind of collaboration is a win-win situation both for students as being better prepared for the job market and for companies as by being able to recruit employees prepared for their needs. The connection of student projects to external companies also had a significant influence on student motivation and commitment, yet it did not have an effect on delivering results faster. Our study is similar, as we use LCDP and project topics matching industry needs, although we do not distribute students into teams for the project.

Eriksson et al. [3] explored the reasons why learners drop out of MOOCs, where a high degree of self-regulated learning is needed. Several factors such as the learner's perception of the course content and course design, social influence from coursemates, and ability to find and manage time effectively, together with a lack of pressure were identified as obstacles to successful course graduation. As our courses are running on SRL strategy, the same obstacles may be encountered by participating students.

The connections between motivation, academic emotions and SRL were investigated by Zheng and Li [31], finding that motivation and academic emotions significantly influence SRL, and that effective use of SRL strategies can significantly improve academic achievement. Dwiare et al. [2] on the other hand delved into the challenges learners face with SRL and features they see helpful in learning management systems to deal with these challenges. Keeping track of time, activities and progress were the main features identified in this study to help to deal with SRL challenges, together with gamification features such as scoreboards.

To the best of our knowledge, there are no works that discuss delivering RAD skills in HE setting using purely online SRL strategy for the mode. Thereby, our contribution tries to fill this gap in existing literature by specifically looking at the suitability of this setting on the example of teaching and exploiting the Oracle APEX LCDP to enable digital transformation and aid digitalisation.

Our previous work has focused around studying and improving students learning gain (e.g., by detecting their inattention moments) focusing and enhancing course content delivery [20,30], establishing a model for fair and individual evaluation of course teamwork [19] but also how to overcome sudden challenges in teaching on the example of the recent pandemics [21], e-learning environment challenges in HE [10], and designing training programs to introduce emerging technologies [11]. In this paper, we advantage of this previous work, and explore teaching low-code and rapid application development in HE to tackle digitalisation challenges (e.g., skill and labour shortage) the world faces.

3   Rapid Application Development Courses

In this section, we provide the backgrounds of the joint project for RAD skills course development, and discuss the implementation of the courses at the School of Information Technologies at Tallinn University of Technology.

3.1   Project Consortium for Course Development

To amplify the reach of advanced digital skills and the importance of high-quality education and training for future ICT professionals, able to tackle the challenges posed by digitalisation, the consortium of the Erasmus+ RAD-Skills project developed foundational (Module 1) and intermediary (Module 2) courses for Rapid Application Development (RAD) at five participating European universities: Vilnius Gediminas Technical University (VilniusTech) in Lithuania, Technological University Dublin (TU Dublin) in Ireland, Tallinn University of Technology (TalTech) in Estonia, Riga Technical University (RTU) in Latvia, and University of Rijeka (UNIRI) in Croatia, in tight cooperation with the Oracle Corporation. The project consortium is coordinated by VilniusTech. Each course (module) was agreed to be of size 3 ECTS and developed in the local language. The Oracle APEX LCDP, with a strong focus on rapid development of web and mobile applications, was provided by Oracle. The use of Oracle APEX, a widely-used industry platform, provisions HE institutions and participating students with digital tools for enhancing the effectiveness and efficiency of the educational experiences for future digital readiness. Before the development of the courses, all teachers completed the training on APEX LCDP provided by Oracle Academy[3] instructors.

The course materials were developed according to learning methods, materials, tools, and innovative digital content provided by Oracle Academy, enabling tight involvement of market players (e.g., Oracle and businesses) for building the digital capacity of partnering universities to use RAD platforms. The exact content of the courses was agreed by the project consortium prior to establishing the course. The aim was to introduce similar courses to five partnering universities in their local language. To support course development, training, and hands-on practice in the cloud, Oracle has provided free access to their Oracle Application Express (APEX) – a cloud-based, low-code development platform that enables users to build scalable, secure enterprise apps, with world-class features deployable anywhere – both for teachers and students. This ensures that students get the most effective education tools and methods with practical, hands-on, engaging activities, and are able to build database-driven web applications for any business or organisation after graduation and transfer to the job market.

3.2   Course Development at TalTech

At TalTech, we addressed the development of foundational and intermediary courses through developing two separate courses: IXX0301 Foundations of Rapid Web Application Development (3 ECTS), and IXX0303 Rapid Application Development for Web (6 ECTS). Both courses start to run at the same time, whereas IXX0301 (Module 1) runs for the first 8 weeks, and IXX0303 runs for the whole semester (16 weeks) consisting of Module 1 and Module 2. Both courses are taught in Estonian. This separation into two courses was established to allow non-ICT students to also participate and obtain basic RAD skills (Module 1). The courses were made freely available to all students of TalTech.

The aim of Module 1 is to provide theoretical knowledge and practical skills for rapid development of web-based applications relying on data stored in databases together with basic knowledge of data presentation methods in a relational data model and Structured Query Language (SQL). The learning objective of Module 1 is that students having completed the module are able to use existing data (e.g., data in spreadsheets), upload it to LCDP and rapidly build simple web applications using wizards. Module 1 ends with a project task of establishing a web-based application by using only LCDP with no coding necessary, i.e., using only graphical interfaces.

Module 2 advances over the topics of Module 1 and goes deep into SQL-language and relational data models, and the specifics of the Oracle APEX low-code platform (e.g., customizing pages, forms, reports, style, navigation, and etc.) to provide a strong basis for rapid web application development skills.

---

[3] https://academy.oracle.com.

In this module, students choose a business use case to solve with the help of Oracle APEX technology, which forms the course project for the module. While Module 1 was intended for all students, Module 2 has a strong focus towards ICT students. Table 1 provides an overview of the topics, elements and activities included in Module 1 and Module 2 to teach RAD skills.

Table 1. RAD-Skills course modules and their content topics.

Module	Topic blocks in Moodle courses	Elements and activities			
		T^*	K^{**}	L^{***}	F^{****}
Module 1	Introduction to Module 1	+	−	−	−
	Introduction to databases	+	+	+	+
	Relational databases	+	+	+	+
	Database normalisation and terminology	+	+	+	+
	Data modelling	+	+	+	+
	Physical data model	+	+	−	+
	Access to Oracle APEX environment	+	−	−	+
	Structured Query Language (SQL): Introduction	+	+	+	+
	App development in APEX (wizard level)	+	−	+	+
Module 2	Introduction to Module 2	+	−	−	−
	APEX course project	+	+	+	+
	Data normalisation (3NF)	+	+	+	+
	Structured Query Language (SQL)	+	+	+	+
	App building in APEX: pages and reports	+	+	P	+
	App building in APEX: forms	+	+	P	+
	App building in APEX: navigation and styles	+	+	P	+

* theoretical knowledge presented as videos and slides.

** knowledge tests to check obtained level of theoretical knowledge.

*** practical tasks on the given topic.

**** topic feedback from students for the given topic.

+: The activity element is switched on for the topic.

−: The activity element is switched off for the topic.

P: The activity element is replaced with project implementation.

The courses were set up on the university's Moodle Learning Management System (LMS). TalTech uses Moodle version 4. Both of the course modules are built up from a flow of topics representing the content – thus a major element in the course structure design is a topic block having the following elements: theory, knowledge tests, practical tasks, and student feedback. Table 1 indicates the use of these elements for the content topics. Each topic block contains theoretical knowledge students of RAD skills should obtain, presented as videos and slides, supported by theoretical knowledge tests, and practical assignments either in the Moodle LMS or on the Oracle APEX platform (Fig. 1). For Module 2 some of the practical tasks are integrated with the course project implementation. On top of the latter, each topic is also equipped with a feedback form, where students are asked to provide feedback on the topic block as a whole. In particular, they are asked to evaluate the difficulty of the topic block, the clarity of provided materials, learning gain and time spent (self-reported) on the block, and provide comments (optional) for topic block improvement. Filling in the feedback form is made compulsory, and is an element of the course flow enforcement – it is required that students pass the previous topic theoretical test and fill in the feedback form before they can proceed with the theoretical test of the next topic. The intended course flow through topic blocks is depicted in blue on Fig. 1 through points 1–4. With this mechanism, we control the course flow and ensure students pass the topics in an intended and logical way. In principle, even though we opted for Moodle LMS maintained by the university, there are no restrictions for setting up the course with the described structure and approach on any other LMS.

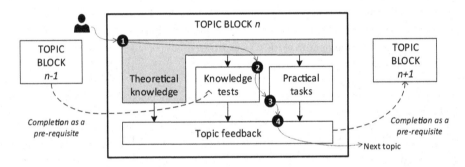

Fig. 1. RAD-Skills course architecture and recommended flow of student actions through elements of topic blocks.

The course topic flow (Fig. 1) starts with obtaining theoretical knowledge either from videos or slides by a student. Next, the student is advised to check the learning gain by performing topic knowledge tests. These knowledge tests can be repeated up to three times, whereas a penalty time of at least a day is applied if the performance falls below a set threshold value. This is to enforce students not to rush and not to 'play a lottery' with the tests, and enforce them to take time for material revision. Knowledge tests are automated. Having obtained theoretical knowledge, students can in parallel start doing the practical tasks, although they are advised not to start with practical tasks before passing theory. The practical tasks are automated, semi-automated and manually checked by lecturers. The latter is also the reason why we have not imposed restrictions on practical tasks, as otherwise lecturers may cause stoppages in the learning flow. For automated and manually checked practical tasks, feedback is provided, and whenever the student's submission does not meet the threshold criteria, it is returned for improvement. The courses also benefit from the activity completion feature of the Moodle LMS, allowing both the lecturers and students to keep track of the progress. The topic block flow ends with a student providing feedback for the topic block.

A self-regulated learning (SRL) strategy [14, 32], which has been recognized as a critical factor in enhancing student engagement and learning outcomes [22, 31] was chosen for the courses at TalTech. Self-regulated learning is a proactive approach where students take the initiative in their learning process [6], involving setting personal learning goals, self-monitoring progress towards these goals, and self-reflecting upon the learning experience, and therefore particularly suitable for RAD courses, where a high degree of independent practical exploration is expected. Moreover, SRL is a critical skill for lifelong learning [5, 25], technology students will face throughout their future careers. With the application of the SRL strategy for the courses, we expect the students to take responsibility and ownership of their learning, set learning goals and monitor progress, identify gaps in obtaining knowledge and skills, and take corrective action, leading to increased motivation and interest, and improved learning outcomes [16]. While implementing the SRL strategy, we let our students to choose their own learning pace within the 8-week and 16-week time-frames of Modules 1 and 2 correspondingly. During the course design, it was decided that this approach provides the benefit of flexibility to students, as the majority of students in Estonia are working at the same time. In addition, we chose not to set any deadlines for tasks and activities but rather compose a logical course flow structure (Fig. 1), where completion of certain tasks is a prerequisite to start another set of tasks – being the only limitation we impose for SRL for the courses. This setup allows us to get better insights into SRL for teaching RAD skills but also guarantees meaningful flow through topics.

4 Study Results

In this section, we discuss the courses running for teaching RAD skills on a foundational level (i.e., Module 1) and answer the set research questions. Our courses (IXX0301 and IXX0303) started to run on 02 February 2024 at School of Information Technologies at TalTech taught in the Estonian language in a remote setting on the SRL concept. Altogether, 65 students applied for the courses by declaring one of the courses in their study plan for spring 2024: 31 students for IXX0301 (Module 1 only) and 35 students for IXX0303 (Modules 1 and 2). Out of the 65 students who declared either of the course 61 signed up for the course in Moodle but only 54 (83%) of them started with course activities in time. The majority of the 54 students (96%) are from ICT curricula (3-year studies) of the School of Information Technologies, joined by a few non-IT students from integrated engineering studies (5-year studies) from the School of Engineering. As all the students need to undergo Module 1 during their studies, the number of students taking Module 1 is 54. The current study is limited only to Module 1 results for both courses IXX0301 and IXX0303, while Module 2 is still ongoing and reporting its results remains a future work.

4.1   RQ1: Self-regulated Learning for RAD Skills

We start answering the first research question by looking at students' task performance and progress on Moodle LMS. Based on how many tasks they have completed, we group them as *lost* – have not completed any task and not logged to the course within 30 days, *passive* – have completed at least two tasks and logged into the course within 30 days, and *active* – have completed several tasks or finished the Module 1. We determine the status based on activity on week 7 (just one week before mid-term and the planned end of Module 1). Table 2 presents the status statistics. We see that almost a quarter of students who remained with the course Module 1 are active, while a bit less than a third are passive but not totally lost for Module 1. A fair amount of 11% (7 students) are considered to have quit the course without any effort. Module 1 is completed by mid-term by 31 students (79% of active students).

Table 2. Student status at performing course Module 1 at week 7.

Determined student status	# students	% students
Active	39	72%
Passive	15	28%
Remaining with course	54	
Lost	7	11%
Total	61	

In order to get insights from students' perspective, we asked students to provide mid-term feedback on their self-regulated learning and challenges they have faced after 7 weeks into the courses. In the anonymous feedback form, we asked the course participants to evaluate 13 statements on their learning experience on a 5-scale agreement level (from *Totally disagree* to *Totally agree*) (Set 1 in Table 3), and evaluate six predefined obstacles for successful implementation of SRL (Set 2 in Table 3), with a possibility to describe additional items they perceived as challenges for SRL. These predefined obstacles were derived from our own expertise and [3,20]. The feedback was collected using Microsoft Forms[4], for which we received 31 responses. To answer RQ1, we analyse this feedback.

The majority (93%) of course Module 1 participants agree that the self-regulated learning format suits them well (Q1), and only some students (7%) would prefer regular class meetings (Q2). Almost all respondents agree that SRL provides freedom to learn whenever they want (Q3) but on the other hand requires strong self-discipline (90%) (Q4). In general, the respondents are satisfied with the course SRL format (Q8), organisation on Moodle LMS (Q9), and the flow and materials structure (Q11). A small number of students (7%) would like to have deadlines assigned to tasks (Q12), whilst 90% like that there were

---

[4] https://forms.office.com.

Table 3. Statements and scales of the feedback survey.

Set	Q#	Scale: *Totally disagree/Somewhat disagree/Neutral/Almost agree/Totally agree*
#1	Q1	The self-regulated learning (SRL) format fits me fell
	Q2	I would prefer a regular scheduled class-meeting
	Q3	The self-regulated learning (SRL) format gives me freedom to study whenever I wish
	Q4	The self-regulated learning (SRL) format requires strong self-disciple
	Q5	I find support from the course forum
	Q6	Students support each-other in the course forum
	Q7	Lecturers are easily available
	Q8	I am satisfied with the self-regulated learning (SRL) format for this course
	Q9	I am satisfied with the course organisation on Moodle LMS
	Q10	I willingly use the feedback option within each topic block
	Q11	The course flow, including materials and structure, is clear
	Q12	I would prefer if each task would have a set deadline
	Q13	I like that there are no specific deadlines in this course and I can choose my own pace
		Scale: *Is not a problem/Somewhat a problem/Neutral/Somewhat challenging/Big challenge*
#2	Q1	Lack of time
	Q2	Lack of motivation
	Q3	The course is more complex than it seemed at first
	Q4	I have declared too many courses for this semester
	Q5	Course topics are not interesting to me
	Q6	I have no previous experience for self-regulated learning

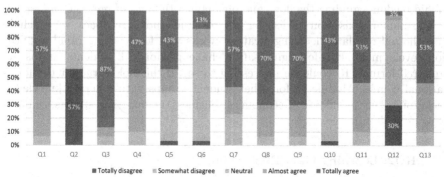

Fig. 2. Students' perception of SRL for RAD skills course (Module 1).

no deadlines set and they can choose their own pace (Q13). Figure 2 depicts the results of the collected feedback on SRL and perception on Module 1.

As SRL is highly dependent on learner motivation, we were also eager to investigate what are the main obstacles for such a learning format (Set 2 in Table 3). For SRL, it is needed that students would monitor themselves, their progress, plan their learning, and keep focus [18]. It is also known that in digital learning each learner has their own learning environment with many distractions, and the learner has to practice higher self-motivation [10]. According to

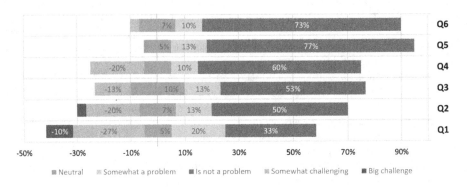

Fig. 3. Evaluation of obstacles for SRL implementation (Module 1)

the respondents, the biggest challenge (37%) is the lack of time (Q1) as also reported by several surveys [3,4,8], into which a high load of courses seems to contribute (Q4). This is followed by motivational issues (23%) (Q2). Interestingly, the complexity of the course (Q3) or topics being boring (Q5) are not considered challenging for managing self-regulated learning. Figure 3 presents the findings for the six predefined obstacles for successful implementation of SRL for our RAD course Module 1. Regarding other outlined obstacles in the survey, two respondents named missing *soft deadlines* as milestones by which something should be done, guiding the flow, and one named the *lack of reminder messages*.

In summary, based on the learner progress and student feedback, we conclude that the self-regulated learning strategy works well for teaching rapid application development skills for digitalisation challenges for ICT students, and is the preferred format. It would be interesting to see, if this holds true for the foundational course (Module 1) for other student groups with different knowledge background, e.g., students of economics, business, or maritime studies, remaining a possible future work.

4.2 RQ2: Learning Gain Reflection

Next, we consider the perceived learning gain reported by learners. In our course design (Sect. 3.2), each topic block is equipped with a feedback activity, where one of the questions asks students to reflect their learning gain. In particular, we ask: *"How much new knowledge/skills did you learn from this topic?"* to be evaluated on a 5-point scale: 0 – nothing, 1 – a little, 2 – moderately, 3 – plenty, and 4 – a lot (the topic was totally new to me). In average, 38 students provided feedback for each topic block.

The analysis (Table 4) shows that students, mostly of ICT, have some knowledge about databases and physical data models, and thereby less learning gain is reflected for these topics, whereas controversially students miss the theoretical grounds on logical database modelling, basics of SQL, and skills of RAD on Oracle APEX LCDP (53% report high learning gain). The learning gain reflection shows the real value the foundational part of the course (Module 1) has provided for students, and mirrors that the topics covered were relevant and useful for future engineers of digital transformation.

Table 4. Reported learning gain regarding new knowledge/skills as value indicator.

Module 1 topic	None	Little	Mod	Plenty	A lot
Introduction to databases	0%	25%	**47%**	22%	6%
Relational databases	2%	10%	**40%**	33%	14%
Database normalisation and terminology	0%	8%	38%	**41%**	13%
Data modelling	0%	9%	34%	**40%**	17%
Physical data model	0%	20%	**37%**	29%	14%
Access to Oracle APEX environment	0%	11%	34%	**46%**	9%
SQL: Introduction	0%	12%	32%	**38%**	18%
App development in APEX (wizard level)	0%	0%	13%	34%	**53%**
Average	0%	12%	35%	36%	16%

4.3 RQ3: RAD Skills Knowledge Improvement

Last, we study the improvement of knowledge of students of the foundational RAD skills course (RQ3). For this, we use the survey developed by the consortium. In this survey, for each module a set of questions is used to measure learners' knowledge before they take the module, and afterwards. For Module 1, this evaluation survey contains 22 questions covering the topics of the module.

We evaluate for each student their learning gain from the foundational course by comparing the scores they have achieved prior to taking Module 1, reflecting their existing knowledge, and after completing the module, reflecting their gained knowledge. The maximum score for the test is 10. The test is based on the benchmark questions provided by Oracle Academy, which they use to measure learning gain. This test was not considered as a part of the course grade, i.e., it did not provide students any points towards the grade. The average recorded score before taking the foundational course was 6.01 (Table 5), while at the end it was 8.18 (for students who had completed), indicating an improvement of

Table 5. Students knowledge improvement for the foundational course (Module 1).

Assessment condition	Min score	Max score	Average score	Standard deviation
Before Module 1	2.73	8.64	6.01	1.68
After Module 1	6.36	9.55	8.18	0.80
Change	133%	11%	36%	-48%

36%. We can observe (Table 5) a positive effect on students' knowledge from the foundational course on the minimum, maximum and average scores, and a negative trend for the deviation of the scores. We conclude that Module 1 delivered online as an SRL course has improved students' knowledge of RAD skills.

5   Conclusions

The rapid development of technology and the need for digitalisation together with a move towards digital transformation has evoked the challenge of expert workforce. To support digital transformation and tackle the problem of high and rapidly growing demand for software developers, low- or no-code platforms are seen as one of the solutions for application building and business automation.

In this paper, we explored self-regulated learning for teaching two novel courses on rapid application development on a foundational level using the Oracle APEX low-code development platform for the task. We were keen to see if self-regulated learning at all and to what extent it is appropriate to educate and prepare young for their future job market on emerging technologies such as rapid application development. Through answering the set research questions, we gained confidence that self-regulated learning is suitable to teach RAD skills for digitalisation challenges and preparing for digital transformation.

As for future work, we will continue monitoring the results of Module 2 and explore further possibilities to improve self-regulated learning through digitalisation (e.g., tools for course flows and SRL management), and thereby improve sustainable education of future generations.

Acknowledgment. This study would not have been possible without the support of the Erasmus+ KA220-HED project *Embracing rapid application development (RAD) skills opportunity as a catalyst for employability and innovation* funded by the European Union.

Disclosure of Interests. The authors have no competing interests to declare that are relevant to the content of this article.

References

1. Gartner Forecasts Worldwide Low-Code Development Technologies Market to Grow 20% in 2023 (2022). https://www.gartner.com/en/newsroom/press-releases/2022-12-13-gartner-forecasts-worldwide-low-code-development-technologies-market-to-grow-20-percent-in-2023. Accessed 01 Mar 2024
2. Dwiarie, A., Nguyen, A., Lamsa, J., Jarvela, S.: Personalized support features learners expect from self-regulated learning analytics. In: 2023 IEEE International Conference on Advanced Learning Technologies (ICALT), pp. 66–67. IEEE Computer Society, Los Alamitos (2023). https://doi.org/10.1109/ICALT58122.2023.00025

3. Eriksson, T., Adawi, T., Stöhr, C.: "Time is the bottleneck": a qualitative study exploring why learners drop out of MOOCs. J. Comput. High. Educ. **29**(1), 133–146 (2017). https://doi.org/10.1007/s12528-016-9127-8

4. Ho, A., et al.: Harvardx and mitx: two years of open online courses fall 2012-summer 2014. SSRN Electron. J. **10**, 1–37 (2015). https://doi.org/10.2139/ssrn.2586847

5. Ifenthaler, D.: Determining the effectiveness of prompts for self-regulated learning in problem-solving scenarios. J. Educ. Technol. Soc. **15**(1), 38–52 (2012)

6. Jossberger, H., Brand-Gruwel, S., van de Wiel, M.W.J., Boshuizen, H.P.A.: Exploring students' self-regulated learning in vocational education and training. Vocat. Learn. **13**(1), 131–158 (2020). https://doi.org/10.1007/s12186-019-09232-1

7. Khorram, F., Mottu, J.M., Sunyé, G.: Challenges & opportunities in low-code testing. In: Proceedings of the 23rd ACM/IEEE International Conference on Model Driven Engineering Languages and Systems: Companion Proceedings. MODELS 2020. Association for Computing Machinery, New York (2020). https://doi.org/10.1145/3417990.3420204

8. Kizilcec, R.F., Halawa, S.: Attrition and achievement gaps in online learning. In: Proceedings of the Second (2015) ACM Conference on Learning @ Scale, L@S 2015, pp. 57–66. Association for Computing Machinery, New York (2015). https://doi.org/10.1145/2724660.2724680

9. Legner, C., et al.: Digitalization: opportunity and challenge for the business and information systems engineering community. Bus. Inf. Syst. Eng. **59**(4), 301–308 (2017)

10. Leoste, J., et al.: Environment challenges of e-learning in higher education–the teachers' perspective. In: Dascalu, M., Marti, P., Pozzi, F. (eds.) SLERD 2022, pp. 143–156. Springer, Singapore (2023). https://doi.org/10.1007/978-981-19-5240-1_10

11. Leoste, J., Õun, T., Loogma, K., San Martín López, J.: Designing training programs to introduce emerging technologies to future workers—a pilot study based on the example of artificial intelligence enhanced robotics. Mathematics **9**(22), 2876 (2021). https://doi.org/10.3390/math9222876

12. Mergel, I., Edelmann, N., Haug, N.: Defining digital transformation: results from expert interviews. Gov. Inf. Q. **36**(4), 101385 (2019). https://doi.org/10.1016/j.giq.2019.06.002

13. Metrôlho, J., Ribeiro, F., Graça, P., Mourato, A., Figueiredo, D., Vilarinho, H.: Aligning software engineering teaching strategies and practices with industrial needs. Computation **10**(8), 129 (2022). https://doi.org/10.3390/computation10080129

14. Paris, S.G., Paris, A.H.: Classroom applications of research on self-regulated learning. Educ. Psychol. **36**(2), 89–101 (2001). https://doi.org/10.1207/S15326985EP3602_4

15. Pastierik, I., Kvet, M.: Oracle application express as a tool for teaching web software development. In: 2023 Communication and Information Technologies (KIT), pp. 1–7 (2023). https://doi.org/10.1109/KIT59097.2023.10297067

16. Payan-Carreira, R., Sebastião, L., Cristóvão, A., Rebelo, H.: How to enhance students' self-regulation. In: Dutton, J. (ed.) The Psychology of Self-Regulation, pp. 211–232. Nova Science Publishers Inc., New York (2022)

17. Picek, R.: Low-code/no-code platforms and modern ERP systems. In: 2023 International Conference on Information Management (ICIM), pp. 44–49 (2023). https://doi.org/10.1109/ICIM58774.2023.00014

18. Pintrich, P.R., De Groot, E.V.: Motivational and self-regulated learning components of classroom academic performance. J. Educ. Psychol. **82**(1), 33–40 (1990). https://doi.org/10.1037/0022-0663.82.1.33
19. Robal, T.: Fair and individualized project teamwork evaluation for an engineering course. In: 2018 28th EAEEIE Annual Conference (EAEEIE), pp. 1–9 (2018). https://doi.org/10.1109/EAEEIE.2018.8534256
20. Robal, T., Zhao, Y., Lofi, C., Hauff, C.: Intellieye: enhancing MOOC learners' video watching experience through real-time attention tracking. In: Proceedings of the 29th on Hypertext and Social Media, HT 2018, pp. 106–114. Association for Computing Machinery, New York (2018). https://doi.org/10.1145/3209542.3209547
21. Ruberg, P., Ellervee, P., Tammemäe, K., Reinsalu, U., Rähni, A., Robal, T.: Surviving the unforeseen – teaching it and engineering students during covid-19 outbreak. In: 2022 IEEE Frontiers in Education Conference (FIE), pp. 1–9 (2022). https://doi.org/10.1109/FIE56618.2022.9962383
22. Russell, J.M., Baik, C., Ryan, A.T., Molloy, E.: Fostering self-regulated learning in higher education: making self-regulation visible. Act. Learn. High. Educ. **23**(2), 97–113 (2022). https://doi.org/10.1177/1469787420982378
23. Sahay, A., Indamutsa, A., Di Ruscio, D., Pierantonio, A.: Supporting the understanding and comparison of low-code development platforms. In: 2020 46th Euromicro Conference on Software Engineering and Advanced Applications (SEAA), pp. 171–178 (2020). https://doi.org/10.1109/SEAA51224.2020.00036
24. Sanchis, R., Garcia-Perales, O., Fraile, F., Poler, R.: Low-code as enabler of digital transformation in manufacturing industry. Appl. Sci. **10**(1), 12 (2020). https://doi.org/10.3390/app10010012
25. Taranto, D., Buchanan, M.T.: Sustaining lifelong learning: a self-regulated learning (SRL) approach. Discourse Commun. Sustain. Educ. **11**(1), 5–15 (2020). https://doi.org/10.2478/dcse-2020-0002
26. Varajão, J.A., Trigo, A., Almeida, M.: Low-code development productivity: "is winter coming" for code-based technologies? Queue **21**(5), 87–107 (2023). https://doi.org/10.1145/3631183
27. Vial, G.: Understanding digital transformation: a review and a research agenda. J. Strateg. Inf. Syst. **28**(2), 118–144 (2019). https://doi.org/10.1016/j.jsis.2019.01.003
28. Waszkowski, R.: Low-code platform for automating business processes in manufacturing. IFAC-PapersOnLine **52**(10), 376–381 (2019). https://doi.org/10.1016/j.ifacol.2019.10.060
29. Yoo, Y., Henfridsson, O., Lyytinen, K.: The new organizing logic of digital innovation: an agenda for information systems research. Inf. Syst. Res. **21**(4), 724–735 (2010). https://doi.org/10.1287/isre.1100.0322
30. Zhao, Y., Robal, T., Lofi, C., Hauff, C.: Stationary vs. non-stationary mobile learning in MOOCs. In: Adjunct Publication of the 26th Conference on User Modeling, Adaptation and Personalization, UMAP 2018, pp. 299–303. Association for Computing Machinery, New York (2018). https://doi.org/10.1145/3213586.3225241
31. Zheng, L., Li, X.: The effects of motivation, academic emotions, and self-regulated learning strategies on academic achievements in technology enhanced learning environment. In: 2016 IEEE 16th International Conference on Advanced Learning Technologies (ICALT), pp. 376–380 (2016). https://doi.org/10.1109/ICALT.2016.128
32. Zimmerman, B.J.: Attaining self-regulation: a social cognitive perspective. In: Boekaerts, M., Pintrich, P.R., Zeidner, M. (eds.) Handbook of Self-Regulation, pp. 13–39. Academic Press, San Diego (2000). https://doi.org/10.1016/B978-012109890-2/50031-7

Data, Data Science, and Computing for Digital Business and Intelligent Systems

Crop Hyperspectral Dataset Unmixing Using Modified U-Net Model

Vytautas Paura[✉] and Virginijus Marcinkevičius

Institute of Data Science and Digital Technologies, Vilnius University, Vilnius,
Lithuania
vytautas.paura@mif.stud.vu.lt, virginijus.marcinkevicius@mif.vu.lt

Abstract. The hyperspectral unmixing procedure allows the extraction
of different material information (endmembers) and their abundances
from pixel spectra of the hyperspectral image for further analysis. An
extensive study of papers on hyperspectral unmixing methods that use
variational autoencoders, deep convolutional networks, or visual transformers shows a lack of diversity in the hyperspectral imaging (HSI)
datasets. In this paper, we propose using a modified U-Net architecture
of a deep convolutional neural network to analyze a new UAV-gathered
HSI dataset for crop health analysis. Secondly, a data analysis methodology was created to extract a set of endmembers with a variation in the
samples from the original HSI data for ground truth creation. Our U-Net
model was modified to extract endmember class data at the bottleneck
layer, and the SoftMax activation function was used during the decoding
phase to extract the abundance map. Multiplication of abundance and
endmember matrices reconstructs the HSI upon which the reconstruction
losses are calculated. We used an image-patching approach to improve
the model's ability to learn endmember data from the HSI dataset. The
model performance was evaluated on our newly created data and openly
available hyperspectral datasets such as *Washington DC Mall*, *Samson*,
and *Urban*.

Keywords: Hyperspectral · Unmixing · UAV crop data ·
convolutional neural networks

1 Introduction

The growing popularity of remote sensing systems and advancements in hyperspectral imaging technologies created a growing interest in using these technologies in various agricultural applications. Most commonly used near-infrared
hyperspectral cameras enable the collection of large amounts of spatial and
spectral information simultaneously. This allows users to quickly analyse large
crop fields, forests or plants directly in a nondestructive way [1]. Additional
applications of hyperspectral imaging in agriculture include crop disease and
stress detection, vegetation monitoring, and plant component identification [2].

© The Author(s), under exclusive license to Springer Nature Switzerland AG 2024
A. Lupeikienė et al. (Eds.): DB&IS 2024, CCIS 2157, pp. 195–210, 2024.
https://doi.org/10.1007/978-3-031-63543-4_13

Hyperspectral imaging technology is still more expensive than the simpler multispectral or RGB camera technologies and has a few drawbacks: a low spatial resolution compared to the multispectral or RGB technologies and higher computational resource costs for data storage and processing. While higher data processing requirements can be solved with better hardware, the low spatial resolution creates a harder problem. In hyperspectral imaging, each of the lower spatial resolution pixels may cover multiple materials on the ground. In turn, the gathered spectral data in these pixels are a mixture of various materials (called endmembers) in different amounts (called abundancies) [3]. Hyperspectral unmixing methods are used to solve this problem. These methods estimate the fractional abundance of each endmember for each pixel in the hyperspectral image. Some variations of hyperspectral unmixing also estimate the number of endmembers used; others extract the endmembers and their abundances. Hyperspectral unmixing is a challenging problem due to data complexity, noise in data collection, environmental factors during data collection, and dataset sizes [4].

In this paper, we propose:

- Methodology of creating hyperspectral unmixing datasets from UAV gathered hyperspectral images of crop fields.
- A modification of popular U-Net deep convolutional neural network for hyperspectral unmixing.
- Comparison of existing hyperspectral unmixing algorithms on most commonly used open hyperspectral unmixing datasets.

2   Related Work

This section describes works related to hyperspectral imaging use cases in agriculture, openly hyperspectral unmixing ch1datasets, and analysis of papers on hyperspectral unmixing algorithms.

2.1   Hyperspectral Imaging in Agriculture

UAV-based hyperspectral remote sensing is used in various agricultural applications, such as crop monitoring, environment analysis, plant classification, and disease detection. The central part of hyperspectral imaging is the new cameras and their sensors capable of collecting hundreds of spectral bands and some spatial information at the same time, compared to the other remote sensing technologies like multispectral imaging, spectroscopy, and RGB imaging [5]. Multispectral imaging collects fewer and broader bands with higher spatial resolution, spectroscopy collects many narrow bands as a single pixel, and RGB imagery collects three colour bands with a large spatial resolution. For various agricultural applications, hyperspectral imaging is used due to the high spectral resolution and large enough spatial resolution [6]. A review on hyperspectral imaging applications [7] distinguishes a few critical use cases of this technology: food quality assessment (plant and animal-based foods), contaminant detection (fungi), fruit diseases, compound distinctions, food type classification by protein, fat and carbohydrate contents.

2.2   Hyperspectral Unmixing Algorithms

This section describes a few of the most common types of hyperspectral unmixing algorithms. These three types of algorithms are [8]:

- Semi-supervised sparse regression modelling.
- Unsupervised non-negative matrix factorization methods.
- Unsupervised deep learning autoencoder neural networks.

Sparse regression algorithms are based on the fact that each pixel in a hyperspectral image will most likely contain only a fraction of all endmembers of the image. Therefore, the abundance matrix will have most of its values equal to zero, it will be sparse matrix upon which sparse regression modeling can be performed. Sparse regression algorithms include methods based on alternating direction method of multipliers (ADMM) [9]; addition of total variation regularization [10]; spatial and spectral data constraints [11]; superpixel based segmentation [12] for more accurate unmixing results.

Non-negative matrix factorization algorithms are based on the hyperspectral image being a product of the endmembers, their abundance, and noise matrices. These matrices will never have negative values since the hyperspectral image is the collection of reflected light, and the lowest values are zeros when no light is gathered. The hyperspectral image matrix can be expressed as a formula:

$$Z = WH + N, \tag{1}$$

where Z is the hyperspectral image, W is the endmember matrix, H is the abundance matrix, and N is the residual data (noise, artefacts, environmental effects). Non-negative matrix factorization methods include blind hyperspectral unmixing with spatial sparsity regularization [13]; endmember constraints and total variation regularization [14]; correntropy-based autoencoder-like algorithm [15].

The last type of the algorithm is autoencoder neural networks that create an artificial neuron bottleneck to compress the data into a latent space, extracting spatial and spectral features from hyperspectral images. Due to the base model architecture design, these types of neural networks can be trained using the difference between the original image and its reconstruction, making the algorithm unsupervised. Autoencoder networks include: generative adversarial network and variational autoencoder combination [16]; a collection of two networks, endmember guided and reconstruction [17]; LSTM based deep neural network [18]; Autoencoder unmixing model based on graph networks [19]; Dual-channel enhanced decoder network [20].

The latest and best results are from autoencoder-type networks, and in turn, a novel transformer-based neural network created by Ghosh et al. [21] was used as the primary experimentation and baseline algorithm in this paper. This paper was chosen as the baseline because of the novel transformer network used, it was one of the best performing hyperspectral unmixing algorithms according to the results achieved by the authors and for the paper code being open source.

2.3 Hyperspectral Datasets

In this section, we analyse freely available hyperspectral datasets most commonly used in study papers on hyperspectral imaging analysis and unmixing algorithms. These datasets are:

- *Synthetic datasets.* A common method of creating accurate hyperspectral unmixing datasets is using a library of various materials' spectral images. The most commonly used is the USGS spectral library [22]. The material spectra are mixed in various ways to create synthetic hyperspectral images with accurate ground truth for accurate algorithm assessment. Multiple paper analysed in previous section use synthetic datasets [9–11,13,14,16,21].
- *Jasper Ridge* [23] - A 512×614 pixels sized hyperspectral image with 224 spectral bands with four endmember classes: '#1 Road', '#2 Soil', '#3 Water' and '#4 Tree'. Papers that use this dataset in experimentation: [12,14,16]
- *Cuprite* [23]. Hypersepctrtal image of size 307×307 pixels and 210 spectral bands with a ground truth consisting of 4, 5, or 6 classes. [13,15]
- *Urban* [23]. A region of 250×190 pixels with 224 spectral bands and a collection of 14 different minerals (endmembers). Endmember spectra are depicted in Fig. 1. Papers that use this dataset in experimentation: [17,18]
- *DC Mall* [23,24]. A scanned area of a part of Washington DC with a size of 1208×307 pixels and 191 spectral bands. Created ground truth for classification has these classes: Roofs, Streets, Paths, Grass, Trees, Water, and Shadows. This dataset was used in this paper's experimentation, and Ghosh et al. [21] paper.

One of the conclusions drawn from the research on existing hyperspectral datasets is that there is a lack of open and freely available agricultural datasets. In this paper, we propose creating an agricultural hyperspectral unmixing dataset from the available UAV data and intend to publish this dataset openly.

3 New Hyperspectral Dataset of Crop's Field

This section describes the new dataset creation methodology and the technologies used to capture and process the data. There is a lack of openly available hyperspectral agricultural data, and in turn, it is rarely used in hyperspectral analysis papers, especially in hyperspectral unmixing. The previous chapter shows that the most common datasets used are synthetic lab-generated or non-agricultural. With the ability to collect agricultural hyperspectral data using UAV and Specim hyperspectral camera [25], an unmixing dataset was created. Hyperspectral dataset collection and pre-processing was done in these steps:

- A crop field was selected for monitoring purposes; in this case, the blueberry field was filmed.

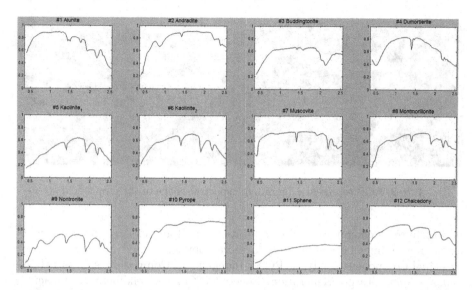

Fig. 1. Cuprite dataset endmember spectra. The graphs show the reflectance values (y-axis) for each of the different materials in specific wavelengths (x-axis) in micrometres Source: [23]

- An UAV flight path was created and uploaded to the drone and a camera for accurate data capture; because of the push broom type camera sensor, the drone has to fly in a straight line while recording.
- Multiple lines were recorded with special calibration surfaces on the ground, and whole data was collected during mid-day to reduce shadows.
- Collected data was processed by manufacturer-provided software from raw data to radiance values in a readable raster format.
- Using special calibration surfaces placed in the field, the data was recalculated to reflectance values.
- The created hyperspectral image was converted to RGB image using CIE 1931 [26] XYZ colour matching functions integrated over the hyperspectral bands for visualization purposes. The created image is shown in Fig. 2.

The collected hyperspectral image is 3177×1024 pixels with 224 spectral bands. Collected spectral wavelengths are 400 to 1000 nm with a spectral width of around 2 nm. The exact wavelengths gathered by the camera will be published with the dataset. The biggest problem in creating the dataset is the lack of accurate ground truth values since we don't exactly know which pixel belongs to which class, and manually labelling more than three million pixels is not feasible. To overcome this problem, an approximation of endmembers and classes was calculated. A special unsupervised method called Vertex Component Analysis (VCA) [27] algorithm was used to extract the endmembers. This algorithm tries to extract possible endmembers given the hyperspectral image and the number of endmembers to extract. This method was chosen due to the best

Fig. 2. RGB representation of hyperspectral image of the crop's field

performance (a combination of computation speed and extraction accuracy) in extracting endmembers compared to more commonly used methods such as: Principal Component Analysis (PCA), Independent Component Analysis (ICA) and Automatic Target Generation Process (ATGA). An endmember extraction experiment was conducted using the steps in the diagram in Fig. 3 to find this dataset's most accurate endmember representation. The experiment was done in these steps:

- A range of numbers from 3 to 50 was selected;
- For each number, the VCA algorithm generated a set of endmembers from the hyperspectral dataset;
- The differences between each endmember and the true hyperspectral data in each pixel were calculated using RMSE. This created a matrix of values of size $3177 \times 1024 \times$ number of endmembers;
- Each pixel was classified by selecting the minimum value from the calculated matrix;
- These classes corresponded to the extracted endmembers;
- RMSE value for the whole dataset was calculated using extracted endmember and real data difference in each pixel;
- For each value from 3 to 50, total RMSE was calculated. The generated graph shows the total RMSE value for each set of endmembers.

The result from the endmember extraction experiment is the number of endmembers and how accurately they can describe the original hyperspectral image. Lower total RMSE indicates a better representation of the original data, while a higher number of endmembers increases the dataset complexity and may result in classes that represent a very small amount of actual data. A combination of the lowest total RMSE with the smallest number of end members is the most optimal combination. It was concluded that the best number of endmembers was 6 or 12. Both of the configurations were used at first, but after an analysis of the number of pixels in each endmember, it was determined that using 12 endmembers, some of the classes have a tiny amount of samples ($< 0.1\%$ of pixels) and would increase the unmixing difficulty significantly. Threfore, for further research, 6 extracted endmembers were used.

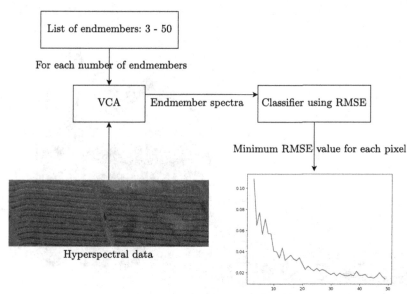

Y axis - average RMSE difference for each pixel compared between hyperspectral data and extracted endmembers. X axis - number of extracted endmembers.

Fig. 3. RGB representation of hyperspectral image used in creating the dataset.

The VCA extracted endmembers were used to classify the whole image to generate the hyperspectral unmixing dataset. The class was set for each pixel using the lowest RMSE value between the pixel spectra and each endmember. With the image classified all the pixel data was gathered for each class, producing a collection of similar pixels. To remove outliers from the dataset, each pixel with a spectral variation in any bands greater than 2-sigma was replaced by a random neighbouring pixel that satisfied this spectral variation rule. A new filtered hyperspectral image was generated with the most significant outliers removed, and a diagram for each of the endmembers and their standard deviations in each spectral band is shown in Fig. 4.

$$RMSE = \sqrt{\frac{1}{N} \sum_{i=1}^{N} (x_i - \hat{x}_i)^2}, \tag{2}$$

Unmixing dataset creation was finalized using these steps:

- A sliding window of 3×3 pixels was selected;
- For each group of 9 pixels (with no overlaps), the singular spectrum was calculated by linearly mixing 9 spectra;
- All of these mixes generated a new artificially mixed hyperspectral image; its size was reduced by 9;
- At the same time, the abundance matrix was calculated from the combination of classes inside each 3×3 window.

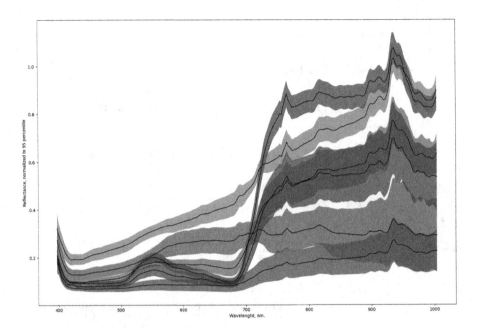

Fig. 4. Six extracted endmembers and the standard deviations in each spectral band in the generated hyperspectral dataset.

The final dataset was 1024×336 pixels and 224 spectral bands, with six endmembers, and the abundance matrix was $1024 \times 336 \times 6$. This created dataset can be used to test hyperspectral unmixing algorithms, their applications in agriculture, and their robustness to UAV field data.

4   Algorithms for Hyperspectral Unmixing

This section describes the algorithms used in the experimentation and our proposed U-Net-based hyperspectral unmixing deep neural network.

The primary model used in creating this paper as the baseline was the unmixing neural network that uses a visual transformer for endmember extraction created by Ghosh et al. [21]. Their model code is implemented in Python using PyTorch neural network creation library and is freely available on https://github.com/preetam22n/DeepTrans-HSU. The implemented code consists of:

– Neural network implementation using PyTorch;
– Various hyperspectral dataset reading and collected parameters for each of the datasets;
– Resulting data visualization wrappers;
– Implementation of a few loss functions used in the model training.

Our proposed model implementation is split into a few parts:

- Convolution encoder that compresses the input hyperspectral image to several select channels with batch normalization in between convolutional operations.
- Recalculation of the compressed data into specified patches.
- Created patch and position embedding is then sent to the visual transformer to extract the possible endmember classes from the data.
- Data is then upscaled and smoothed to generate the abundance estimation.
- Upscaled abundance map is then reconstructed back to the size of the input image.
- A one cycle [28] learning rate scheduler was used to slow training at the start and end of the training process.

This model architecture returns both the calculated abundance matrix and the reconstructed hyperspectral image, with endmembers being the weights of the convolutional decoder layer. The created model is then trained using multiple metrics between the input and reconstructed images, making this process completely unsupervised. Only the model hyperparameters must be provided, including the number of endmembers to extract, patch size to be used, weights for each of the losses, learning rate to use and the number of epochs to train. Two metrics used in training are reconstruction error (RE) (Eq. 3) and spectral angle distance (SAD) (see Eq. 4). These metrics were used for training in the paper by Ghosh et al. [21]. For a detailed explanation of these metrics, refer to the original paper.

$$L_{RE}(I, \widehat{I}) = \frac{1}{W \cdot H} \sum_{i=1}^{H} \sum_{j=1}^{W} (\widehat{I}_{ij} - I_{ij})^2 \tag{3}$$

$$L_{SAD}(I, \widehat{I}) = \frac{1}{R} \sum_{i=1}^{R} \arccos \left(\frac{\left\langle I_i, \widehat{I}_i \right\rangle}{\|I_i\|_2 \|\widehat{I}_i\|_2} \right) \tag{4}$$

With research conducted on existing hyperspectral unmixing algorithms and using the above-mentioned model as the baseline for experimentation, a new model was proposed for hyperspectral unmixing with its architecture based on U-Net deep convolutional autoencoder [29]. The original U-Net model created by Ronneberger et al. [29] was used for biomedical image segmentation, and its base architecture has been adapted to many different applications since then. We chose this architecture as the base of our model because of the autoencoder nature of the model that compresses data into small latent space to extract features from the data at various scales during the compression. Figure 5 shows the original U-Net model architecture diagram.

The transformer model created by Ghosh et al. had a few downsides that were discovered during testing:

- Original model was used only on square images;
- The whole image was used as the input in the model that determined the size of model layers. In turn, a large input dataset needed to be compressed, or

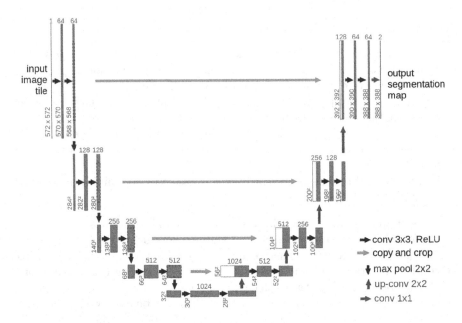

Fig. 5. U-Net model architecture and layers. Source: [29]

the transformer latent space needed to be reduced due to reaching the limits of available GPU VRAM.

– A set of manually tuned hyperparameters was provided for each dataset tested in the paper. A new set of parameters must be generated to use new datasets.

The first problem was solved directly in the original code to use rectangular images and not only squares. This was done only on the data reading part of the code without any changes to the model itself. Optimizations and model improvements may be possible when using rectangular data as input to the transformer patching algorithm used in the model. Running this model with our new dataset, a few iterations of training were conducted to get a set of parameters that gave valid results without hitting VRAM limits or other errors (e.g., input data shape must be divisible by the patch size provided). A manual solution to the second and third problems was found.

To solve all the problems, we propose a new hyperspectral unmixing model that combines ideas from the U-Net model architecture and the transformer-based unmixing model created by Ghosh et al. The original U-Net was used for segmentation, and modifications in architecture were needed for endmember and abundance matrix extraction and image reconstruction. Figure 9 shows our new proposed model architecture diagram.

The main changes from the U-Net and transformer models were:

– Splitting the hyperspectral image into smaller same-size images to reduce the overall size of the model, enabling usage of augmentations (e.g. mirroring and rotations) on the input data and training the model by selecting these image patches in random order;

- Splitting the compressed data into endmember and abundance extraction sub-networks;
- A model architecture dependant on fewer hyperparameters;
- Addition of cosine similarity loss was used to encourage the model to extract less similar endmembers.

5   Hyperspectral Unmixing Models Comparison

This section describes the experimentation to test the newly created hyperspectral unmixing model and the existing transformer model using the created dataset. The testing methodology from the paper by Ghosh et al. was selected to create the experiment baseline. Full experimentation steps are listed below:

- Selection of a few existing datasets used in testing the transformer neural network created by Ghosh et al. This included *Samson* and *Washington DC* datasets.
- Newly created dataset adaptation to existing model and running a few test passes to gather a set of hyperparameters.
- Newly created model adaptation to existing data pipeline developed by Ghosh et al. to keep the testing between the datasets and models consistent.
- For model training reconstruction error (RE, Eq. 3) and spectral angle distance (SAD, Eq. 4) were used as losses, and an additional cosine similarity loss (Eq. 5) was added to the new proposed model.
- For testing the results, root mean squared error (RMSE, Eq. 2) and SAD metrics were used.

$$\cos(\theta) = \frac{A \cdot B}{\|A\| \|B\|} \tag{5}$$

RMSE, SAD and RE results by running our new proposed model and the transformer model developed by Ghosh et al. with 3 selected datasets are provided in Table 1, where the agricultural dataset is our newly created dataset. Extracted endmembers compared with the ground truth endmembers are provided as separate graphs for each of the six combinations of the two models and three datasets tested. Figures 6, 7, and 8 show the extracted and ground truth endmembers for each of the classes, models and datasets. In these graphs, the x-axis is the wavelength array index values, and the y-axis is the normalized reflectance values (Fig. 9).

Table 1. RMSE, SAD and RE metric results of our proposed and the transformer models for different datasets, including our newly created agricultural hyperspectral dataset. Bold values show better results for each dataset and metric between the two models.

Dataset:	Agricultural	Agricultural	DC Mall	DC Mall	Samson	Samson
Model:	Transformer	Our model	Transformer	Our model	Transformer	Our model
RE	0.3129	**0.0754**	**0.0253**	0.0451	0.1651	**0.0401**
mean RMSE	0.5054	**0.3625**	0.3853	**0.3832**	0.6027	**0.5215**
mean SAD	**0.4135**	0.6632	0.3002	**0.1928**	**0.2411**	0.7880

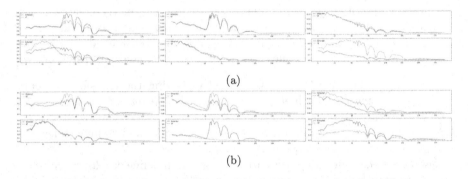

(a)

(b)

Fig. 6. These graphs show extracted and ground truth endmember for each class in the DC Mall dataset. The result in figure (a) was acquired by our proposed new model, and in figure (b) was acquired by the transformer model developed by Ghosh et al.

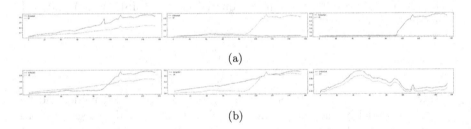

(a)

(b)

Fig. 7. These graphs show extracted and ground truth endmember for each class in the Samson dataset. The result in figure (a) was acquired by our proposed new model, and in figure (b) was acquired by the transformer model developed by Ghosh et al.

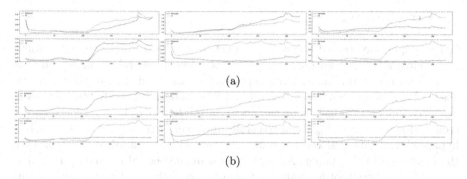

(a)

(b)

Fig. 8. These graphs show extracted and ground truth endmember for each class in our newly created agricultural hyperspectral dataset. The result in figure (a) was acquired by our proposed new model, and in figure (b) was acquired by the transformer model developed by Ghosh et al.

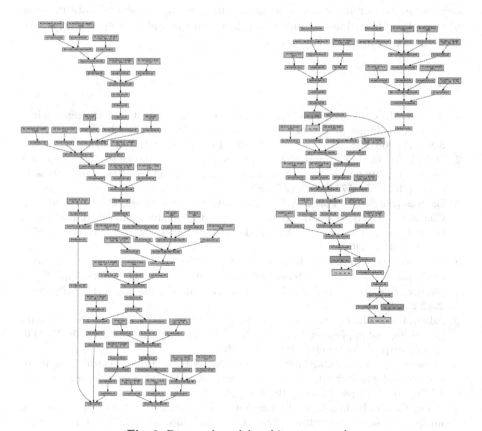

Fig. 9. Proposed model architecture graph.

6   Conclusion

In this paper, we created a new hyperspectral unmixing dataset in agriculture. The main goal of the new dataset is to test any hyperspectral unmixing datasets on agricultural data. This testing type would indicate if the algorithm can be used in lower-resolution hyperspectral agricultural data (e.g., satellite data). Any other hyperspectral analysis or classification methods can be used for accurate crop and food monitoring by successfully unmixing agricultural data. The raw hyperspectral data and the generated dataset will be published together with the code used in this paper. An agricultural hyperspectral unmixing dataset is a valuable testing tool for unmixing algorithms if they are to be used in this domain because some algorithms may need specific optimization for different types of data for optimal performance. Our proposed U-Net base convolutional deep neural network model improves unmixing agricultural datasets and performs similarly in other datasets. From the extracted endmember graphs, more accurate methods may be required to use unmixed hyperspectral data in other analysis algorithms. Further algorithm development and testing of newly published unmixing methods is planned.

References

1. Ahmad, M., et al.: Hyperspectral image classification-traditional to deep models: a survey for future prospects. IEEE J. Select. Topics Appl. Earth Observ. Remote Sens. **15**, 968–999 (2022). https://doi.org/10.1109/jstars.2021.3133021
2. Dale, L. M., et al.: Hyperspectral imaging applications in agriculture and agro-food product quality and safety control: a review. Appl. Spectrosc. Rev. (2013).https://doi.org/10.1080/05704928.2012.705800
3. Bioucas-Dias, J.M., Plaza, A., Camps-Valls, G., Scheunders, P., Nasrabadi, N., Chanussot, J.: Hyperspectral remote sensing data analysis and future challenges. IEEE Geosci. Remote Sens. Magaz. **1**(2), 6–36 (2013). https://doi.org/10.1109/MGRS.2013.2244672
4. Bioucas-Dias, J.M., et al.: Hyperspectral unmixing overview: geometrical, statistical, and sparse regression-based approaches. IEEE J. Select. Topics Appl. Earth Observ. Remote Sens. **5**(2), 354–379 (2012). https://doi.org/10.1109/JSTARS.2012.2194696
5. Adão, T., et al.: Hyperspectral imaging: a review on UAV-based sensors, data processing and applications for agriculture and forestry. Remote Sens. **9**(11), 1110 (2017). https://doi.org/10.3390/rs9111110
6. Mahesh, S., Jayas, D.S., Paliwal, J., White, N.D.G.: Hyperspectral imaging to classify and monitor quality of agricultural materials. J. Stored Prod. Res. **61**, 17–26 (2015). https://doi.org/10.1016/j.jspr.2015.01.006
7. Wang, C., Liu, B., Liu, L., et al.: A review of deep learning used in the hyperspectral image analysis for agriculture. Artif. Intell. Rev. **54**, 5205–5253 (2021). https://doi.org/10.1007/s10462-021-10018-y
8. Paura, V., Marcinkevicius, V.: Benchmark for hyperspectral unmixing algorithm evaluation. Informatica **34**(2), 285–315 (2023). https://doi.org/10.15388/23-INFOR522

9. Bioucas-Dias, J.M., Figueiredo, M.A.T.: Alternating direction algorithms for constrained sparse regression: application to hyperspectral unmixing. In: 2010 2nd Workshop on Hyperspectral Image and Signal Processing: Evolution in Remote Sensing (2010). https://doi.org/10.1109/WHISPERS.2010.5594963

10. Iordache, M., Bioucas-Dias, J.M., Plaza, A.: Total variation spatial regularization for sparse Hyperspectral unmixing. IEEE Trans. Geosci. Remote Sens. **50**(11), 4484–4502 (2012). https://doi.org/10.1109/TGRS.2012.2191590

11. Zhang, S., Li, J., Li, H.-C., Deng, C., Plaza, A.: Spectral–spatial weighted sparse regression for hyperspectral image unmixing. IEEE Trans. Geosci. Remote Sens. **56**(6), 3265–3276 (2018). https://doi.org/10.1109/TGRS.2018.2797200

12. Su, H., Jia, C., Zheng, P., Du, Q.: Superpixel-based weighted collaborative sparse regression and reweighted low-rank representation for hyperspectral image unmixing. IEEE J. Select. Topics Appl. Earth Observ. Remote Sens. **15**, 393–408 (2022). https://doi.org/10.1109/JSTARS.2021.3133428

13. Wang, X., Zhong, Y., Zhang, L., Xu, Y.: Spatial group sparsity regularized nonnegative matrix factorization for hyperspectral unmixing. IEEE Trans. Geosci. Remote Sens. **55**(11), 6287–6304 (2017). https://doi.org/10.1109/TGRS.2017.2724944

14. Wang, J.-J., Wang, D.-C., Huang, T.-Z., Huang, J.: Endmember constraint nonnegative tensor factorization via total variation for hyperspectral unmixing. In: 2021 IEEE International Geoscience and Remote Sensing Symposium IGARS (2021). https://doi.org/10.1109/IGARSS47720.2021.9554468

15. Feng, X.-R., Li, H.-C., Liu, S., Zhang, H.: Correntropy-based autoencoder-like NMF with total variation for hyperspectral unmixing. IEEE Geosci. Remote Sens. Lett. **19**, 1–5 (2022). https://doi.org/10.1109/LGRS.2020.3020896

16. Borsoi, R.A., Imbiriba, T., Bermudez, J.C.M.: Deep generative endmember modeling: an application to unsupervised spectral unmixing. IEEE Trans. Computat. Imaging **6**, 374–384 (2020). https://doi.org/10.1109/TCI.2019.2948726

17. Han, Z., Hong, D., Gao, L., Zhang, B., Chanussot, J.: deep half-siamese networks for hyperspectral unmixing. IEEE Geosci. Remote Sens. Lett. **18**(11), 1996–2000 (2021). https://doi.org/10.1109/LGRS.2020.3011941

18. Zhao, M., Yan, L., Chen, J.: LSTM-DNN based autoencoder network for nonlinear hyperspectral image unmixing. IEEE J. Select. Topics Signal Process. **15**(2), 295–309 (2021). https://doi.org/10.1109/JSTSP.2021.3052361

19. Chen, J., Li, J., Gamba, P.: A multi-tasks autoencoder hyperspectral unmixing model with information gain based on graph network. In: 2023 13th Workshop on Hyperspectral Imaging and Signal Processing: Evolution in Remote Sensing (WHISPERS), Athens, pp. 1–5 (2023). https://doi.org/10.1109/WHISPERS61460.2023.10430667

20. Shu, S., Huang, T.-Z., Huang, J.: Dual-channel enhanced decoder network for blind hyperspectral unmixing. IEEE Geosci. Remote Sens. Lett. **21**, 5500405(1–5) (2024). https://doi.org/10.1109/LGRS.2023.3338193

21. Ghosh, P., Roy, S.K., Koirala, B., Rasti, B., Scheunders, P.: Hyperspectral unmixing using transformer network. IEEE Trans. Geosci. Remote Sens. **60**, 553511(1–16) (2022). https://doi.org/10.1109/TGRS.2022.3196057

22. Kokaly, R.F., et al.: USGS Spectral Library Version 7. In: Survey, U.S. Data Series (2017). https://doi.org/10.3133/ds1035

23. Hyperspectral Datasets. http://lesun.weebly.com/hyperspectral-data-set.html. Accessed 15 Mar 2024

24. Hyperspectral Images - MultiSpec. https://engineering.purdue.edu/~biehl/MultiSpec/hyperspectral.html. Accessed 15 Mar 2024

25. Specim AFX10 Hyperspectral Camera. https://www.specim.com/products/specim-afx10/. Accessed 15 Mar 2024
26. CIE 1931 Color Space. https://en.wikipedia.org/wiki/CIE_1931_color_space/. Accessed 10 Mar 2024
27. Nascimento, J.M.P., Dias, J.M.B.: Vertex component analysis: a fast algorithm to unmix hyperspectral data. IEEE Trans. Geosci. emote Sens. **43**(4), 898–910 (2005). https://doi.org/10.1109/TGRS.2005.844293
28. OneCycleLR.   https://pytorch.org/docs/stable/generated/torch.optim.lr_scheduler.OneCycleLR.html. Accessed 12 Mar 2024
29. Ronneberger, O., Fischer, P., Brox, T.: U-net: convolutional networks for biomedical image segmentation. arXiv preprint arXiv:1505.04597 (2015)

Evaluation of Deep Learning-Based Models for Recognition of Skydiving Formations

Algimantas Skuodis[✉][iD] and Olga Kurasova[iD]

Vilnius University, Institute of Data Science and Digital Technologies,
Akademijos str. 4, Vilnius 08412, Lithuania
algimantas.skuodis@mif.stud.vu.lt, olga.kurasova@mif.vu.lt

Abstract. This study explores the feasibility of employing deep-learning models to perform approximate live judging for 4-way formation skydiving, a discipline where skydivers perform predefined formations in free fall. Given the time and effort required to judge these formations, our research aims to explore a more instantaneous method for approximate scoring. We created a novel dataset from twelve skydiving competitions and the first six skydiving formations, resulting in 2,946 frames annotated with formation names. We have selected and evaluated the effectiveness of several deep learning architectures, including ResNet-50, EfficientViT, FastViT, and several ConvMixer configurations, in classifying these formations. Our findings reveal that selected pretrained deep-learning models could be used to classify skydiving formations and can extract enough features to achieve high classification accuracy, with the ConvMixer_768_32 model achieving the highest overall F1 score of 0.9865. These results indicate the potential of deep learning applications in automated judging of formation skydiving competitions with potential improvements in spectator experience. Despite the promising outcomes, limitations such as the dataset's scope and disregard for inference time highlight areas for future research.

Keywords: Deep Learning · Image Classification · Skydiving · Competitions · ResNet · Vision Transformers · ConvMixer

1 Introduction

Deep learning has become a powerful paradigm in the machine learning domain, demonstrating remarkable achievements in various applications such as image recognition, natural language processing, and speech synthesis. The ability of deep neural network models to automatically learn hierarchical representations from data has led to significant advancements in solving complex problems. One critical aspect of utilizing deep learning models is their evaluation, ensuring robust performance across diverse datasets.

This work presents a comparative analysis of some well-known deep-learning models within the context of a novel skydiving dataset. Skydiving as a sport

A. Lupeikienė et al. (Eds.): DB&IS 2024, CCIS 2157, pp. 211–226, 2024.
https://doi.org/10.1007/978-3-031-63543-4_14

has many disciplines. One of them is the 4-way formation skydiving. In this discipline, competitors have to repeat randomly selected formations (in this discipline called randoms and blocks) during free fall in a limited amount of time. Two types of competitions exist: indoor and outdoor. In indoor competitions, skydivers perform formations in a wind tunnel, filmed by stationary cameras. In the case of the outdoor competition, the cameraman jumps with the 4-way team and films all the formations. In both cases, the video is judged by a group of judges who count how many formations were performed in the designated time. Usually, competitions consist of ten competition jumps, called rounds. The main problem of such judging is that it is time-consuming and cannot be done live because the video is handed over to the judges only after the jump. So, there is a time gap between the competition round and the moment when the scores of that particular round are announced. This means that neither the spectators nor the competitors know the result of the jump. This lag between the jump and the results removes some competition attractiveness, especially for the spectators. Especially during the indoor competition, when spectators can see the round themselves just outside of the glass wall of the wind tunnel but have no idea about even the approximate result. Thus, whether it is possible to use deep learning models to perform approximate live judging for the 4-way formation skydiving is questioned. To understand this, it is crucial to evaluate currently existing well-known deep learning models with the novel skydiving dataset and evaluate their feature extracting and classification capabilities.

The primary objectives of this work are as follows:

- Identify deep learning models most commonly used for feature extraction in similar tasks related to image classification and human pose detection.
- Create a skydiving dataset for such evaluation.
- Evaluate selected deep learning models within the created skydiving dataset.

This paper is organized as follows. Section 2 presents the motivation behind selecting specific deep learning models. Section 3 introduces the novel skydiving dataset, describes selected deep learning models in more detail and provides information about the experiment environment, scoring, and evaluation. Results are presented and discussed in Sect. 4. Conclusions, limitations, and future works are provided in Sect. 5.

2 Related Works

In the context of current knowledge, no deep-learning models have been applied to the classification of skydiving formations, and no research has been done on this topic. After analyzing the most recent and most referenced publications related to human pose estimation, it can be seen that several strategies could be used to create a deep learning model to perform approximate live judging for the 4-way formation skydiving competition. One strategy would be to use models adapted to perform human pose detection. Two commonly known high-level strategies for a human pose or multi-pose detection are top-down and bottom-up. In the top-down case, initially, persons are detected in the image, and then, for each detected person, body parts are estimated for pose detection. Oppositely, in the bottom-up approach, the critical body parts are first detected and then grouped into person instances.

In both cases, whether it's top-down or bottom-up, those models are based on or in some way use image feature extractors based on deep residual networks [7] or, more recently, vision transformers and their modifications.

Compositional Human Pose Regression [14] and DeepPose [16] use top-down regression-based human pose estimation strategies and Convolutional neural network (CNN) based methods that use deep convolutional neural networks, such as AlexNet [9], GoogleNet [15], ResNet-50 [7], to extract image features and then regress body joint coordinates. Another example is presented in [11]. It used Faster-RCNN [13] for person detection and ResNet [7] for pose keypoint detection from dense heatmaps with novel Non-Maximum-Suppression (NMS) to combine outputs and obtain highly localized keypoint predictions. FastPose [22] proposed an end-to-end multitask network that simultaneously performs human detection, pose estimation, and person re-identification tasks, RestNet-18 and ResNet-50 [7] were used as a backbone of Scale-normalized Image and Feature Pyramids (SIFP). DeeperCut architecture [8] proposed several improvements to DeepCut [12]. In the new architecture, strong body part detectors based on current advances in deep learning (ResNet [7]) were added that, taken alone, already allow obtaining competitive performance on pose estimation benchmarks.

Recently, vision transformers (ViTs) have started to be applied to human pose estimation tasks with great potential and state-of-the-art performance. Some use CNN as a backbone, but others [21] use the plain vision transformers. The authors of [21] try to answer the question: how well the plain vision transformer can do pose estimation? Vision transformers have shown great potential in many vision tasks. Thus, different vision transformer structures have been used to estimate human pose. According to [21], most of them adopt CNN as a backbone and then use a transformer of structures to refine extracted features and model the relationship between the body key points. To find the answer to the previous question, a baseline model called ViTPose is presented in [21]. The presented model demonstrated its potential on the MS COCO Keypoint dataset, where ViTPose obtained state-of-the-art performance.

However, visual transformers have limitations: they require significant computational resources, making them computationally expensive compared to traditional convolutional neural networks. The quadratic memory complexity of attention mechanisms leads to large memory requirements and long training and inference times. Authors of [17] try to investigate whether the transformer architecture of ViTs or different image input representations (compared to convolutional neural networks) are responsible for significantly better performance of the visual transformers.

3   Development and Evaluation Methodology

The research question is whether it is possible to classify skydiving formations using feature extractors, often used in human pose estimation architectures, like ResNet [7], EfficientViT [10], FastViT [18] and, even if it was not used in human pose estimation recently, but has strengths of ViTs - ConvMixer [17]. And how accurate such classification could be.

In 4-way formation skydiving, there are 16 formations named 'A', 'B', 'C', 'D', 'E', 'F', 'G', 'H', 'J', 'K', 'L', 'M', 'N', 'O', 'P', 'Q' and 22 blocks named by numbers 1–22, which are two consecutive formations with some transition. In the case of the blocks, the beginning and end formations are the same in some cases, which should be addressed later. So, in total, there are 60 formations.

It is common that after skydiving competitions, videos of the jumps are published on various sites [1–3]. Videos of the jumps from 12 competitions were selected to create a dataset. Those videos were accessible on the mentioned sites. Each competition consists of up to 10 rounds and various teams (Table 1).

Table 1. Skydiving competitions from which video files were extracted.

Competition	Rounds	Teams
Airspace2022	10	36
Eloy2022	10	25
Tanay2021	6	13
Eloy2019	10	20
FlyspotOpen2021	10	6
FlyspotOpen2022	10	11
DIPC2021	10	6
USPANationals2022	10	12
SwissNationals2022	8	3
USPANationals2022Advanced	10	15
1STDITC2021	10	7
AbhuDhabiFirstOpen2022	6	4

Timestamps of each formation from video files were acquired by processing metadata provided with corresponding video files or applying image recognition methods to get judging signals displayed in the video frame. In total, 26436 frames with various formations were captured (Fig. 1). The dataset was annotated with the formation name and region of interest in the frame (Fig. 3).

This paper's experimental investigation is limited to the first six skydiving formations (named 'A,' 'B,' 'C,' 'D,' 'E,' and 'F'). Each captured frame has to be reviewed manually to correct possible errors when automatically getting frames from the video. This is a time-consuming process. Thus, evaluation was limited

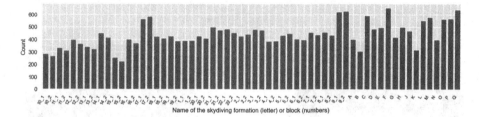

Fig. 1. Number of examples for each formation: formations are named by letters, and blocks are numbered with underscore numbers identifying the start and end of the block.

to the first six formations mentioned above. In total, the experimental dataset with six formations consists of 2,946 images. It was split uniformly at random to training and validation datasets with a split ratio of 8/2. A count of formation examples in the training validation dataset can be seen in Figs. 2a, 2b. Sample formations from this dataset can be seen in Fig. 3. All images have three color channels and the same aspect ratio. During the training or inference, all images were transformed to 224 × 224 size.

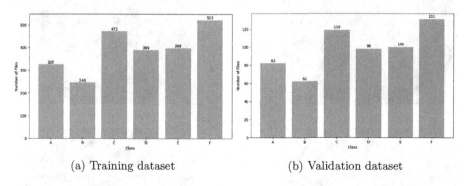

(a) Training dataset   (b) Validation dataset

Fig. 2. Number of files of each class in training and validation datasets.

3.1 Models Selected for the Experiments

Pytorch Image Models (timm, [4]) were used for model training and evaluation. Several well-known deep learning models were selected for the classification experiments: ResNet-50 [7], several variations of ConvMixer [17], EfficientViT [10], FastViT [18]. Those exact models were selected because, as stated in Sect. 2, ResNets and ViTs are often used as backbones and feature extractors in many human pose estimations. ConvMixer is a different architecture that uses the input representation of ViTs but does not use transformer architecture, thus eliminating some of ViT's weaknesses. Considering all of that, deep learning models presented in [7,10,17,18] are good candidates for such evaluation.

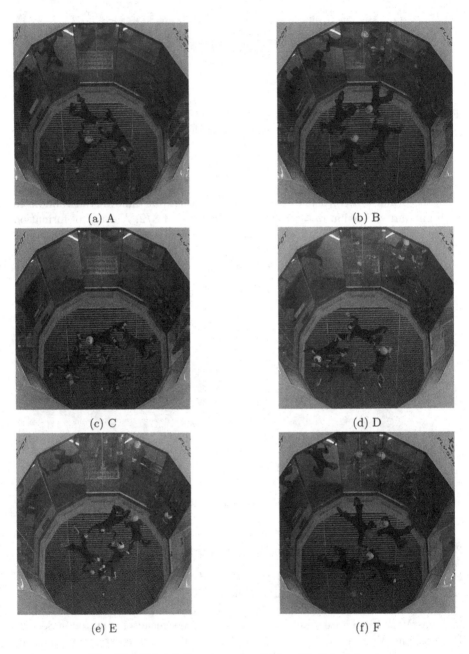

(a) A

(b) B

(c) C

(d) D

(e) E

(f) F

Fig. 3. A-F formation examples from validation dataset.

Deep Residual Networks. Deep residual networks (ResNets) [7] are foundational models for many computer vision tasks. Hence, their modifications are often used as a processing step or a backbone of the human pose estimation models to extract image features for body parts or keypoint detection. The main idea of ResNet is its residual blocks. Each block has a shortcut connection (also called skip connection) that allows the input of the block to be added to its output, helping to mitigate the vanishing gradient and deep network degradation problems. Mathematically, it would mean $y = x + \mathcal{F}(x)$, where x is the input of the layer, y is the output of the layer, and $\mathcal{F}(x)$ is residual mapping of the layer. Shortcut connection performs identity mapping, adding its output to the layer's output. Inside the residual layer, there might be several weight layers and ReLU (rectified linear unit) activation function. Figure 4 provides a building block of residual learning. For this experiment, ResNet-50 was selected. ResNet-50 is named like that because it has 50 layers with weights (Fig. 5):

- 7×7 kernel convolution layer,
- 3×3 max pool layer,
- 16 residual blocks, each consisting of 3 convolution layers,
- 1×1 global average pooling layer,
- n-dimensional fully connected layer where n is the number of classes.

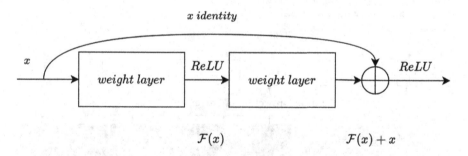

Fig. 4. A building block of residual learning.

Visual Transformers. EfficientViT [10] and FastViT [18] are based on Vision Transformers class models, usually called just ViTs. Vision transformers were introduced in [6]. Transformers were introduced in [19] and have since become the choice model for natural language processing (NLP) tasks. In computer vision tasks, convolutional neural networks were dominant. Still, after the success of transformers in NLP, researchers started investigating how to combine CNN with transformers or apply plain transformers to vision tasks.

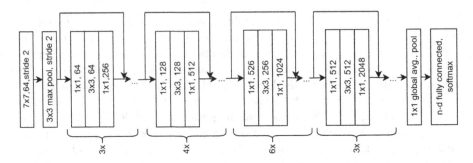

Fig. 5. Architecture of ResNet50.

The idea of vision transformers was to split images into 16×16 size patches and treat them as a sequence of word representations. In the case of color images with three color layers, each patch was flattened to a 768-dimensional vector ($16 \times 16 \times 3$) and then, after adding positional embedding, was passed to the transformer. The general architecture of ViT is presented in Fig. 6.

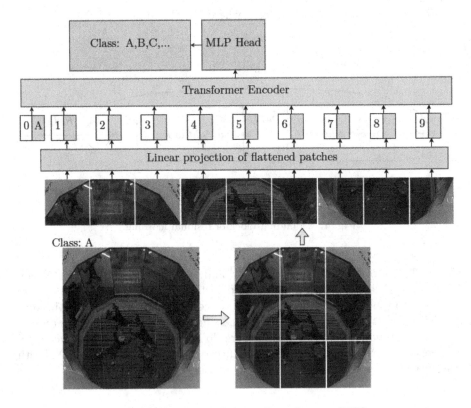

Fig. 6. Architecture of Vision Transformers (ViT).

According to the design of [6], the transformer encoder block of ViT consists of alternating layers of multi-head self-attention and multi-layer perception (MLP) blocks with layer normalization applied before every block and residual connections after every block (see Fig. 7).

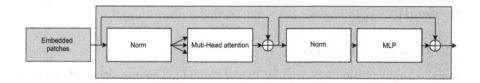

Fig. 7. Transformer Encoder.

After visual transformer architecture was introduced in [6], many variants of visual transformers started to appear. For example, a good list of visual transformer variants can be found here [20]. Even though visual transformers outperform classical convolutional architectures in accuracy, this performance does not come without a cost. Usually, ViT model sizes are higher than those of classical convolutional architectures. Larger model sizes require higher computational costs. Thus, there is extensive and resource-hungry training and longer inference time. Some of the latest works concentrated on fighting those problems, especially targeting long inference time, a massive problem regarding mobile or real-time applications.

In this work, EfficientViT [10] and FastViT [18] were chosen as they are trying to fight those problems. For example, EfficientViT [10] proposed a new efficient building block for the vision transformer, which consists of an efficient sandwich layout, cascaded group attention module, and parameter relocation strategy. Compared to common CNN MobileNets, EfficientViT obtained from 1.4% to 1.9% better top-1 classification accuracy on ImageNet-1k while running from 2.5x to 3.0x faster [10].

FastViT [18] is a hybrid vision transformer that uses structural reparametrization to obtain lower memory access costs and increase capacity. FastViT uses RepMixer, a token mixer that reparametrizes a skip connection, which helps alleviate memory access costs. FastViT obtained the best accuracy-latency tradeoff compared to recent state-of-the-art models on desktop-grade GPUs and mobile devices [18].

ConvMixer. On the other hand, authors of [17] raised a question: is the performance of ViTs due to the inherently more powerful transformer architecture, or is it at least partly due to using patches as the input representation? They presented ConvMixer architecture, which directly operates on patches (like all ViTs), maintains an equal resolution and size representation throughout all layers, and does no downsampling of the representation at successive layers. But unlike ViT's, ConvMixer does all the operations via standard convolutions. Basically, the model itself consists of a patch embedding layer and a number of fully convolutional blocks. Patch embedding with patch size p was implemented as convolution with h output channel, p kernel size and p stride. The ConvMixer block consists of depthwise convolution followed by pointwise convolution. Block is applied several times and is finished by global average pooling and softmax classifier [17].

3.2 Data Augmentation

Random augmentation was used for model training. The magnitude of augmentation was set to 9 with magnitude variance as a Gaussian distribution with a standard deviation of 0.5. Two random augmentations were used from the following possible augmentations: 'AutoContrast', 'Equalize', 'Invert', 'Rotate', 'Posterize', 'Solarize', 'SolarizeAdd', 'Color', 'Contrast', 'Brightness', 'Sharpness', 'ShearX', 'ShearY', 'TranslateXRel', 'TranslateYRel'.

3.3 Transfer Learning

After initial experiments with poor results with non-pre-trained models, it was clear that achieving reasonable results within a reasonable amount of time would be time-consuming, if not impossible. Thus, transfer learning was utilized. Luckily, Pytorch Image Models provides pre-trained variants of the selected models. All selected pretrained models were pre-trained on the ImageNet-1k dataset [5] and were provided by Pytorch Image Models.

3.4 Scoring and Evaluation

Models were evaluated using per-class accuracy and weighted F1 scores. In the domain of deep learning multi-class classification tasks, the assessment of model performance goes beyond just overall accuracy. Per-class accuracy and weighted F1 score are two metrics that offer a more nuanced evaluation by considering a model's performance across individual classes within a dataset.

Per-class accuracy is the proportion of correct predictions in the total number of predictions, which can be expressed by:

$$A = \frac{1}{N} \sum_{i=1}^{N} 1(\hat{y}_i = y_i), \tag{1}$$

where A is class accuracy, N is number of total predictions, $\hat{y}_i$ predicted label of i-th data instance, y_i true label of i-th data instance.

The weighted F1 score is used to assess the model's accuracy due to a slightly different number of instances in each class. First, the F1 score for each class is calculated by:

$$F1 = 2 \times \frac{precision \times recall}{precision + recall}, \tag{2}$$

where precision is the number of true positive results divided by the number of all positive results (including those identified incorrectly), and recall is the number of true positive results divided by the number of samples that should have been identified as positive (Eq. (3)).

$$Precision = \frac{TP}{TP + FP}, Recall = \frac{TP}{TP + FN}, \tag{3}$$

where TP is true positive - instances that are actually positive and are correctly predicted as positive, FP is false positive - instances that are actually negative but are incorrectly predicted as positive and FN is false negative - instances that are actually positive but are incorrectly predicted as negative.

Then, the F1 weighted score is calculated by multiplying each per class F1 score by the class weight, which is true instances for the class divided by the total number of instances (Eq. 4).

$$F1_{weighted} = \sum_{i=1}^{N} w_i \times F1_i, \tag{4}$$

where $F1_i$ is F1 score of the class i, w_i is the weight of the class i and N is the number of classes.

3.5   Environment

Experiments were performed on the Vilnius University High Performance Computing (HPC) GPU node. GPU node consists of 3 NVIDIA DGX-1 servers containing NVIDIA Tesla V100 32GB SMX2 GPU's. The models were trained using Pytorch Image Models command line training scripts executed on the mentioned servers as batch jobs using Slurm Workload Manager. Each batch job requested 2 GPUs and was scheduled to run for 300 epochs with a step learning rate scheduler, scheduler warmups, and batch sizes 64 or 128.

4   Results

Classification results of the trained models are presented in Tables 2 and 3. Model training and evaluation were performed on several ConvMixer variants with different hidden dimensions d (dimensions of patch embeddings) and depths h (number of repetitions of ConvMixer layers), named ConvMixer_d_h. "M0" for EfficientViT and "MA36" for FastViT specify the architecture variant of the mentioned models, and their descriptions can be found in [10] and [18].

Two models were trained without transfer learning, and the rest were trained using models pre-trained on the ImageNet-1k dataset. That is indicated with "Pretrained" "TRUE" or "FALSE" in Tables 2 and 3. The size and parameter count of the corresponding model are provided. The per-class classification accuracy for each corresponding model and the weighted average F1 score are presented.

Loss curves of the four best-performing models are presented in Fig. 8. As shown in Fig. 8, 300 epochs are enough to train the classifier for six formations. In all cases, training could have been stopped earlier, after about 100 epochs. Learning curves also show a significant effect of applied random augmentation: training loss is higher than validation loss. According to Tables 2 and 3, achieving high classification results on the skydiving dataset with six classes is possible. The best results in the tables are marked in bold. It can be seen that in all cases, models previously pre-trained in ImageNet-1k achieved a higher F1 score. ConvMixer_768_32 achieved the best overall F1 score of 0.9865, even compared to other ConvMixer variations. While it has fewer hidden dimensions than other variants (768), it has a bigger depth (32), i.e., a larger number of ConvMixer layers. Thus, it can better classify accurately, corresponding to results provided in [17].

Figure 9 shows confusion matrices of the best four models. Looking at the confusion matrices (Fig. 9), it can be seen that most of the errors were classifying D and E formations. Those two formations are expected to have the most similarities compared to all other formations (Fig. 3). Similar-looking formations will have a higher error rate in classification. To overcome that, fine-tuning of the selected models should be performed.

Table 2. Results on the validation dataset after training on various models (part 1).

Model	ResNet50	ConvMixer _1536_20	EfficientViT _m0	ConvMixer _1024_20
Pretrained	FALSE	FALSE	TRUE	TRUE
Parameters	23,520,326	50,098,182	2,157,594	23,364,614
Accuracy of				
class A	0.4390	0.8415	0.9390	0.9634
class B	0.1129	0.4355	0.8548	0.9839
class C	0.6471	0.2857	0.8908	0.9832
class D	0.4286	0.7959	0.7653	0.9082
class E	0.5600	0.7800	0.9400	0.9700
class F	0.1527	0.7939	0.8550	0.9924
F1 score (weighted)	0.3778	0.6415	0.8731	0.9677

5   Summary and Conclusions

This work raised the question of whether it is possible to use deep-learning models to perform approximate live judging for 4-way formation skydiving. To answer this question, deep learning models, most commonly used for feature extraction in similar tasks related to image classification and human pose detection, were identified. A skydiving dataset for such evaluation was created. And

Table 3. Results on the validation dataset after training on various models (part 2).

Model	ResNet50	FastViT _ma36	ConvMixer _1536_20	ConvMixer _768_32
Pretrained	TRUE	TRUE	TRUE	TRUE
Parameters	23,520,326	42,858,306	50,098,182	20,345,862
Accuracy of				
class A	0.9634	**0.9756**	0.9634	**0.9756**
class B	0.9677	0.9839	**1.0000**	**1.0000**
class C	0.9748	0.9832	**1.0000**	0.9916
class D	0.9184	0.9286	0.9286	**0.9592**
class E	0.9700	0.9600	**0.9900**	**0.9900**
class F	**1.0000**	0.9924	0.9924	1.0000
F1 score (weighted)	0.9678	0.9712	0.9797	**0.9865**

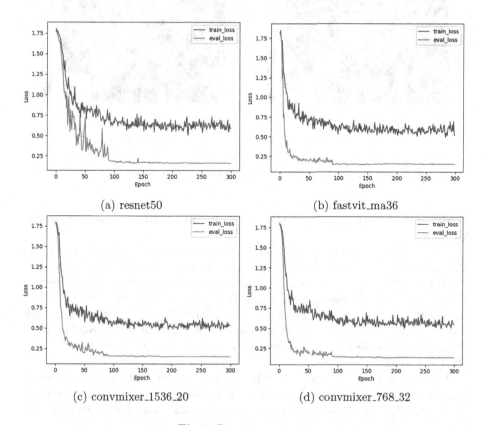

(a) resnet50

(b) fastvit_ma36

(c) convmixer_1536_20

(d) convmixer_768_32

Fig. 8. Learning curves.

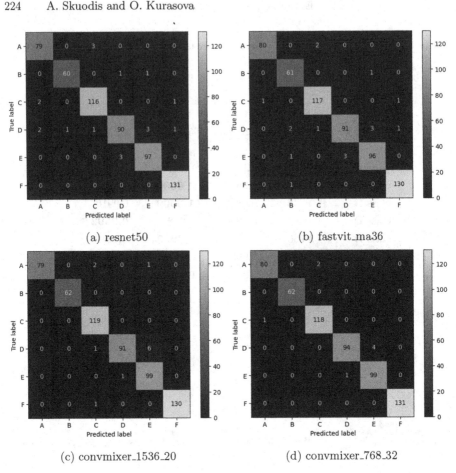

(a) resnet50   (b) fastvit_ma36

(c) convmixer_1536_20   (d) convmixer_768_32

Fig. 9. Confusion matrix of four best models according to weighted F1 score.

finally, selected deep-learning models were evaluated within the created skydiving dataset.

The results of evaluation of ResNet-50 [7], several variations of ConvMixer [17], EfficientViT [10] and FastViT [18] deep-learning models on the skydiving dataset suggest that selected pre-trained deep-learning models could be used to classify skydiving formations and can extract enough features to achieve high classification accuracy. According to result Tables 2 and 3, achieving a high classification score on the skydiving dataset with six classes is possible. ConvMixer_768_32 achieved the best overall F1 score of 0.9865, even compared to other ConvMixer variations.

While this work provides valuable insights into evaluating deep learning-based models on the skydiving dataset, it is essential to acknowledge certain limitations that should be considered. First, evaluation was performed on a skydiving dataset limited to the first six formations. Increasing the formation count to the real-world scenario might significantly affect results. Second, evaluations do not consider inference time, which would be crucial to the real-world application of such models in the skydiving scoring system.

Identified limitations provide future work and research directions. First, the skydiving dataset has to be expanded to the full version with all possible skydiving formations. The evaluation performed in this work could be recreated using a full-size dataset and compared to the results. As in this work, the confusion matrix of the results from the full-size dataset should show more errors with similar-looking skydiving formations. This real-world application problem will have to be solved in future works. Second, models could be evaluated using inference time. We could assume that bigger models with a higher number of parameters will have worse inference time but better accuracy. This dilemma should be considered when choosing a deep learning model for a skydiving scoring system.

Acknowledgments. The authors are thankful for the high-performance computing resources provided by the Information Technology Research Center of Vilnius University.

A   Online Resources

The dataset is available online on GitHub - https://github.com/voidsky/skyd ivingdataset6.

References

1. Fai 1st and 2nd Category Results Portal. (2024).http://results.worldskydiving. org/. Accessed 2 Feb 2024
2. InTimeScoring. (2024). https://www.intimescoring.com/. Accessed 2 Feb 2024
3. OmniScore. (2024). https://omniskore.com/. Accessed 2 Feb 2024
4. Pytorch Image Models (timm) — timmdocs. (2024). https://timm.fast.ai/. Accessed 2 Feb 2024
5. Deng, J., Dong, W., Socher, R., Li, L.J., Li, K., Fei-Fei, L.: ImageNet: a large-scale hierarchical image database. In: 2009 IEEE Conference on Computer Vision and Pattern Recognition, pp. 248–255 (2009). ISSN:1063-6919
6. Dosovitskiy, A., et al.: An image is worth 16x16 words: transformers for image recognition at scale. arXiv preprint arXiv:2010.11929 [cs] (2021)
7. He, K., Zhang, X., Ren, S., Sun, J.: Deep residual learning for image recognition. arXiv preprint arXiv:1512.03385 [cs] (2015)
8. Insafutdinov, E., Pishchulin, L., Andres, B., Andriluka, M., Schiele, B.: Deeper-Cut: a deeper, stronger, and faster multi-person pose estimation model (2016). arXiv:1605.03170
9. Krizhevsky, A., Sutskever, I., Hinton, G.E.: ImageNet classification with deep convolutional neural networks. In: Advances in Neural Information Processing Systems, vol. 25. Curran Associates, Inc. (2012)

10. Liu, X., Peng, H., Zheng, N., Yang, Y., Hu, H., Yuan, Y.: EfficientViT: memory efficient vision transformer with cascaded group attention. arXiv preprint-arXiv:2305.07027 [cs] (2023)
11. Papandreou, G., et al.: Towards accurate multi-person pose estimation in the wild. arXiv preprint arXiv:1701.01779 (2017)
12. Pishchulin, L., et al.: DeepCut: joint subset partition and labeling for multi person pose estimation. arXiv preprint arXiv:1511.06645 (2016)
13. Ren, S., He, K., Girshick, R., Sun, J.: faster r-CNN: Towards real-time object detection with region proposal networks. arXiv preprint arXiv:1506.01497 (2016)
14. Sun, X., Shang, J., Liang, S., Wei, Y.: Compositional human pose regression. arXiv preprint arXiv:1704.00159 (2017)
15. Szegedy, C., et al.: Going deeper with convolutions. arXiv preprint arXiv:1409.4842 (2014)
16. Toshev, A., Szegedy, C.: DeepPose: human pose estimation via deep neural networks. In: 2014 IEEE Conference on Computer Vision and Pattern Recognition, pp. 1653–1660 (2014)
17. Trockman, A., Kolter, J.Z.: Patches Are All You Need? arXiv preprint arXiv:2201.09792 [cs] (2022)
18. Vasu, P.K.A., Gabriel, J., Zhu, J., Tuzel, O., Ranjan, A.: FastViT: a fast hybrid vision transformer using structural reparameterization. arXiv preprint arXiv:2303.14189 [cs] (2023)
19. Vaswani, A., et al.: Attention Is All You Need. arXiv preprint arXiv:1706.03762 [cs] version: 1 (2017)
20. Wang, P.: lucidrains/vit-pytorch (2024). https://github.com/lucidrains/vit-pytorch. Accessed 2 Feb 2024
21. Xu, Y., Zhang, J., Zhang, Q., Tao, D.: ViTPose: simple vision transformer baselines for human pose estimation. arXiv preprint arXiv:2204.12484 [cs] version: 3 (2022)
22. Zhang, J., et al.: FastPose: towards real-time pose estimation and tracking via scale-normalized multi-task networks (2019)

Comparative Analysis of Various Data Balancing Techniques for Propaganda Detection in Lithuanian News Articles

Ieva Rizgelienė[(✉)] [iD] and Gražina Korvel[iD]

Institute of Data Science and Digital Technologies, Faculty of Mathematics and Informatics,
Vilnius University, Vilnius, Lithuania
ieva.rizgeliene@mif.vu.lt

Abstract. With the increased use of social networks, spreading propaganda has become more accessible, making developing propaganda detection methods crucial. However, only some datasets are available specifically for automatic propaganda detection, and the situation is particularly dire for low-resource languages such as Lithuanian. In this paper, balancing techniques are proposed as a solution to mitigate this limitation. Four balancing techniques, SMOTE, SMOTE-ENN, SMOTE-TOMEK and ADASYN, were evaluated for classification performance using LR, XGB, SVM, and RF models. The results showed that all data balancing techniques significantly improve the classification performance of machine learning models when the models are trained and tested on the same dataset. At the same time, SMOTE, SMOTE-TOMEK and ADASYN effectively improve performance when tested using new-unseen data, with the ADASYN technique proving to be superior.

Keywords: Propaganda detection · News articles · Data balancing · Machine learning

1 Introduction

In the age of information war, explicit and implicit propaganda spreads globally through social media and networks. Propaganda aims to sway public opinion using biased or misleading information, while organized propaganda employs troll factories and bots as information warfare tools [1]. Working towards a more informed and critical society involves analyzing and identifying propaganda sources. Propaganda constantly evolves, adapts, and transforms, making detection a challenging field. Machine learning plays an important role in propaganda detection and classification. By analyzing large amounts of data and identifying patterns, machine learning algorithms can detect potential propaganda material and manipulation techniques [2, 3]. These algorithms can be trained to identify propaganda in a variety of media, including text [4], images [5], and video [6]. While machine learning algorithms can be a powerful tool for detecting potential propaganda, it is important to consider the potential limitations. One of the main limitations is data availability. The model can effectively detect and classify propaganda in

A. Lupeikienė et al. (Eds.): DB&IS 2024, CCIS 2157, pp. 227–236, 2024.
https://doi.org/10.1007/978-3-031-63543-4_15

news articles that target high-resource languages. Low-resource languages, such as the Lithuanian language under consideration in this article, are challenging.

Researchers have given relatively little attention to detecting propaganda in the Lithuanian language, which emphasizes the need for further exploration and investigation in this area. Propaganda detection in Lithuanian text has been the focus of interdisciplinary research [7, 8]. However, the task of automatic propaganda detection has only been addressed for the partially related phenomenon of verbal aggression [9]. A hate speech classifier for social media texts has also been developed [10, 11]; all relevant sources are listed in [12]. Our paper focuses explicitly on applying machine learning algorithms to text data, particularly within the context of Lithuanian news articles, for automatic propaganda detection.

To fill the gap left by the lack of sufficient data, the researchers use different methods of data augmentation and balancing. Data augmentation is a strategy widely used in machine learning to artificially increase the size and diversity of training datasets. This is done through various methods such as synonym replacement [13], back translation [14], generative augmentation [14], or augmentation through reinforcement learning-guided conditional generation [15]. An imbalance in class distribution can be addressed through oversampling or undersampling [16, 17]. This approach is a potential solution for low-resource languages to overcome the uneven distribution of data across classes and paves the way for more accurate propaganda detection models. Following this, various augmentation techniques could be applied to enrich the dataset further. Our paper addresses the problem of dataset balancing for the Lithuanian language. We investigate the effectiveness of the adaptive synthetic sampling approach (ADASYN) [18], synthetic minority oversampling technique (SMOTE) and its improved variants SMOTE-ENN (SMOTE + Edited Nearest Neighbors) and SMOTE-TOMEK (SMOTE + Tomek links) in balancing our dataset [19]. We are testing how these techniques improve model performance.

The cornerstone of our experimental design is to assess not only the direct impact of data balancing methods on model accuracy but also the ability of the model to generalize to unseen data [20, 21]. This aspect is crucial to ensure that models maintain their performance robustness when confronted with new datasets that reflect real-world variability in propaganda content. By training models on balanced datasets and testing them on unseen datasets, we aim to explore the role of data balancing in improving models' performance on known data and their predictive capabilities on new data. By taking this dual approach, our research aims to identify the most effective methods of data balancing to address the challenges posed by data limitations in low-resource languages while highlighting the importance of model generalization in the dynamic and heterogeneous field of propaganda detection.

The remainder of the paper is organized as follows. It starts with describing the data balancing techniques, and Sect. 3 delves into the classification methods employed. Section 4 outlines the experimental setup, meticulously describing the dataset and the preprocessing steps. Subsequently, Sect. 5 presents the experimental results, offering a critical analysis of the performance metrics obtained from applying the discussed classification methods on the balanced datasets. The paper concludes with synthesizing the key findings.

2 Data Balancing Techniques

Four data balancing techniques were employed to address the uneven distribution of data across classes in the textual dataset: SMOTE (Synthetic Minority Over-sampling Technique), SMOTE-ENN (SMOTE + Edited Nearest Neighbors), SMOTE-TOMEK (SMOTE + Tomek Links), and ADASYN (Adaptive Synthetic Sampling Approach).

SMOTE is an approach where the minority class is over-sampled by taking each sample and introducing synthetic examples along the line segments connecting any of the k minority class nearest neighbours [19]. Depending on the amount of over-sampling required, neighbours are chosen randomly. Synthetic samples are generated as follows: (i) calculating the difference between the feature vector and its nearest neighbour; (ii) multiplying this difference by a random number between 0 and 1 and then adding it to the feature vector [19].

SMOTE-ENN is a hybrid approach that combines SMOTE and ENN (Edited Nearest Neighbors) in a single pass over the data [22]. The SMOTE-ENN method first oversamples the minority class using SMOTE and then uses the ENN to clean up the noise in the sample [23]. The ENN algorithm has the following steps: (i) identifying the k nearest neighbors for each sample x, regardless of class, (ii) calculating the Euclidean distance between each sample x and its k nearest neighbors, (iii) for each sample x, if the majority of its k nearest neighbors belong to the opposite class, then x is flagged as noise, (iv) removing all samples flagged as noise.

SMOTE-TOMEK is another hybrid approach, that combines SMOTE and Tomek links for sampling. After the data is sampled with SMOTE method, it is resampled one more time with Tomek links, which is a data cleaning technique [24], where Tomek link is a pair of minimally distanced neighbors (x_i, x_k), belonging to different classes.

ADASYN is an approach that uses a weighted distribution for different minority class examples according to their level of difficulty in learning [18]. Generating synthetic samples involves the following steps: (i) for each minority class sample, calculating its density distribution, which reflects the learning difficulty of the sample; (ii) determining the number of synthetic samples, emphasizing areas where the minority class is harder to learn; (iii) through interpolation between a given minority class example and one of its nearest neighbours within the same class, generate synthetic samples until the desired class balance is achieved.

3 Classification Methods

To evaluate the effectiveness of various balancing techniques, four different machine-learning models were used to detect propaganda in the Lithuanian language: LR (Logistic Regression), XGB (Extreme Gradient Boosting), SVM (Support Vector Machine), and RF (Random Forest). LR is a linear classification model that uses a logistic function to map input features to a probability score [25]. XGB is a scalable gradient-boosting framework that uses decision trees as base learners for classification tasks [26]. SVM is a classifier that finds the optimal hyperplane and maximizes the distance between data points belonging to different classes [27]. RF is an ensemble learning approach that combines multiple decision trees to make predictions. Each tree is trained on a random subset, and the predictions of the trees are aggregated for the final decision [28]. The selection of these four machine learning algorithms over others, such as neural networks, was due to the small size of the dataset.

4 Experimental Setup

Two datasets, anonymized for privacy reasons and renamed as Dataset 1 and Dataset 2, were used for this task. Both datasets consist of articles from two different non-credible Lithuanian news data sources. These sources were selected based on journalistic research conducted by the Lithuanian National Radio and Television [29], which identified unreliable news outlets that spread propaganda and disinformation. These portals were crawled and entered into an annotation tool where three experts labelled articles as propaganda or non-propaganda using a cross-annotation method [30]. Propaganda articles were considered to be those that employed propaganda techniques [31].

1021 articles were labeled for this research, with the annotation process ongoing. Dataset 1 contained 910 articles (604 non-propaganda, 306 propaganda) and Dataset 2 had 111 articles (59 non-propaganda, 52 propaganda). Text data was preprocessed by converting to lowercase, removing punctuation, lemmatizing and removing stopwords. Finally, the TF-IDF technique was used to vectorize the text data.

To estimate the influence of different data balancing techniques for propaganda classification performance, four machine learning models given in Sect. 3 were trained on Dataset 1 using 10-fold cross-validation. To evaluate the classification performance on new, unseen data, all the models were trained on Dataset 1 and tested on Dataset 2. For both experiments, machine learning models were trained five times: (i) without any balancing technique, (ii) using the SMOTE technique, (iii) using the SMOTE-ENN technique, (iv) using the SMOTE-TOMEK technique and (v) using the ADASYN technique. The Imbalanced-learn Python library was used for calculations with default parameters. The sampling strategy involved augmenting the minority class observations until both classes had equivalent cases. This was achieved by generating synthetic samples based on the five nearest neighbours.

5 Experimental Results

This section discusses and summarizes the results of applying the data balancing techniques outlined in Sect. 2. Two metrics were chosen to evaluate model performance: Accuracy (ACC), which measures the overall rate of correct predictions, and the F1 score, the harmonic mean of precision and recall, assessing model performance in imbalanced datasets. The standard deviation of accuracy and the F1 score are also added to measure the variability of the model's performance metrics across the ten different folds.

Table 1 shows the results of a 10-fold cross-validation classification for four different machine learning models trained on Dataset 1 using various balancing techniques. Overall, data balancing significantly enhances model performance. The highest accuracies were achieved in XGB (0.96), SVM (0.94), and RF (0.93) models using SMOTE-ENN, with XGB also achieving the top F1 score (0.91). However, this technique introduced the highest variability in results, as seen in the high standard deviations. The lowest F1 score was 0.53, observed in the LR model and SMOTE-ENN technique. In contrast, techniques like SMOTE, SMOTE-TOMEK, and ADASYN yielded more consistent results with lower variability, achieving an average accuracy and F1 score of 0.89.

Table 1. Classification performance of ML models (trained on dataset 1) using different data balancing techniques and 10-fold cross-validation.

Balancing technique	Metric	LR	XGB	SVM	RF
No balancing	Mean ACC	0.72	0.79	0.72	0.75
	Std. dev. (ACC)	0.05	0.03	0.05	0.05
	Mean F1 score	0.57	0.74	0.58	0.62
	Std. dev. (F1)	0.08	0.04	0.08	0.06
SMOTE	Mean ACC	0.88	0.86	**0.89**	0.86
	Std. dev. (ACC)	0.04	0.03	0.03	0.03
	Mean F1 score	0.88	0.85	**0.89**	0.84
	Std. dev. (F1)	0.04	0.03	0.03	0.04
SMOTE-ENN	Mean ACC	0.88	**0.96**	**0.94**	**0.93**
	Std. dev. (ACC)	0.07	0.05	0.06	0.06
	Mean F1 score	0.53	**0.91**	0.85	0.8
	Std. dev. (F1)	0.15	0.09	0.14	0.19
SMOTE-TOMEK	Mean ACC	0.88	0.86	**0.89**	0.85
	Std. dev. (ACC)	0.04	0.03	0.03	0.03
	Mean F1 score	0.88	0.85	**0.89**	**0.87**
	Std. dev. (F1)	0.04	0.03	0.03	0.03
ADASYN	Mean ACC	**0.89**	0.85	**0.89**	0.86
	Std. dev. (ACC)	0.03	0.03	0.03	0.03
	Mean F1 score	**0.89**	0.85	**0.89**	0.85
	Std. dev. (F1)	0.03	0.03	0.03	0.03

Table 2 details the class distribution before and after applying balancing techniques. Initially, there were 306 propaganda and 604 non-propaganda cases. Both SMOTE and SMOTE-TOMEK equalized classes to 604 each, indicating no effect from Tomek-links in these cases. This may be because after the generation of the SMOTE synthetic sample, no Tomek relationships were found between nearest neighbors of opposite classes. The SMOTE-ENN technique reduced numbers to 238 propaganda and 35 non-propaganda cases, causing overestimation in the propaganda class and high F1 score variability. ADASYN slightly increased the number of propaganda cases to 634, while non-propaganda cases remained at 604.

Table 3 shows the classification performance results when models were trained on Dataset 1 balanced with the balancing technique and tested on Dataset 2 without any balancing. The SMOTE-ENN technique resulted in the worst results, as it oversampled the propaganda class and undersampled the non-propaganda class, causing models to overfit in the propaganda class. Conversely, models trained with SMOTE,

Table 2. Class distribution in dataset 1 after application of data balancing techniques.

Balancing technique	Propaganda	Not propaganda
No balancing	306	604
SMOTE	604	604
SMOTENN	238	35
SMOTOMEK	604	604
ADASYN	634	604

SMOTE-TOMEK, and ADASYN techniques outperformed models trained with unbalanced dataset, demonstrating improved classification of unseen news articles. In this case, SMOTE and SMOTE-TOMEK achieved identical results, indicating no impact from Tomek links. The best performance was with the LR model using ADASYN, achieving 0.72 accuracy and a 0.71 F1 score. The superiority of the ADASYN technique is also demonstrated by the results of all the classification algorithms used.

Table 3. Classification performance of models (training with dataset 1, testing with dataset 2) with different balancing techniques

Balancing technique	Metric	LR	XGB	SVM	RF
No balancing	Accuracy	0.56	0.66	0.56	0.6
	F1 score	0.45	0.64	0.45	0.51
SMOTE	Accuracy	0.7	0.69	**0.59**	**0.63**
	F1 score	0.69	0.68	**0.51**	0.52
SMOTE-ENN	Accuracy	0.47	0.5	0.47	0.47
	F1 score	0.32	0.5	0.32	0.32
SMOTE-TOMEK	Accuracy	0.7	0.69	**0.59**	0.61
	F1 score	0.69	0.68	**0.51**	0.55
ADASYN	Accuracy	**0.72**	**0.7**	**0.59**	0.61
	F1 score	**0.71**	**0.69**	**0.51**	**0.55**

To illustrate the separation of the data between the two classes, "propaganda" and "non-propaganda", the t-SNE (t-distributed Stochastic Neighbor Embedding) method was used. Figure 1 displays class distributions before and after applying four sampling techniques in dataset 1. Graph (a) illustrates overlapping data, indicating poor separation. Graphs (b) and (d), for SMOTE and SMOTE-TOMEK, respectively, show similar class separations, aligning with previous findings from Tables 2 and 3. Graph (c), for SMOTE-ENN, highlights the substantial removal of non-propaganda cases. Graph (e), for ADASYN, demonstrates the most effective class separation. Figure 2 shows the data distribution between two classes in Dataset 2, indicating no clear separation between them in this dataset either. It also confirms that the distribution between classes differs between Dataset 1 and Dataset 2.

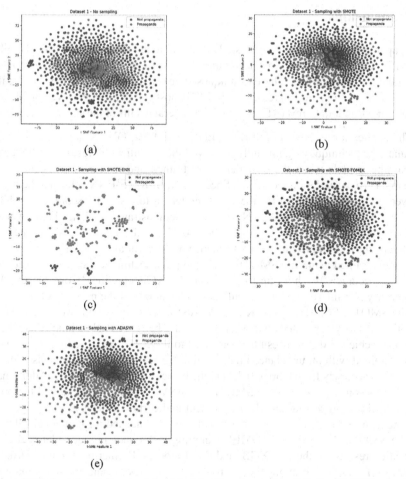

(a)

(b)

(c)

(d)

(e)

Fig. 1. t-SNE class distribution in dataset 1. (a) without sampling, (b) after SMOTE sampling, (c) after SMOTENN sampling, and (d) after SMOTOMEK sampling, (d) after ADASYN sampling

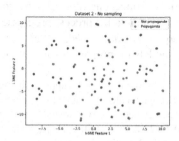

Fig. 2 t-SNE class distribution in dataset 2.

6 Conclusions

The paper presents the results of a study that examined the SMOTE, SMOTE-ENN, SMOTE-TOMEK, and ADASYN techniques for addressing dataset balancing problems in Lithuanian news articles. These techniques were evaluated based on the classification performance of Logistic Regression (LR), XGBoost (XGB), Support Vector Machine (SVM), and Random Forest (RF) models. The general results of the study are as follows:

- The application of SMOTE, SMOTE-ENN, SMOTE-TOMEK, and ADASYN data balancing techniques significantly improved the classification results of all machine learning models when these models were trained and tested on the same dataset using a cross-validation technique. Specifically, SMOTE-ENN achieved the highest average accuracy of 0.96 for the XGB model. In terms of F1 score, the SMOTE, SMOTE-TOMEK and ADASYN techniques demonstrated a balanced improvement, increasing the average F1 scores to above 0.85 for all models. This indicates their effectiveness in improving the performance of different algorithms.
- Models trained using the SMOTE-ENN sampling technique can achieve very high model accuracy, reaching up to 0.96 with the XGB classifier. However, this high accuracy is primarily due to a significant undersample of the majority class.
- The SMOTE, SMOTE-TOMEK, and ADASYN techniques improve model classification results when tested on new, unseen data. The ADASYN technique and the LR model achieved the best results. Compared to the results achieved when the model was trained with an unbalanced dataset, the ADASYN technique increased the LR model's accuracy from 0.56 to 0.72 and the F1 score from 0.45 to 0.71. Additionally, using the same parameters as SMOTE, ADASYN slightly oversampled the propaganda class, suggesting the algorithm identified certain articles as challenging and generated extra synthetic samples beyond what was needed for numerical balance.
- The SMOTE and SMOTE-TOMEK sampling techniques produce identical classification results for the LR, XGB, and SVM models. Furthermore, data distribution across classes after applying these sampling techniques remains the same, indicating that Tomek links had no noticeable effect following sampling with SMOTE for this specific case.

In the future, we plan to continue our research on propaganda detection in the Lithuanian language. As the data annotation process progresses and high-quality Lithuanian textual propaganda corpora are developed, we aim to enhance our research by incorporating deep learning models for propaganda technique detection.

Acknowledgments. We are grateful for the financial support provided by the Lithuanian Government Priority Research Program (implemented through the Lithuania Research Council) "Building Societal Resilience and Crisis Management in the Context of Contemporary Geopolitical Developments" under grant number S-VIS-23-8. Project title: 'Propaganda and Disinformation Research: Machine Learning Based Automatic Detection, Impact and Societal Resilience'.

Disclosure of Interests The authors have no competing interests to declare that are relevant to the content of this article.

References

1. Prier, J.: Commanding the trend: social media as information warfare. Strat. Stud. Q. **11**(4), 50–85 (2017). http://www.jstor.org/stable/26271634
2. Choraś, M., et al.: Advanced Machine Learning techniques for fake news (online disinformation) detection: a systematic mapping study. Appl. Soft Comput. **101**, 107050 (2021)
3. Khanday, A.M.U.D., Khan, Q.R., Rabani, S.T.: Identifying propaganda from online social networks during COVID-19 using machine learning techniques. Int. J. Inf. Technol. **13**, 115–122 (2021)
4. Barrows, M., Haig, E., Conduit, D.: Sentiment and objectivity in Iranian state-sponsored propaganda on twitter. IEEE Trans. Comput. Soc. Syst. (2023)
5. Killi, C.B.R., Balakrishnan, N., Rao, C.S.: Deep fake image classification using VGG-19 model. Ingénierie des Systèmes d'Information **28**(2) (2023)
6. Panda, S.K., Diwan, T., Kakde, O.G., Tembhurne, J.V.: Improvised detection of deepfakes from visual inputs using light weight deep ensemble model. Multimedia Tools Appl. **82**(13), 20101–20118 (2023)
7. Zelenkauskaite, A.: Bots, trolls, elves, and the information war in Lithuania: theoretical considerations and practical problems. In: Information Wars in the Baltic States: Russia's Long Shadow, pp. 123–140. Springer International Publishing, Cham (2022)
8. Kasperienė, R., Krilavičius, T.: Content analysis methods for estimating the dynamics of Facebook groups. In: CEUR Workshop Proceedings [Electronic Resource]: IVUS 2019, International conference on information technologies, Kaunas, Lithuania, 25 Apr 2019. Aachen: CEUR-WS, 2019, vol. 2470. CEUR-WS, Aachen (2019)
9. Ruzaitė, J.: How Do Haters Hate? Verbal Aggression in Lithuanian Online Comments. Discourse and Conflict: Analysing Text and Talk of Conflict, Hate and Peace-Building, 115–145 (2021)
10. Kankevičiūtė, E., Songailaitė, M., Zhyhun, B., Mandravickaitė, J.: Lithuanian hate speech classification using deep learning methods. Autom. Technol. Bus. Process./Avtomatizaciâ Tehnologiceskih i Biznes-Processov **15**(3) (2023)
11. Kankevičiūtė, E., Songailaitė, M., Mandravickaitė, J., Kalinauskaitė, D., Krilavičius, T.: A comparison of deep learning models for hate speech detection (2022)
12. Petrauskaitė, R., Amilevičius, D., Dadurkevičius, V., Krilavičius, T., Raškinis, G., Utka, A., Vaičenonienė, J.: CLARIN-LT: Home for Lithuanian Language Resources. CLARIN. The Infrastructure for Language Resources. deGruyter, Berlin (2022)
13. Feng, Z., Zhou, H., Zhu, Z., Mao, K.: Tailored text augmentation for sentiment analysis. Expert Syst. Appl. **205**, 117605 (2022)
14. Shorten, C., Khoshgoftaar, T.M., Furht, B.: Text data augmentation for deep learning. J. Big Data **8**, 1–34 (2021)
15. Liu, R., Xu, G., Jia, C., Ma, W., Wang, L., Vosoughi, S.: Data boost: text data augmentation through reinforcement learning guided conditional generation. arXiv preprint arXiv:2012.02952 (2020)
16. Madani, M., Motameni, H., Mohamadi, H.: KNNGAN: an oversampling technique for textual imbalanced datasets. J. Supercomput. **79**(5), 5291–5326 (2023)
17. Prusa, J., Khoshgoftaar, T.M., Dittman, D.J., Napolitano, A.: Using random undersampling to alleviate class imbalance on tweet sentiment data. In: 2015 IEEE International Conference on Information Reuse and Integration, pp. 197–202. IEEE (2015)
18. He, H., Bai, Y., Garcia, E.A., Li, S.: ADASYN: adaptive synthetic sampling approach for imbalanced learning. In: 2008 IEEE International Joint Conference on Neural Networks (IEEE World Congress on Computational Intelligence), Hong Kong, 2008, pp. 1322–1328. https://doi.org/10.1109/IJCNN.2008.4633969

19. Chawla, N.V., Bowyer, K.W., Hall, L.O., Kegelmeyer, W.P.: SMOTE: synthetic minority over-sampling technique. J. Artif. Intell. Res. **16**, 321–357 (2002)
20. Linzen, T.: How can we accelerate progress towards human-like linguistic generalization? arXiv preprint arXiv:2005.00955 (2020)
21. Qiao, F., Peng, X.: Uncertainty-guided model generalization to unseen domains. In: Proceedings of the IEEE/CVF Conference on Computer Vision and Pattern Recognition, pp. 6790–6800 (2021)
22. Batista, G.E.A.P.A., Prati, R.C., Monard, M.C.: A study of the behavior of several methods for balancing machine learning training data. SIGKDD Explor. Newsl. **6**(1), 20–29 (2004). https://doi.org/10.1145/1007730.1007735
23. Beckmann, M., Ebecken, N.F., Pires de Lima, B.S.: A KNN undersampling approach for data balancing. J. Intell. Learn. Syst. Appl. **7**(04), 104–116 (2015)
24. Tomek, I.: Two modifications of CNN. IEEE Trans. Syst. Man Cybern. **6**, 769–772 (1976)
25. LaValley, M.P.: Logistic regression. Circulation **117**(18), 2395–2399 (2008)
26. Chen, T., Guestrin, C.: Xgboost: a scalable tree boosting system. In: Proceedings of the 22nd International Conference on Knowledge Discovery and Data Mining, pp. 785–794 (2016)
27. Stitson, M.O., Weston, J.A.E., Gammerman, A., Vovk, V., Vapnik, V.: Theory of support vector machines. Univ. London **117**(827), 188–191 (1996)
28. Breiman, L.: Random forests. Mach. Learn. **45**, 5–32 (2001). https://doi.org/10.1023/A:101 0933404324
29. LRT tyrimas. Lietuvos „penktoji kolona": Rusijos propagandą platina šeimos gynėjai, sektos ir knygų apie Staliną leidėjai - LRT
30. Stollenwerk, F., et al.: Text Annotation Handbook: A Practical Guide for Machine Learning Projects (2023). arXiv:2310.11780
31. https://propaganda.qcri.org/annotations/definitions.html

Synthesizing Vibration Signals Using Generative Adversarial Networks

Tadas Žvirblis[1](✉)[iD] and Donatas Pučinskas[2]

[1] Institute of Data Science and Digital Technologies, Vilnius University, Vilnius,
Lithuania
tadas.zvirblis@mf.vu.lt
[2] Institute of Computer Science, Vilnius University, Vilnius, Lithuania
donatas.pucinskas@mif.stud.vu.lt

Abstract. This work evaluates the applicability of GANs in generating synthetic time series data. Hypoid gear vibration data was used as
experimental data to test models. GANs for time series can be divided
into two different types: discrete type (discrete time series) and continuous type (continuous time series). In time series, there are complex
time-dependent features and their attributes, for example, when using
biometric data, ECG characteristics will depend on the age and health
of the individual. TimeGAN is a generative time series model that combines unsupervised learning using GAN with supervised autoregressive
learning. TimeGAN model performace was evaluated using predictive
score and visualization using PCA and tSNE analysis for original and
synthetic data. The best predictive score was 0.062, however visual evaluation using tSNE and PCA analysis revealed that generated data was
not sufficiently similar to the real. It can be concluded that the application of GANs to time series presents difficulties that are not present
in image generation models. Continuing this work could lead to testing
other time series GANs in the future, e.g. DoppelGANger whose synthetic data structure does not require complex reconstruction.

Keywords: generative adversarial network · deep neural network ·
deep learning parameters · data augmentation · synthetic data

1 Introduction

In recent years, machine learning models are getting bigger and bigger, the
number of parameters is growing exponentially. This creates a problem of data
scarcity, as more data is needed to train the models. For most problem areas,
there are usually public repositories from which the necessary data can be
obtained. However, time series datasets of sufficient size are not so readily available. Often, this is an actual problem that is solved by data processing methods,
data transformations [3, 4].

One of the more recent approaches to the problem of time series data scarcity
is the generation of synthetic data using a generative adversarial network (GAN)

© The Author(s), under exclusive license to Springer Nature Switzerland AG 2024
A. Lupeikienė et al. (Eds.): DB&IS 2024, CCIS 2157, pp. 237–246, 2024.
https://doi.org/10.1007/978-3-031-63543-4_16

presented by Ian Goodfellow in 2014 [3,4]. GAN is one of the most revolutionary models of the last decade, which is widely applied to solving computer vision problems, generating photos, etc. However, this model is not only applied to the generation of synthetic pictures, GANs are increasingly applied in the field of time series data [1]. Some examples of data include stock prices, exchange rates, sales data, biomedical measurements, astronomical data, and weather data collected over a period of time [9].

GANs have recently become very popular and powerful tools for data augmentation and data synthesis, including time series data. The architecture of GANs learns the distribution of data by extracting key features of the data. A trained generator of this architecture can then synthesize completely new data. Currently, there are many different uses of GANs architectures for time series data [6–8]. One of the most advanced time series GANs architectures TimeGAN [12] adds two new encoder and recovery networks to the conventional generator and discriminator architecture. This architecture was then explored by synthesizing sinusoidal, stock market, energy forecast, and lung cancer time series data.

Conditional GANs contribute to traditional architectures by incorporating conditional information into the training process. This allows the network to be trained to generate more accurate data based on specific inputs, such as classes of data. The conditional GAN time series architecture TSGAN [10] achieved better results in synthesizing time series data for classification tasks than other GAN architectures. The TSGAN architecture was tested on 70 datasets and compared with the WGAN architecture [5]. The accuracy of the synthesized data of the TSGAN architecture was better than that of the WGAN architecture by about 11%.

There are many different ways to perform time series data augmentations, but not all data augmentations can be applied to specific data sets. This work will aim to apply data augmentation methods to conveyor belt tension signal data and investigate the influence of these methods on the classification accuracy of machine learning algorithms.

The aim of this work is to evaluate the applicability of GANs in generating synthetic hypoid gear vibration data. In order to generate synthetic hypoid gear vibration data, this paper will examine the scientific literature describing GANs and their applicability with an emphasis on time series applications. This work aims to create a GAN capable of synthesizing hypoid gear vibration signal data.

2   Methodology

2.1   An Overview of GANs

GANs is a machine learning technique used in both semi-supervised and unsupervised learning scenarios. The essence of this method is two competing networks, the generator G and the discriminator D. It is important to note that the generator has no access to the input data and the only way it can learn is through interaction with the discriminator (Fig. 1).

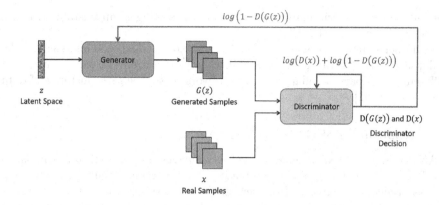

Fig. 1. A typical architecture of a GAN [11].

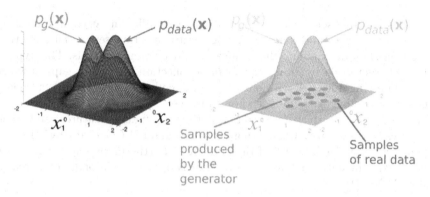

Fig. 2. Probability distribution of real and synthetic data, in the optimal case the probabilities will overlap evenly [2].

Formally, the discriminator D is trained to achieve the maximum probability of correctly labeling both the training data and the data generated by the generator G. At the same time, G is trained to achieve the maximum value of $\log(1 - D(G(z)))$, where $G(x)$ represents the probability of the input x belong to real data. This allows us to define this problem as a min max optimization problem with a value function

$$\min_G \max_D V(G, D) = \mathbb{E}_{x \sim p_{data}(x)}[\log D(x)] + \mathbb{E}_{x \sim p_z(z)}[\log(1 - D(G(z)))], \quad (1)$$

where p_{data} is the probability distribution of the real data and p_z is the distribution of the data generated by G. It is easy to see that the generator G is optimal when the discriminator D is most uncertain about the outcome or in other words when $p_{data}(x) = p_z(x)$ which is identical discriminator probability estimate of 0.5 for all data from x.

However, this balance between generator and discriminator is very difficult to achieve, as a decrease in the value of the generator can affect the decrease in the value of the discriminator and vice versa, resulting in an unstable training process for the GAN (Fig. 2).

Another common problem with GANs is regime collapse. This refers to the collapse of the generator and the ability to generate only a small amount of different data (partial collapse) or, in the worst case, the same instance of data (full collapse) [2].

2.2 Application of GANs to Time Series

GANs are widely used to generate synthetic images that are difficult or indistinguishable from real images. For this reason, most efforts are focused on improving GANs in media generation. However, there is a growing consensus in the scientific community that these networks can be applied much more widely than just image generation and manipulation. This led to a move towards generating time series data using GANs [1].

GANs for time series can be divided into two different types: discrete type (discrete time series) and continuous type (continuous time series). Discrete time series consist of data points that are separated by time intervals. This type of data is characterized by an infrequent data collection interval or gaps in which data are missing due to disruptions in the data collection process. In continuous time series, a value exists for each point in time.

In time series, there are complex time-dependent features and their attributes, for example, when using biometric data, ECG characteristics will depend on the age and health of the individual. Furthermore, long-term dependencies exist in data that are not necessarily fixed-dimensional compared to image GANs [1].

2.3 TimeGAN: Generative Time Series Model

TimeGAN is a system that combines unsupervised learning with supervised learning. Much attention is paid to generating data while preserving temporal dynamics. TimeGAN integrates an unsupervised GAN together with a supervised autoregressive model. The system consists of four parts: an embedding function, a recovery function, a generator, and a discriminator [12]. The main innovation of TimeGAN is to train the autoencoder components (embedding and recovery functions) together with competing components (generator and discriminator). In this way, TimeGAN simultaneously learns to encode features, generate their representations, and iterate through time. The embedding network provides the latent space in which the generator operates. Latent dynamic time signatures of real and generated data are synchronized by supervised loss (Fig. 3).

The TimeGAN model is evaluated according to three criteria. Visualization in PCA and tSNE analysis for original and synthetic data. Discriminant evaluation is a quantitative metric that assesses whether synthetic and real data are indistinguishable. This metric is implemented by training a time series classification model (an optimized two-layer long-term memory model). Predictive score

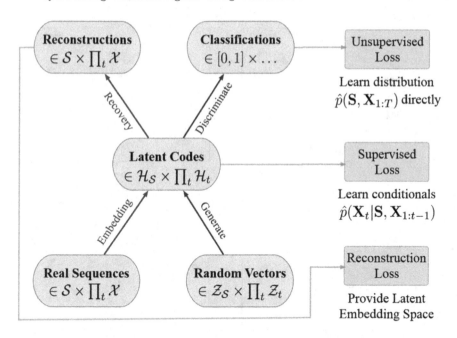

Fig. 3. Block diagram of TimeGAN architecture [12].

determines whether synthetic data is as useful when used for forecasting. This metric is determined by training a sequence prediction model (a two-layer long-short-term memory model). TimeGAN is tested on a variety of data sets: sine waves, stock price data, energy consumption data, and lung cancer symptom data. This model is compared with other time series GANs such as RCGAN, CRNNGAN, and WaveGAN [12].

3 Results and Discussion

The vibration data of the hypoid gear was collected experimentally by examining the signal changes under different conditions. During the measurements, the engine revolutions were changed, five different speeds were selected: 1000, 2000, 3000, 4000 and 5000. The torques were also changed: 25, 50, 75, 100 and 125 Nm. Combinations of each of these parameters were used to measure hypoid gears with different levels of damage. Measurements were made with the following damages: condition 0 gear without damage, condition 1 gear with damage to one gear tooth, conditions 2, 3 and 4 gear with greater damage to one tooth, conditions 5 and 6 gear with damage to two and three teeth. Measurements were made for 5 s with a sampling rate of 51200 Hz. Two tests were performed for each parameter value [13].

Two selections of the dataset were analyzed for training the TimeGAN model. The first case is to train the model with the full data set, the second is to select vibration data collected with fixed playing condition, RPM and torque parameters. The vibration measurements were taken independently of each other, and

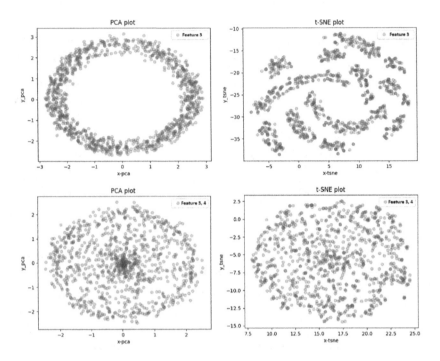

Fig. 4. PCA and tSNE analysis for data: third game conditions only; for the general conditions of the third and fourth games.

by combining the data into a common set, the TimeGAN model can learn certain data dependencies between different trials that have no real meaning. Also, problems can be caused by the large size of the total data set, which would increase the training time of the model, thus hindering the optimization of the model's hyperparameters. To confirm this hypothesis, PCA and tSNE analysis were performed for both cases of the data set (Fig. 4). Analysis of the overall data set failed to group the data into distinct clusters, meaning that no common features were detected in the data set. This differs from the analysis performed on a dataset from a single experiment, where the high-level features of the data have a more pronounced structure.

Training GANs is complex and unstable, requiring extensive optimization of model hyperparameters. This is another reason why only the third condition game, 3000 RPM and 75 Nm torque data set was selected for further model training. The data parameters are selected taking into account the dependence of the classification accuracy of the CNN2D model and the values of the data parameters [13].

3.1   Optimization of tSNE Parameters

The tSNE analysis parameters specified in the original TimeGAN repository code were not applied to the drive vibration data and therefore did not provide a significant result. However, the python sklearn.manifold.TSNE class provides

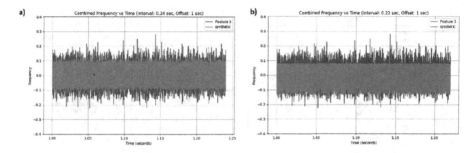

Fig. 5. Drive vibration data: a) sequences connected to each other; (b) Data reconstructed from sequences.

a number of parameters on which the analysis results depend. Parameters such as confusion, learning rate and number of iterations had the greatest influence on the result. These parameters were optimized until significant results were obtained from the tSNE analysis.

Before training the TimeGAN model on the data, certain transformations are performed. The data is flipped to maintain chronological order, then the data is split into sequences of the specified length and finally rescaling is applied to the range from 0 to 1. This means that the generated data is of the same structure, i.e. an array of short data sequences. The principle of splitting into sequences is to scroll the window of the specified sequence length one by one over the entire length of the original sequence. In order to generate a sequence of the original data length concatenated from much shorter sequences.

The idea of reconstruction is to apply inverse data transformations to the generated data. Flipping the data and rescaling it back to the original scale was easy to implement. The idea of sequence concatenation is to take advantage of the fact that during sequence splitting, each element of the original sequence becomes the first element of a short sequence. For this reason, concatenation of a sequence is done by sequentially concatenating the first elements of each shorter sequence. However, in the graph of Fig. 5b, we can see that after visualizing the reconstructed data, the data is not exactly restored. It is not exactly clear what the reason for this is. There is a possibility that this problem could be solved if the quality of the data generated by TimeGAN was improved. However, in the graph of Fig. 5a, we can see that concatenating the sequences to each other is a good way to reconstruct the sequence. The data reconstructed in this way may have some features of erroneous data at the junction point of the sequences, but it is well suited for visual evaluation of the generated data.

3.2 Training Experiments

The original hyperparameter values were chosen for model training, with one exception, the sequence length was chosen to be 2560. This sequence length was chosen to retain a larger amount of significant time dependencies. However, this

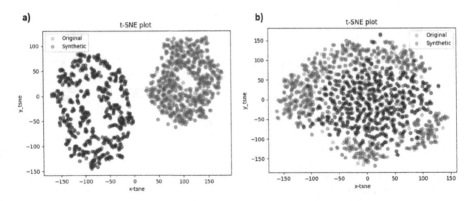

Fig. 6. tSNE analysis: (a) data generated after 1000 epochs; (b) data generated after 500 epochs.

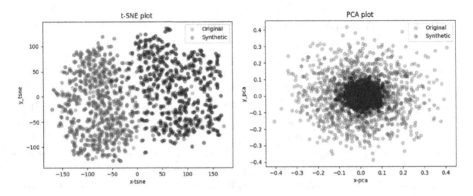

Fig. 7. Experiment 5 performed tSNE and PCA analysis after 1500 co-training steps.

solution presented an unexpected problem after training the model, the memory limit was exceeded when trying to generate synthetic data. Then there was an attempt to increase the limit, but when the RAM limit was set to 100 GB, the data generation still exceeded the allowed limit. The reason for the large memory usage is that the data structure is changed after data preparation for training, i.e. instead of the initial data form (256000, 1), sequences are created that share a large part of the elements, the processed data form is (253440, 2560, 1). The next problem was the long duration of training the model, the training of the model had to be stopped after 30 h, because the allowed time limit would have been exceeded. For this reason, a smaller sequence length and 25% of the original data were used for subsequent training trials.

In the following training trial, the sequence length was reduced to 256. This change allowed us to train the model and evaluate the quality of the generated data. As we can see in Fig. 6, the quality of the generated data after 500 co-training steps is better than the quality of the data after 1000 training steps. This demonstrates the instability of training GANs when the model starts to optimize parameters that interfere with the generation of better quality data. The predictive metric after 1000 training steps is 0.093.

Next, hyperparameters of the model such as batch size, sequence length, number of model dimensions and layers were optimized. The large number of combinations of model hyperparameters to be optimized made it difficult to discover the best combination. This task was complicated by the fact that training the model for too long can mean worse results. One of the tested optimizations for training the model was changing the architecture of the memory cell from GRU to LSTM. This change significantly shortened the training time, but there was a problem such as the collapse of the embedding network mode.

The best prediction metric achieved in the training trials is 0.62. However, in the tSNE and PCA analysis of the synthetic and original data generated during this test (Fig. 7), we can see that the static characteristics of the data are not maintained and the quality of the data is not acceptable.

4   Conclusions

In this work GANs and their application to time series data was explored. The theoretical operating principle and architecture of GANs are described. The application of GANs to time series data and the associated issues and obstacles are reviewed. One of the problems addressed is the difficulty in evaluating the data generated by GANs, and some evaluation methods applied to time series data are described. TimeGAN architecture, operating principle, evaluation metrics, main innovations and differences from other models are analyzed and described. The environment used to train the TimeGAN model and the problems encountered while trying to train it are described. tSNE and PCA analysis was performed on the data, which required the optimization of tSNE parameters, the results were compared and it was decided to use the data of one game type. The original TimeGAN model code has been extended with new functionalities that are relevant for model training using drive vibration data. The problem of reconstruction of synthetic data generated by the TimeGAN model is examined and several alternatives are presented. Conducted TimeGAN training experiments using hypoid gear vibration data. Optimized model hyperparameters in an attempt to generate synthetic data as close as possible to real data and specified problem situations during training. During test 5, the best predictive metric estimate of 0.062 was achieved, but during the visual evaluation of the data and after performing tSNE and PCA analysis, it was determined that the generated data are not sufficiently similar to the real ones.

It can be concluded that the application of GANs to time series presents difficulties that are not present in image generation models. One such problem is non-standardized and complex quality assessment of synthetic data. Also, the structure of the data generated by TimeGAN is not adapted to the generation of a long data sequence, there are problems in reconstructing a complete sequence from the short generated sequences, and choosing a longer sequence length hyperparameter increases the amount of training data and the training time significantly.

Continuing this work could lead to testing other time series GANs in the future, e.g. DoppelGANger whose synthetic data structure does not require complex reconstruction. To implement a comprehensive search of TimeGAN hyperparameters, which would allow choosing the best combination from a large number of hyperparameters to be optimized. Also, the generated data was used in the classification of gear failures and to evaluate whether the synthetic data increases the accuracy of the classification.

Acknowledgement. This paper has received funding under postdoctoral fellowship project from the Research Council of Lithuania (LMTLT), agreement No. [S-PD-22-81].

References

1. Brophy, E., Wang, Z., She, Q., Ward, T.: Generative adversarial networks in time series: a survey and taxonomy. arXiv preprint arXiv:2107.11098 (2021)
2. Creswell, A., White, T., Dumoulin, V., Arulkumaran, K., Sengupta, B., Bharath, A.A.: Generative adversarial networks: an overview. IEEE Signal Process. Mag. **35**(1), 53–65 (2018)
3. Goodfellow, I., et al.: Generative adversarial nets. Adv. Neural Inf. Process. Syst. **27** (2014)
4. Goodfellow, I., et al.: Generative adversarial networks. Commun. ACM **63**(11), 139–144 (2020)
5. Hartmann, K.G., Schirrmeister, R.T., Ball, T.: Eeg-gan: Generative adversarial networks for electroencephalograhic (EEG) brain signals. arXiv preprint arXiv:1806.01875 (2018)
6. Huang, T., Chakraborty, P., Sharma, A.: Deep convolutional generative adversarial networks for traffic data imputation encoding time series as images. Int. J. Transp. Sci. Technol. **12**(1), 1–18 (2023)
7. Iglesias, G., Talavera, E., González-Prieto, Á., Mozo, A., Gómez-Canaval, S.: Data augmentation techniques in time series domain: a survey and taxonomy. Neural Comput. Appl. **35**(14), 10123–10145 (2023)
8. Mogren, O.: C-rnn-gan: continuous recurrent neural networks with adversarial training. arXiv preprint arXiv:1611.09904 (2016)
9. Ramponi, G., Protopapas, P., Brambilla, M., Janssen, R.: T-cgan: conditional generative adversarial network for data augmentation in noisy time series with irregular sampling. arXiv preprint arXiv:1811.08295 (2018)
10. Smith, K.E., Smith, A.O.: Conditional GAN for timeseries generation. arXiv preprint arXiv:2006.16477 (2020)
11. Vint, D., Anderson, M., Yang, Y., Ilioudis, C., Di Caterina, G., Clemente, C.: Automatic target recognition for low resolution foliage penetrating SAR images using CNNs and GANs. Remote Sens. **13**(4), 596 (2021)
12. Yoon, J., Jarrett, D., Van der Schaar, M.: Time-series generative adversarial networks. Adv. Neural Inf. Process. Syst. **32** (2019)
13. Žvirblis, T., Petkevičius, L., Vaitkus, P., Šabanovič, E., Skrickij, V., Kilikevičius, A.: Investigation of deep neural networks for hypoid gear signal classification to identify anomalies. In: 2020 IEEE 8th Workshop on Advances in Information, Electronic and Electrical Engineering (AIEEE), pp. 1–6. IEEE (2021)

Author Index

A. Lupeikienė et al. (Eds.): DB&IS 2024, CCIS 2157, p. 247, 2024.
https://doi.org/10.1007/978-3-031-63543-4

Printed in the United States
by Baker & Taylor Publisher Services